IMAGES
of America

AROUND PRATTSBURGH

I0805887

On the Cover: Taken in the early 1940s, this image offers a look of how the area's ancestors were able to clear the "big swamp" of all its trees and find the fertile soil that remained. Many bountiful crops have been grown on this 700-acre muck. At first, almost everything was done completely by hand. Today, very large pieces of equipment are used to plant and harvest the crops. Several growers owned the muck, and today, with modern equipment, it is owned by one or two with onions being the main crop. The earliest residents would be amazed at how the crops are harvested now. (Courtesy of the Prattsburgh Historical Society.)

IMAGES
of America

AROUND PRATTSBURGH

Lenora J. Applebee

ARCADIA
PUBLISHING

ISBN 978-0-7385-7692-3

Published by Arcadia Publishing
Charleston, South Carolina

Printed in the United States of America

Library of Congress Control Number: 2011937793

For all general information, please contact Arcadia Publishing:
Telephone 843-853-2070
Fax 843-853-0044
E-mail sales@arcadiapublishing.com
For customer service and orders:
Toll-Free 1-888-313-2665

Visit us on the Internet at www.arcadiapublishing.com

This book is dedicated to the brave people who wanted a better life in a new place—a place that is now celebrating 200 years of rich history.

Contents

ACKNOWLEDGMENTS

Since the Prattsburgh Historical Society was founded in 1988, many volunteers have worked to preserve the history of Prattsburgh. So many who worked to establish the historical society and build the photograph collection archives have passed on, leaving this treasure of stories and information about the town's history for future generations, making this book possible. All of the images appearing in the first six chapters of this are property of the Prattsburgh Historical Society. The images in the Pulteney chapter are courtesy of the town of Pulteney historian, Sharon Daggett. The images in the Wheeler chapter are courtesy of the town of Wheeler historian, Melvin Partridge, unless otherwise noted.

Thank you to Arcadia Publishing editor Erin for her expert guidance (when requested) and prodding (when needed). Also, thanks to Rich Simpson for his long hours of scanning the images and Angela Einwachter for typing many pages for the book.

Finally, thank you to my husband, George, for your love and encouragement, not just on this project, but in everything.

Introduction

As we celebrate the town of Prattsburgh's bicentennial anniversary, it is important to look not only at the history of its buildings and the beauty of its surroundings, but also, and most notably, at the incredible people who have called Prattsburgh home. From the founding fathers to the residents occupying this great place today, one thing is certain: a common bond of pride in our community holds each generation together.

This small and beautiful township bestows a sense of pride upon all of us, and whether born and raised here or blessed to move into this region later in life, this place is like no other in our great country. Surely, there are many rural towns that are fine examples of the foundations of America, but there is only one Prattsburgh—a picturesque town whose beauty takes one's breath away and whose townspeople are more than just neighbors, they are family!

When thinking of Prattsburgh, one immediately thinks of the people who call it home and their belief that small-town life is paradise. As the current superintendent of schools for the Prattsburgh Central School District, I have the opportunity to witness amazing people selflessly serving this community on a daily basis. The incredible generosity, the tireless work ethic, the random acts of kindness in placing others before themselves, the pride in traditions, and the loyalty to the Prattsburgh name are evident to anyone who participates in life in our community.

As Prattsburgh enters its third century, the future is very bright. The sense of patriotism toward our country is represented in our local values. As we use history's teachings to maintain our ideals, this small town with the big spirit will carry on and succeed. In the midst of challenging times, this town will move forward and not only survive, but also continue as a model to other communities as we work together and take care of each other on a daily basis.

As you journey through this commemorative book, enjoy the documented memories and proud history of the past 200 years. And remember that Prattsburgh is not just a place, but also a way of life!

Respectfully,
Joseph L. Rumsey
Superintendent of Schools
Prattsburgh Central School District

One

Home is Where the Heart Is

When the first settlers came to Prattsburgh, there was nothing here but vast forests. They came on foot or by oxen cart, carrying with them all the possessions they had. With a lot of hard work and determination, they began to build dwellings and a new life. Their first homes were basic log shelters, which utilized the ample natural resources at hand.

As the town grew, so too did the desire to build homes suited to raising families and living comfortable lives. The homes featured here offer a sampling of the outstanding craftsmanship displayed by the town's fathers. Each home was essentially a showcase for the person building it, displaying artful details such as vast open staircases, finely detailed woodwork, and intricately plastered ceilings.

Most of these homes have stood the test of time, providing Prattsburgh's current residents with an important connection to their history. As a tribute to these adventurous families, this book offers a glimpse of their accomplishments.

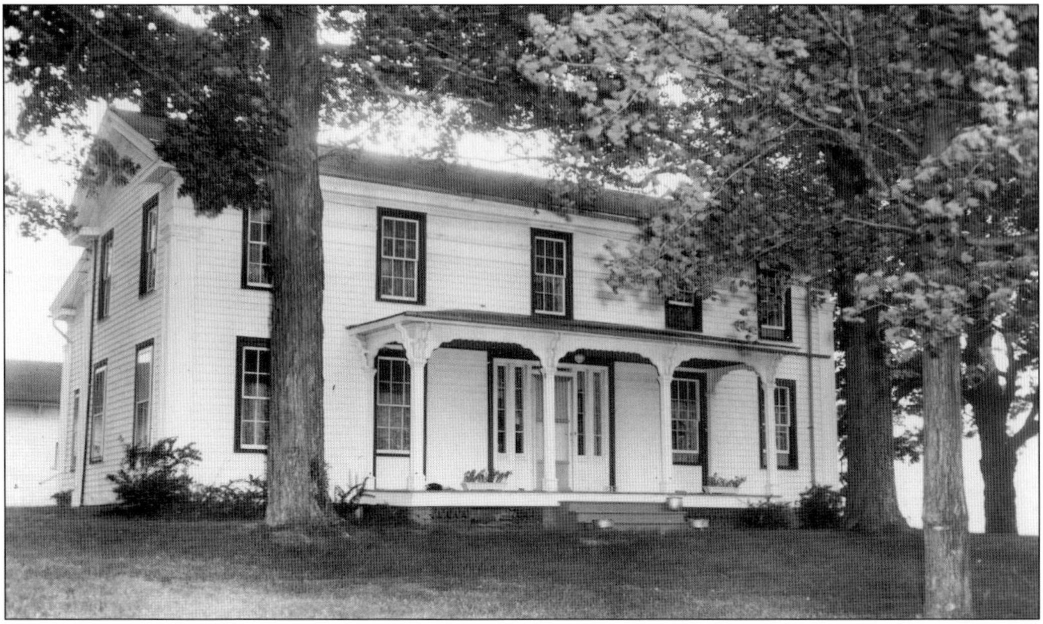

Capt. Joel Pratt purchased the town in 1802 from the Pulteney estate, moving his family here in 1805 to live in a small cabin. The town was officially established in 1813 and named for Captain Pratt. He built this home in 1817 on what is now State Route 53, where he lived with his wife, Mary, daughter Anna, and five sons, Elisha, Harvey, Joel Jr., Ira, and Dan. Pratt's descendants lived in the same home until 1936.

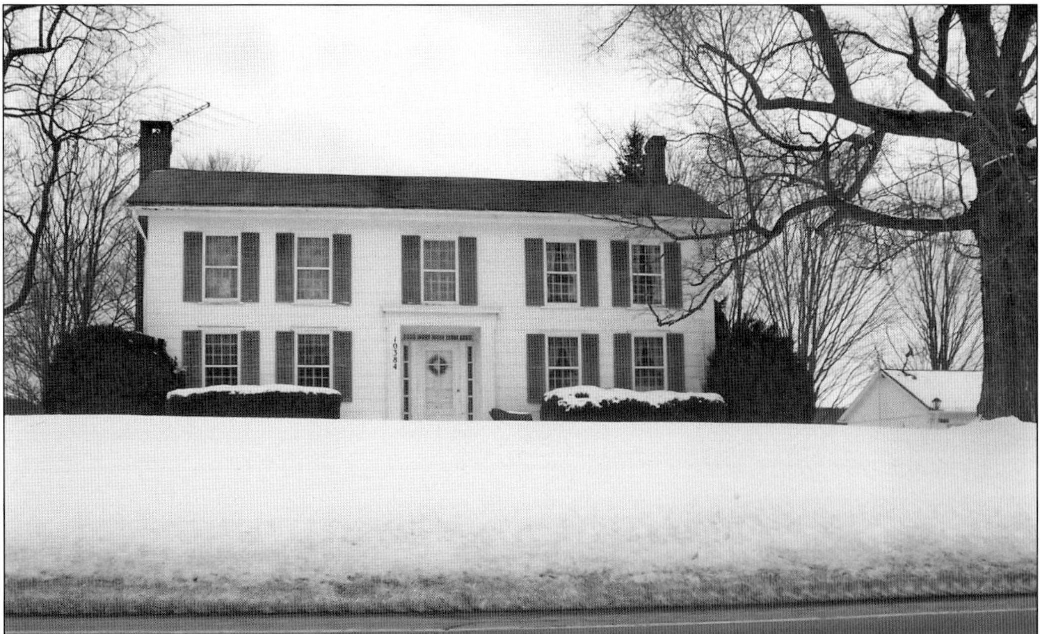

Jared Pratt, Prattsburgh's first settler and nephew to Capt. Joel Pratt, built this house on State Route 53. It was the first permanent home to be built in the town. His daughter Marcella was the first white child to be born in Prattsburgh. Pratt's home was the site of the first religious service held in Prattsburgh, by Rev. John Niles.

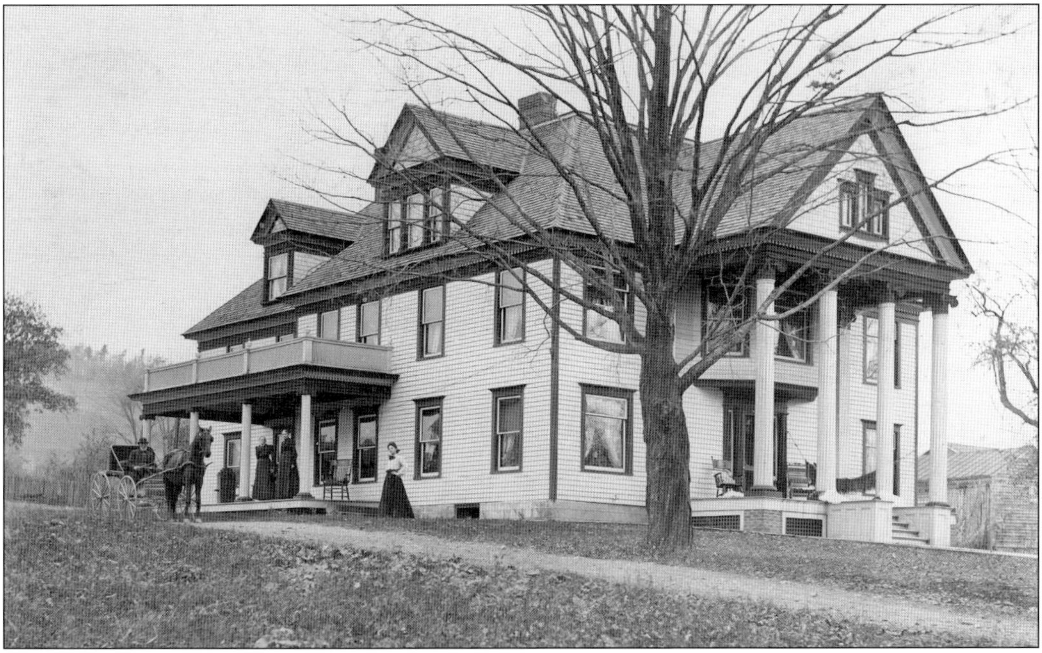

Built by John Ringrose, this was the home of Joel Pratt Jr., son of Capt. Joel Pratt. There was a sawmill in back of the barn. The lumber for the house came from this mill. The mill also did custom sawing and used a steam engine for power. Joel Pratt Jr. was the town's first supervisor in 1814.

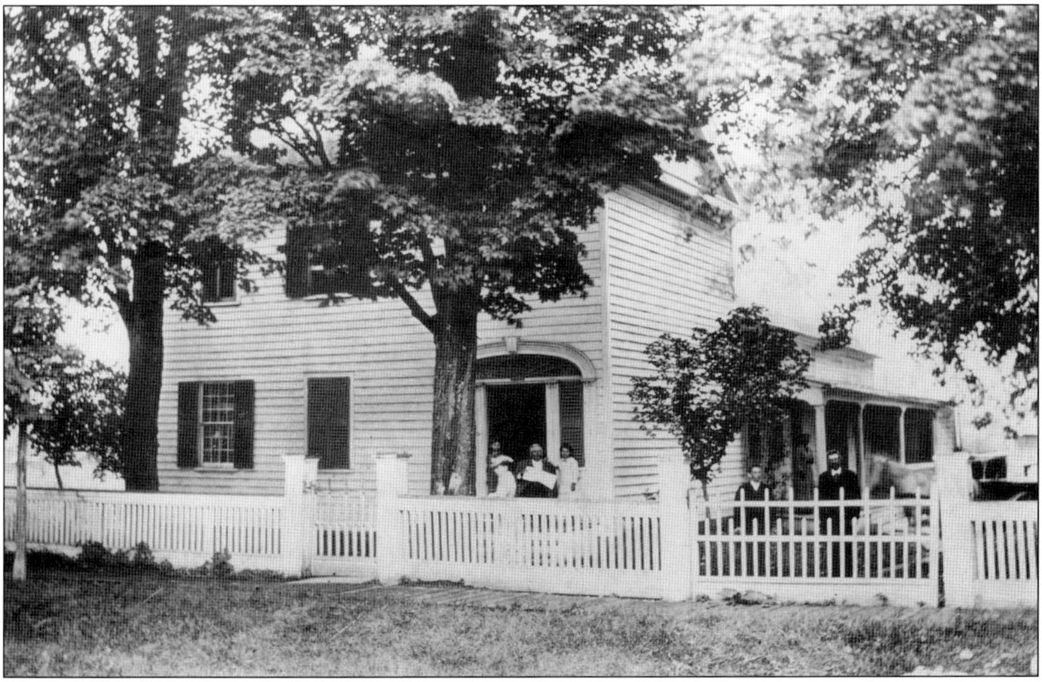

Carpenter Stephen Prentiss, Narcissa Prentiss's father, built this house on North Main Street in 1828. It was a wedding gift from Capt. Joel Pratt to his daughter Anna Pratt for her marriage to Burrage Rice. Paul Cook Howe, the editor of the *Prattsburgh News*, later occupied the home.

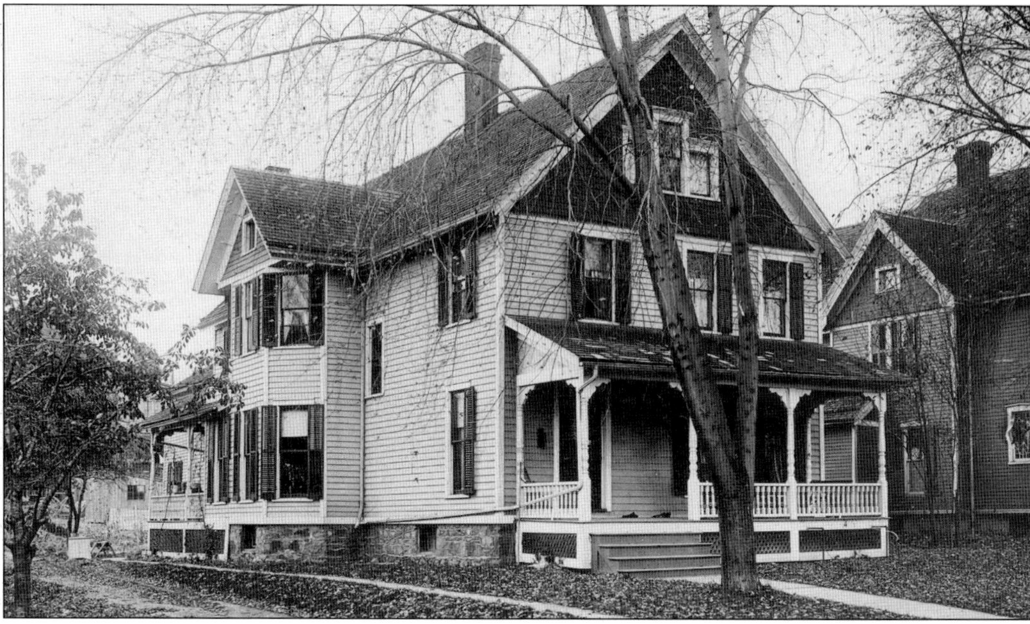

William B. Pratt, grandson of Elisha Pratt, built this house at 74 South Main Street in 1893. William B. Pratt was an officer of the Prattsburgh State Bank and on a committee of the Prattsburgh Fair Association. He also was chairman of the first committee considering the building of a railroad between Prattsburgh and Kanona.

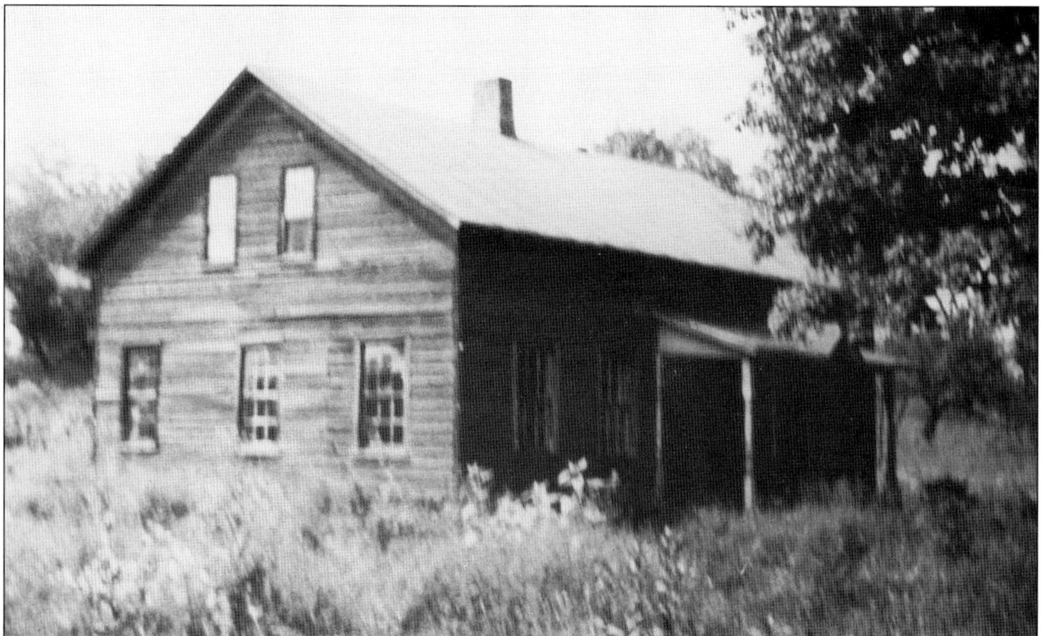

Built in 1805 by Judge Stephen and Clarissa Ward Prentiss, this is the home where Narcissa Prentiss was born in 1808. It was a small, one-and-a-half-story home where Narcissa lived along with her eight other siblings. Narcissa eventually married Dr. Marcus Whitman and became one of the first white women to cross the Rockies. Tragically, Narcissa and her husband were massacred at the hands of the Cayuse Indians while doing missionary work.

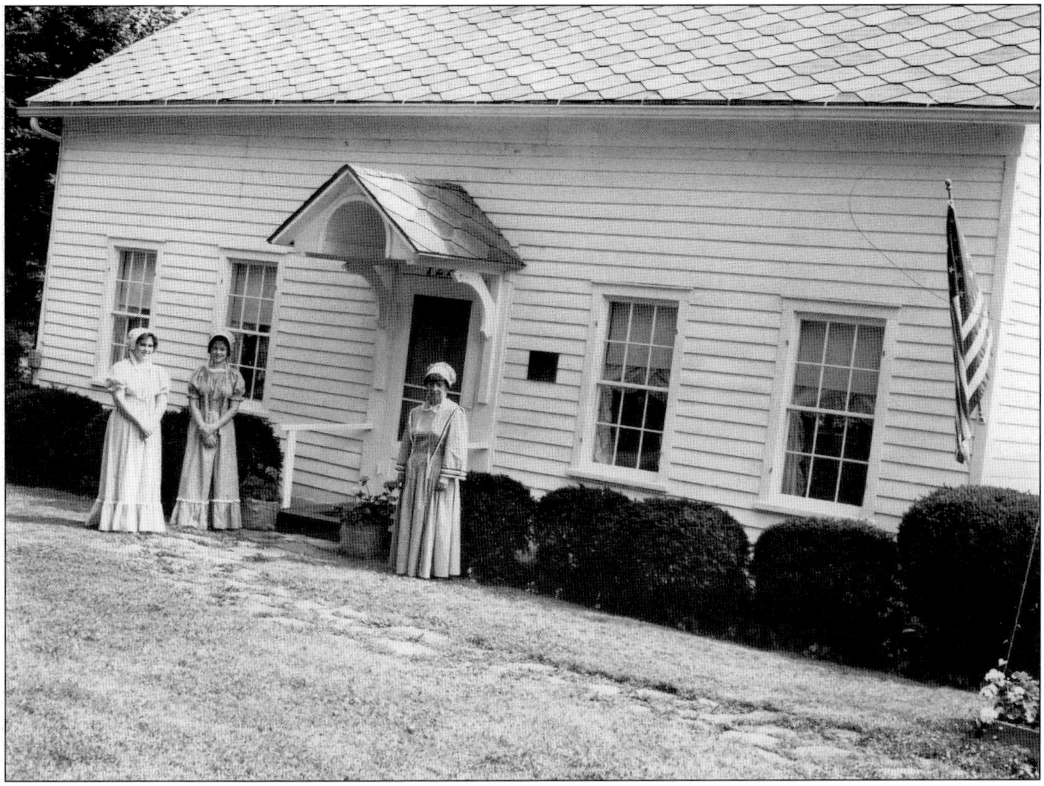

The Prentiss house originally was on the corner of Routes 74 and 75. It was moved to its present location so another home could be built on the corner by a Mr. Higby. A visit to this local landmark allows visitors the opportunity to become acquainted with one of America's most fascinating and ultimately tragic couples, Narcissa and Marcus Whitman. The house is open to the public seasonally for tours.

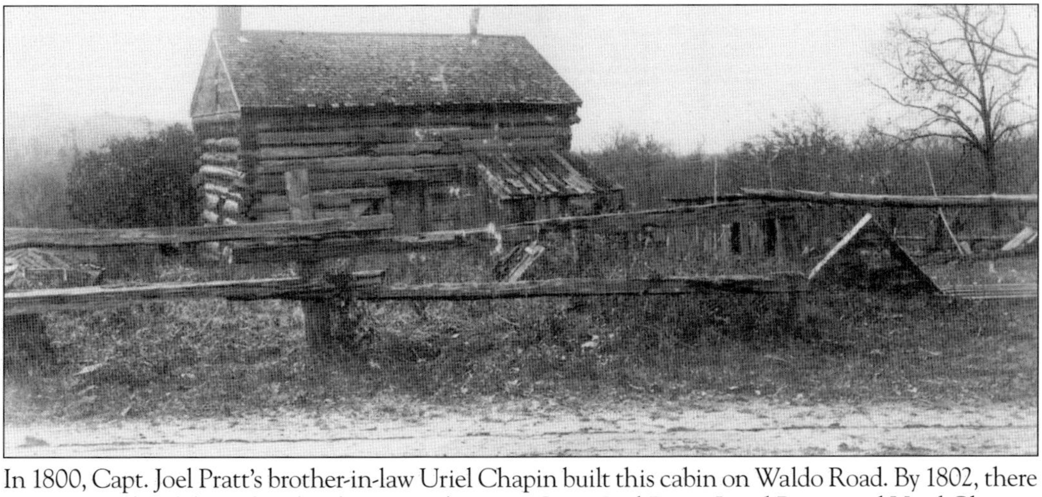

In 1800, Capt. Joel Pratt's brother-in-law Uriel Chapin built this cabin on Waldo Road. By 1802, there was a triangle of three families living in the area, Capt. Joel Pratt, Jared Pratt, and Uriel Chapin. The rest of the area that would eventually become Prattsburgh was still virgin wilderness.

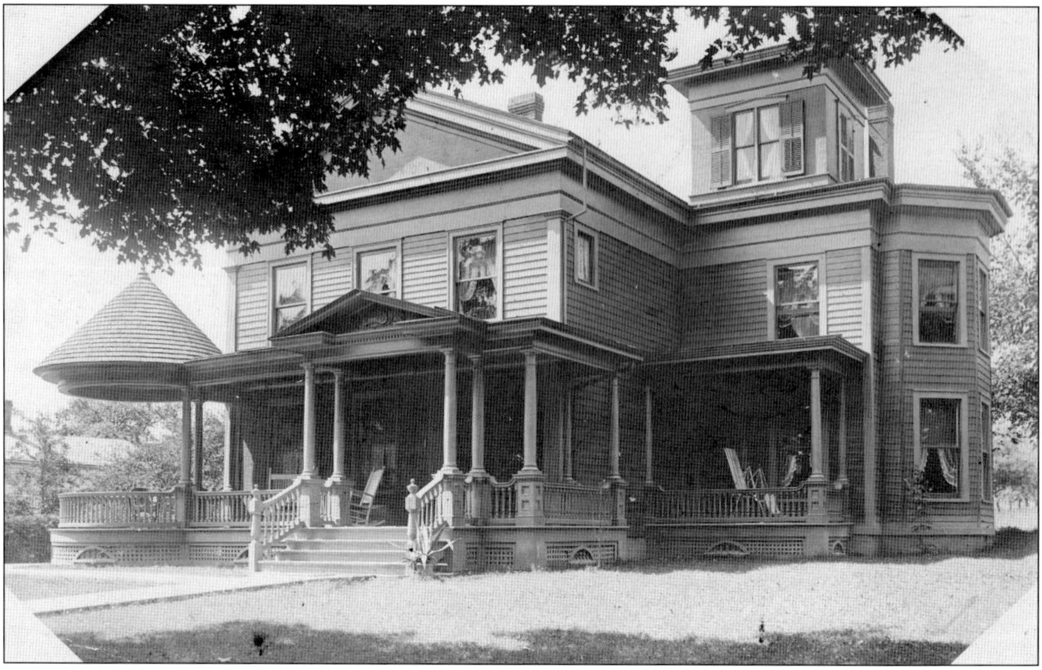

Originally belonging to the Van Valkenburgh family, this house was located at the corner of Main and Chapel Streets. Martin Pinney purchased land so he could build his big brick house and sold this house to W.F. McLean. McLean then moved it to 54 South Main Street, which is where it sits to this day. McLean was president of the bank. The house was heated by steam and had hot and cold running water with a lavatory and toilet on the first and second floors. It also boasted a billiard room on the second floor. (Courtesy of Stacy Bottoni.)

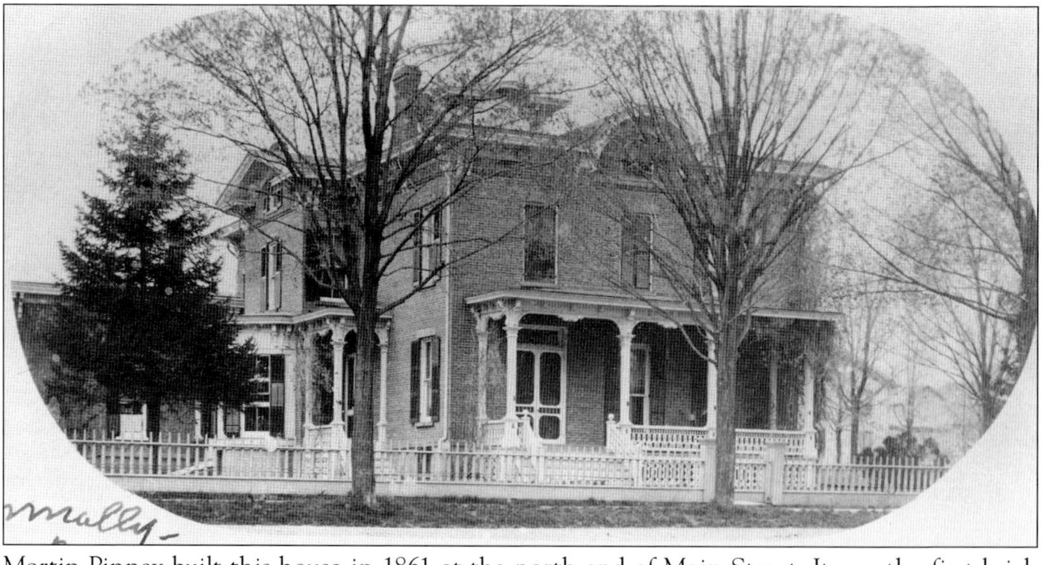

Martin Pinney built this house in 1861 at the north end of Main Street. It was the first brick building constructed in the village. The original house on this lot was partly moved to South Main Street. Pinney had a store in the front and lived in the back apartment. Years later, this building became the post office for the town. The building was torn down to make way for the grocery store.

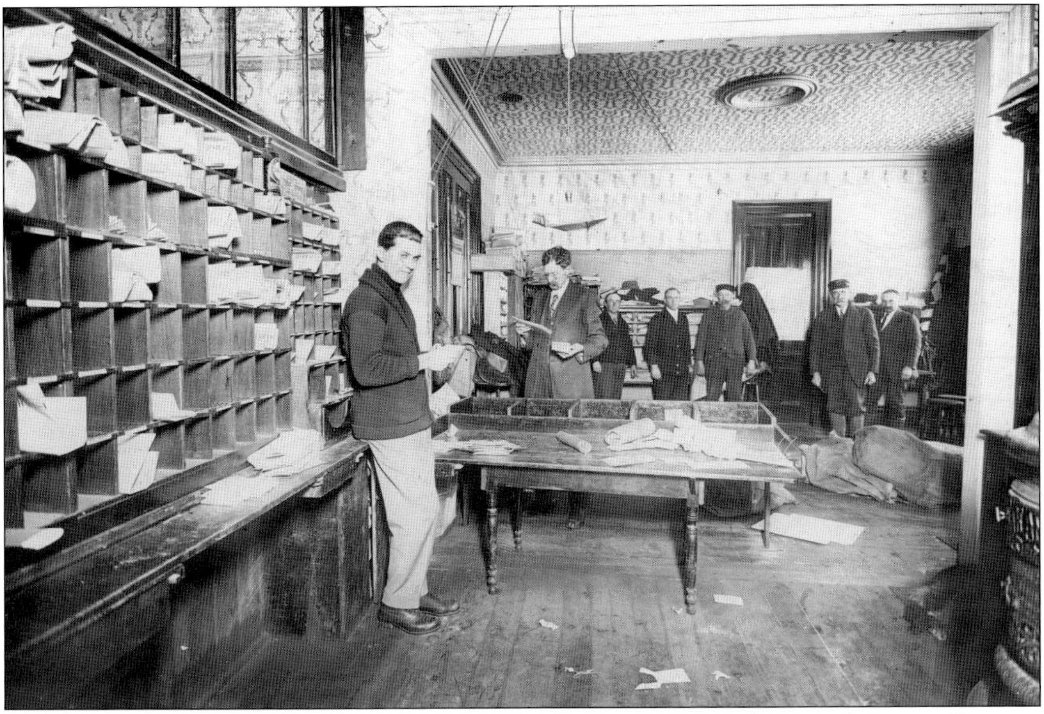

The Prattsburgh Post Office was once located in the Martin Pinney house. This post office was established in 1824. Samuel Rice was the first postmaster. The post office was originally established in 1808 by postmaster Joel Pratt Jr. and was located in the Kremlin Building.

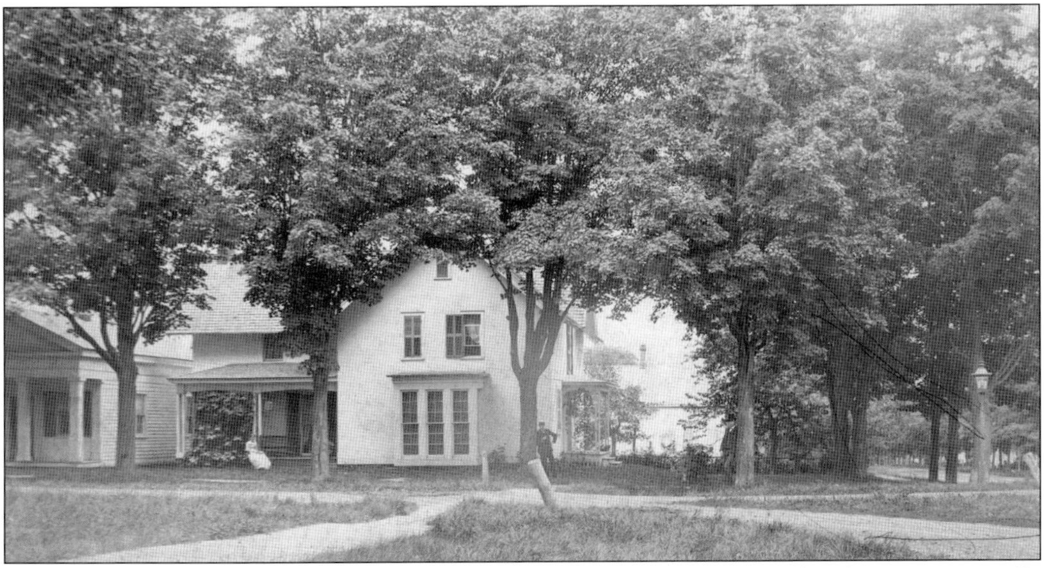

This house at 1 North Main Street was one of the first to be built in Prattsburgh. It was originally a log house, built by Henry Allis. Henry Allis donated land for what was to become Allis Street. Allis was not known for his work ethic and spent many a lazy afternoon fishing on his pond at the east end of Howe Street.

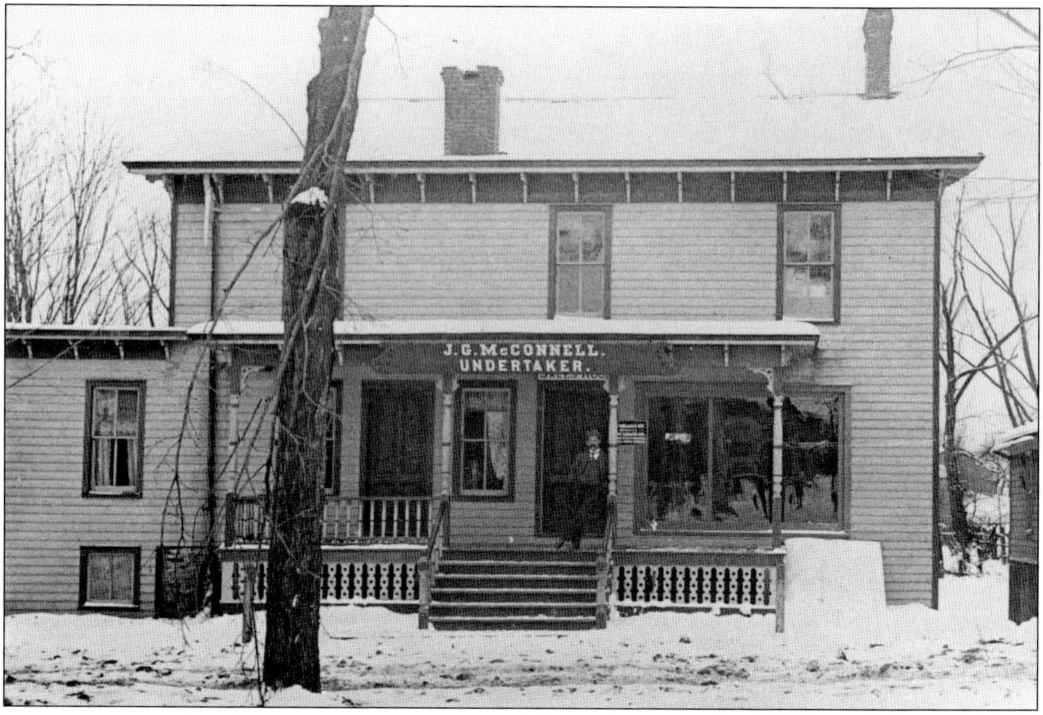

Known as the oldest house in Prattsburgh, the Old Red Shop on Mechanic Street was built in 1811 and part of it was used as a dwelling for the family of Erastus Skinner. It was later owned by Joseph G. McConnell, who ran it as a furniture store and funeral home.

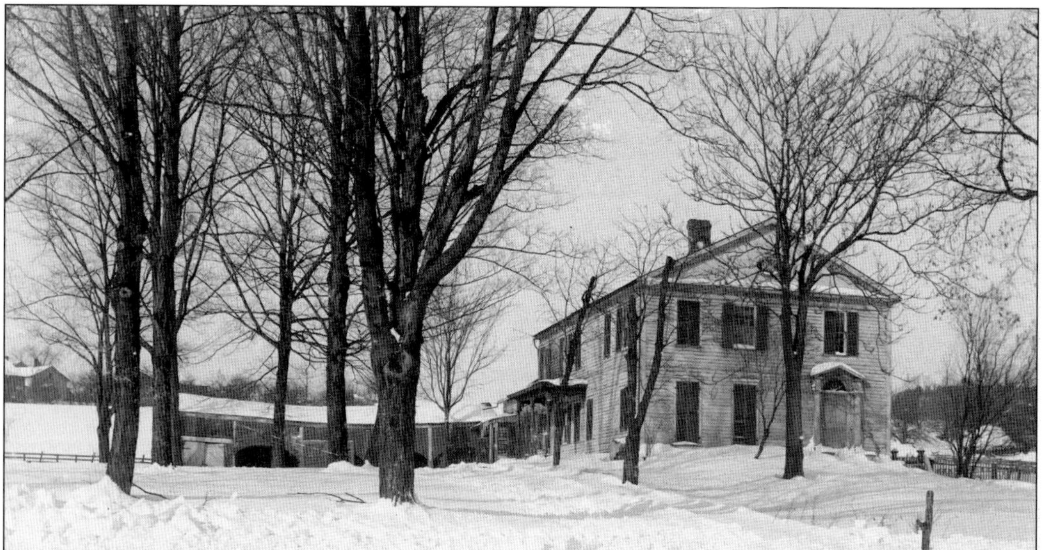

This house on North Main Street was completed in 1818 by Judge Robert Porter. It was the only painted house between Bath and Geneva, giving it the name "Lilly of the Valley." Highly educated, Porter came to Prattsburgh in 1806, buying up a large tract of land. He built the first gristmill in the area. The prominent Robert Porter held many elected positions in town and was eventually elected associated judge of Steuben in 1814. The home was moved farther north on Main Street around 1897 by horses and purchased by Edward Watkins.

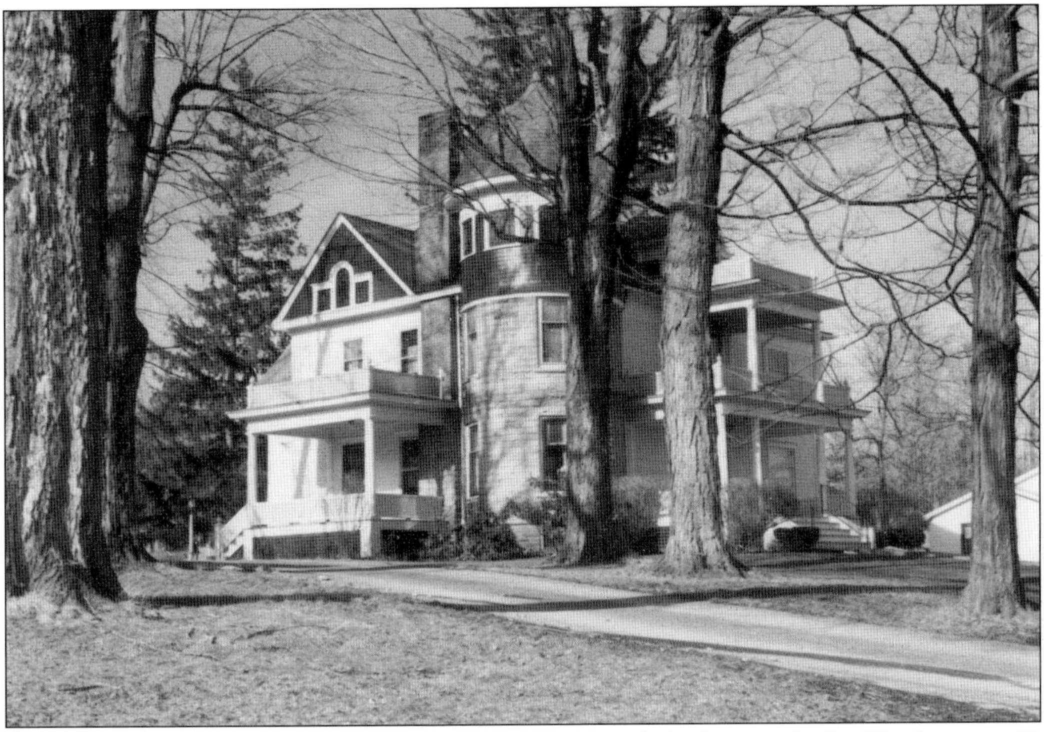

This house was built by William G. Dean in 1899 as a gift for his new bride. The house at 32 North Main Street was built in the Romanesque Villa style and features a castle-like tower, high roofs, and multiple porches. This rare style was promoted by outstanding architect Henry Holoson Richardson. William Dean was a director of the Prattsburgh State Bank in 1904.

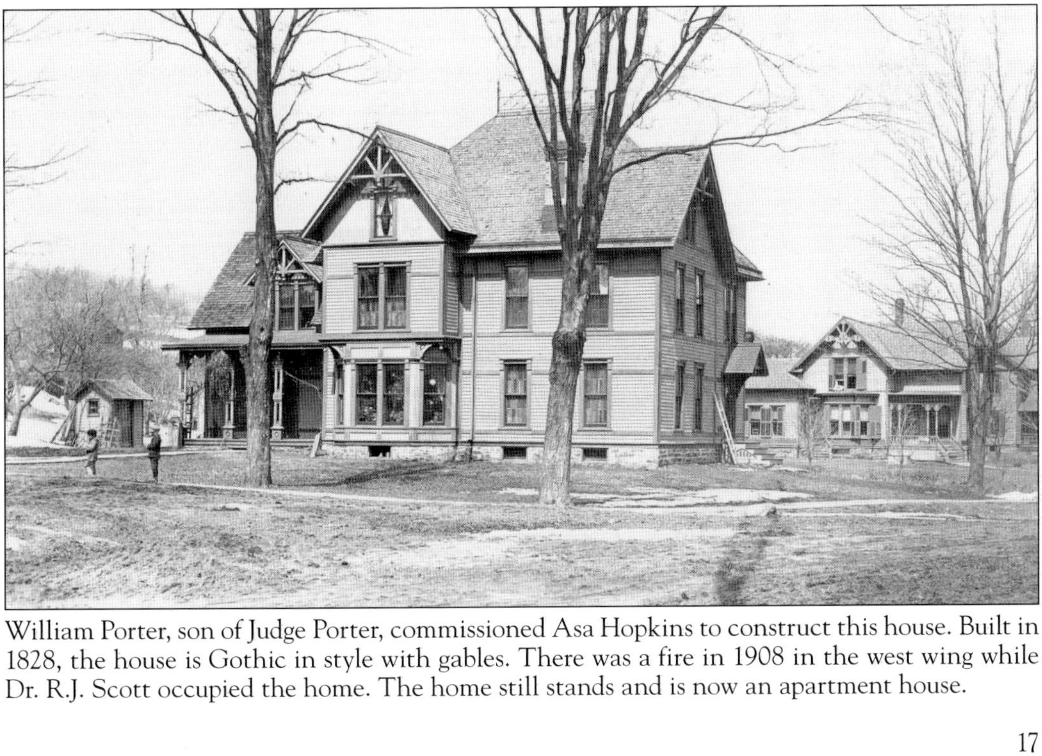

William Porter, son of Judge Porter, commissioned Asa Hopkins to construct this house. Built in 1828, the house is Gothic in style with gables. There was a fire in 1908 in the west wing while Dr. R.J. Scott occupied the home. The home still stands and is now an apartment house.

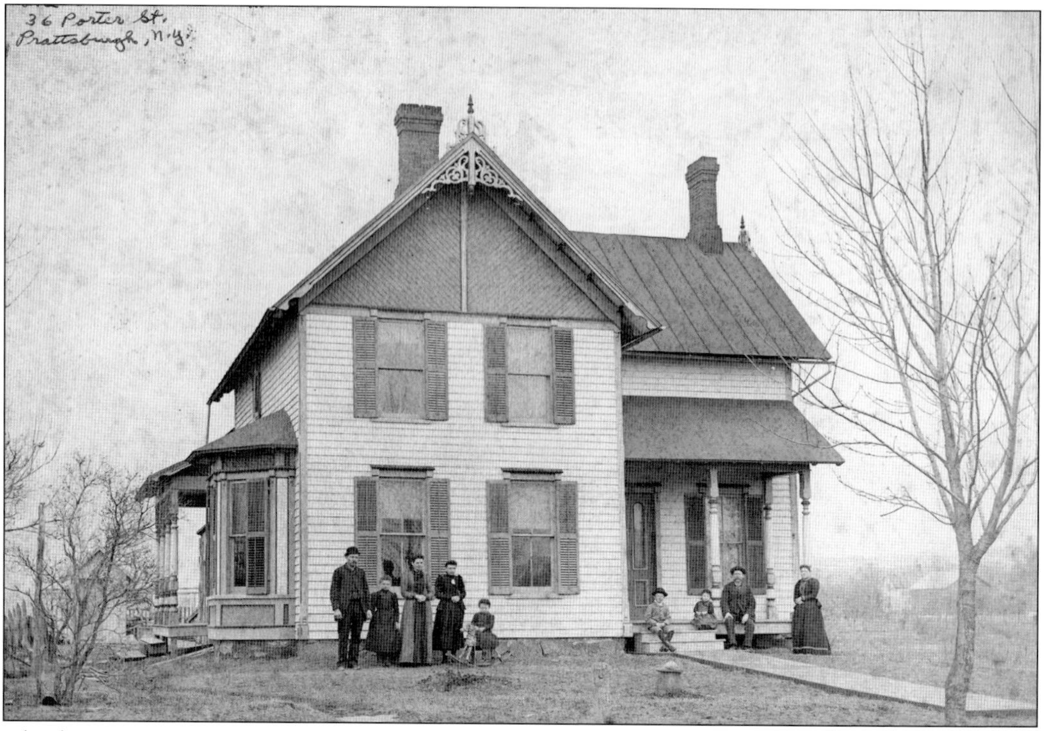

Charles Smith, a machinist, had a big shop out back of his home here. He was very talented and could make most anything people needed, including the steam engine that powered his shop and the boat, *The Wanderer*, he helped make. He was the inventor of a valve that would automatically close the flow of gas when fickle nature should see fit to suspend the supply. He had it patented and soon had an order for 2,000 valves. Prattsburgh businesses pledged money so that he could purchase the necessary machinery for the valves to be manufactured in Prattsburgh.

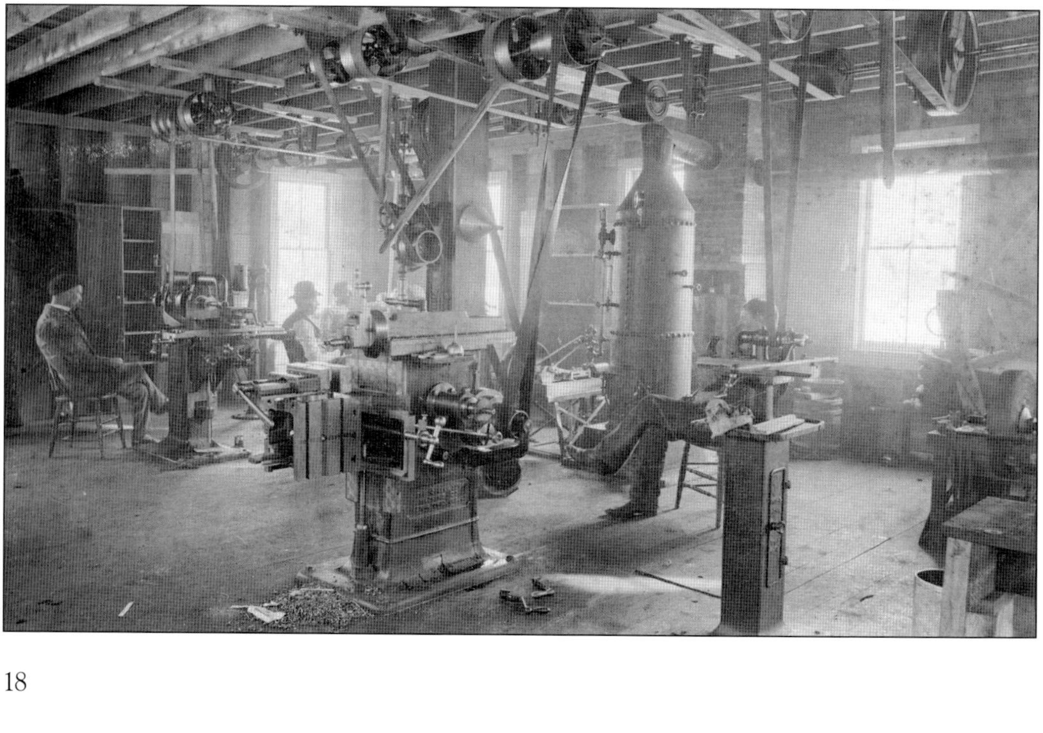

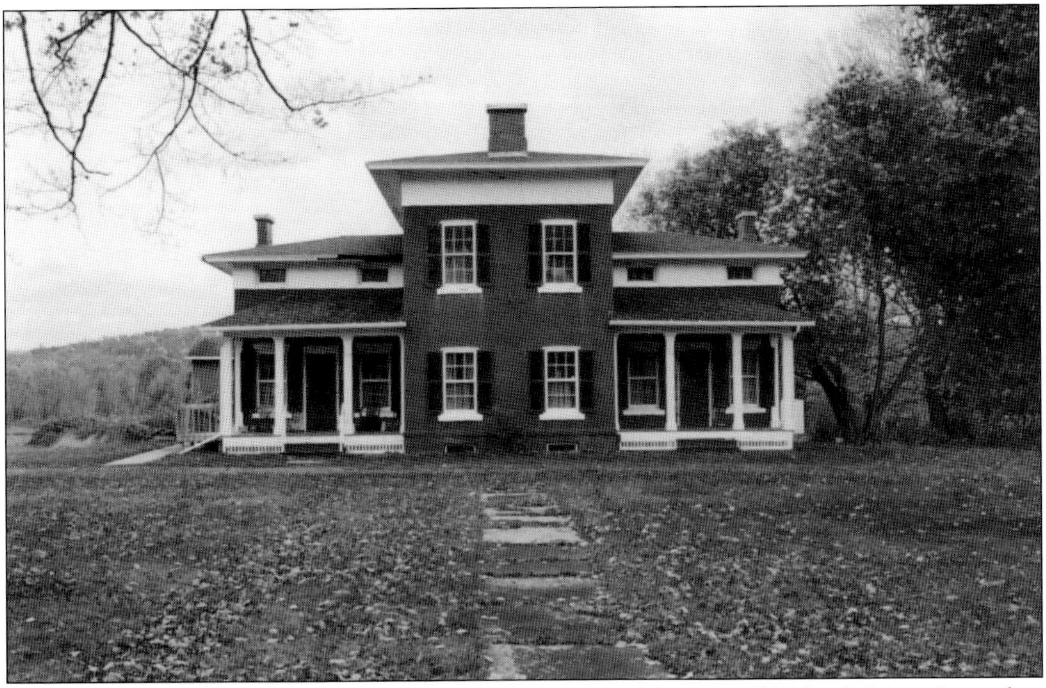

Built in 1834 by Otis Sheppard, this brick, Greek Revival house at 59 North Main Street has 12-inch-thick walls. The redbrick was shipped by way of the Great Lakes through canals to Pulteney Landing. From there, they were transported to Prattsburgh by an ox team.

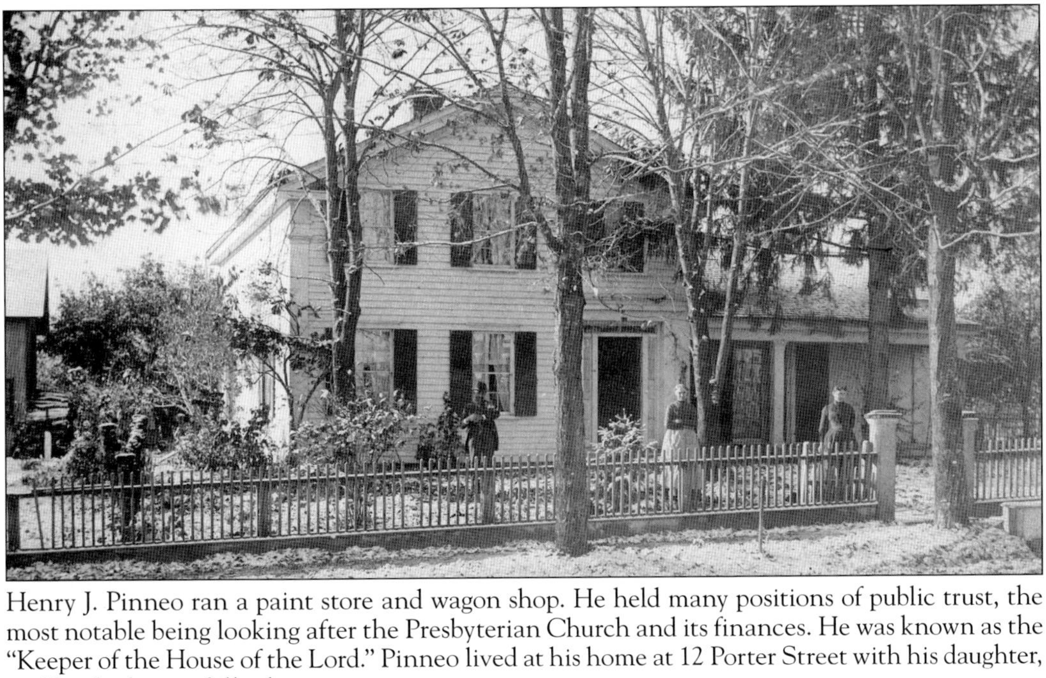

Henry J. Pinneo ran a paint store and wagon shop. He held many positions of public trust, the most notable being looking after the Presbyterian Church and its finances. He was known as the "Keeper of the House of the Lord." Pinneo lived at his home at 12 Porter Street with his daughter, and he died peacefully there.

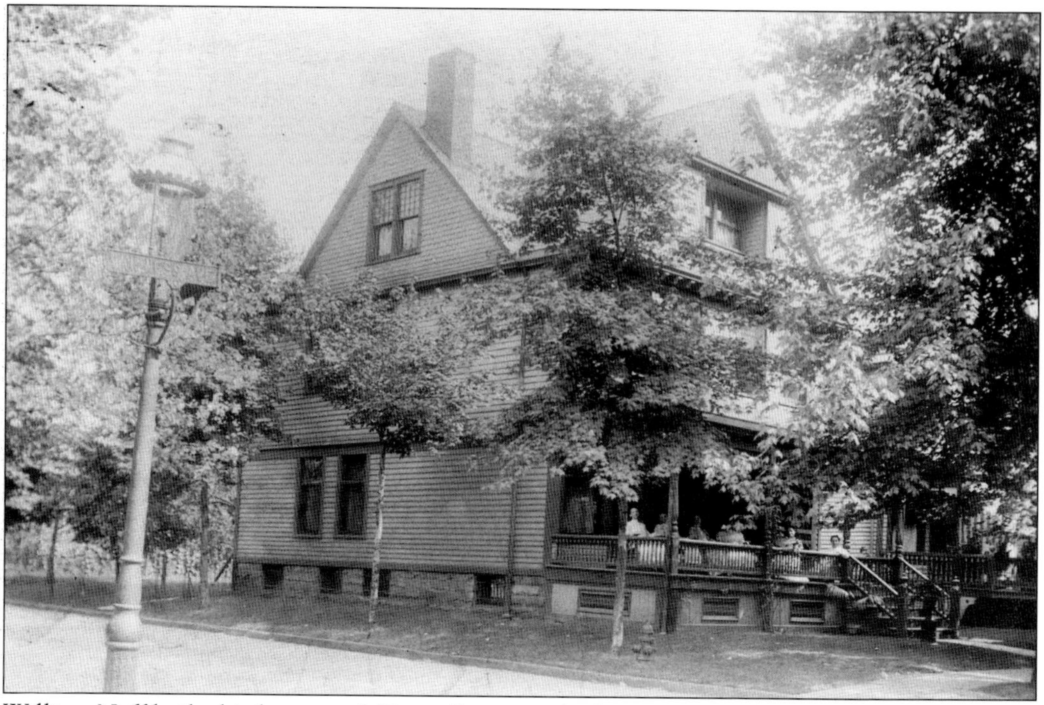

William Neff built this house at 9 Howe Street in the late 1890s for himself and later sold it to Jennie Wixom Howell, who lived there until her death. It was then sold to Floyd Braisted, who occupied it until 1946. William Neff was a well-known carpenter, as evidenced by this house. Neff built many of the other homes in Prattsburgh.

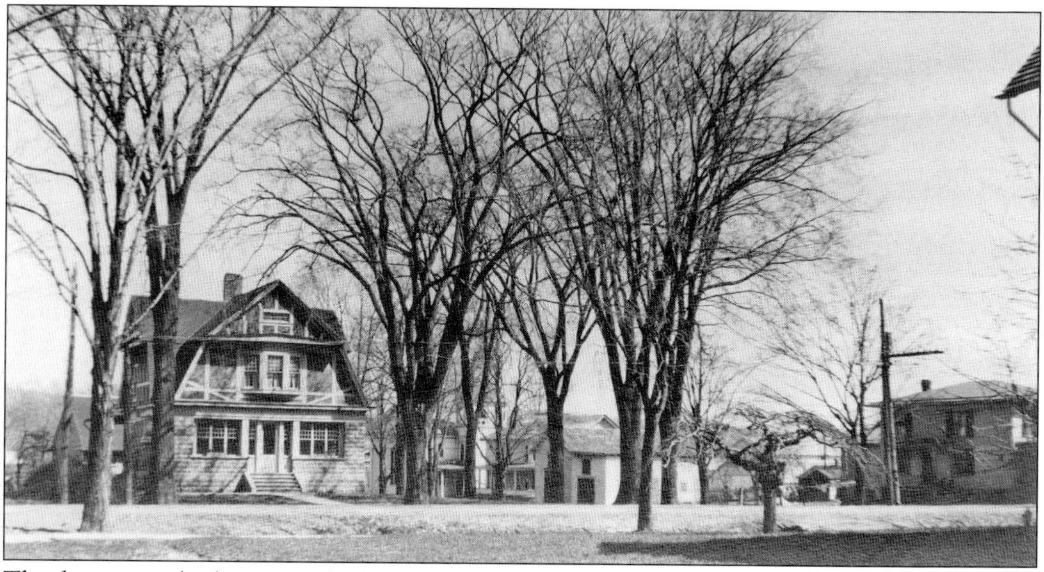

This house was built in 1909 by local druggist George E. Hayes on 27 North Main Street. He originally lived next door but sold that to Samuel Hayes after building this new home.

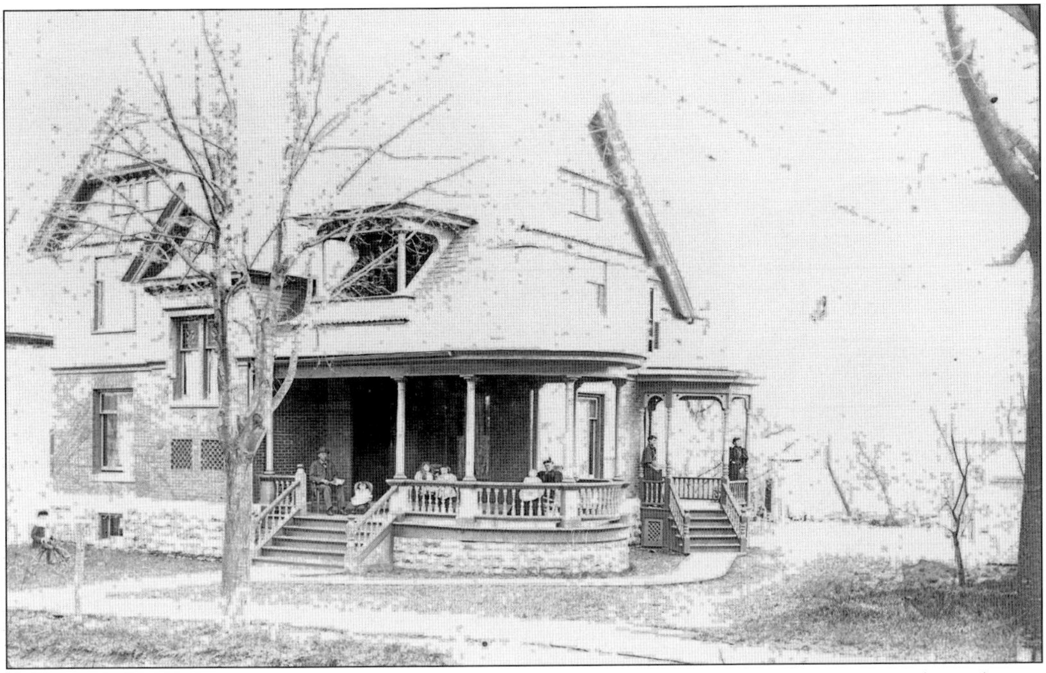

This house was built in 1897 for the chef at the local hotel on the corner of Main and Mechanic Streets. The Currans were of Irish descent. The original house on that site was moved to the lower end of Mechanic Street and is now known as the Beamish house.

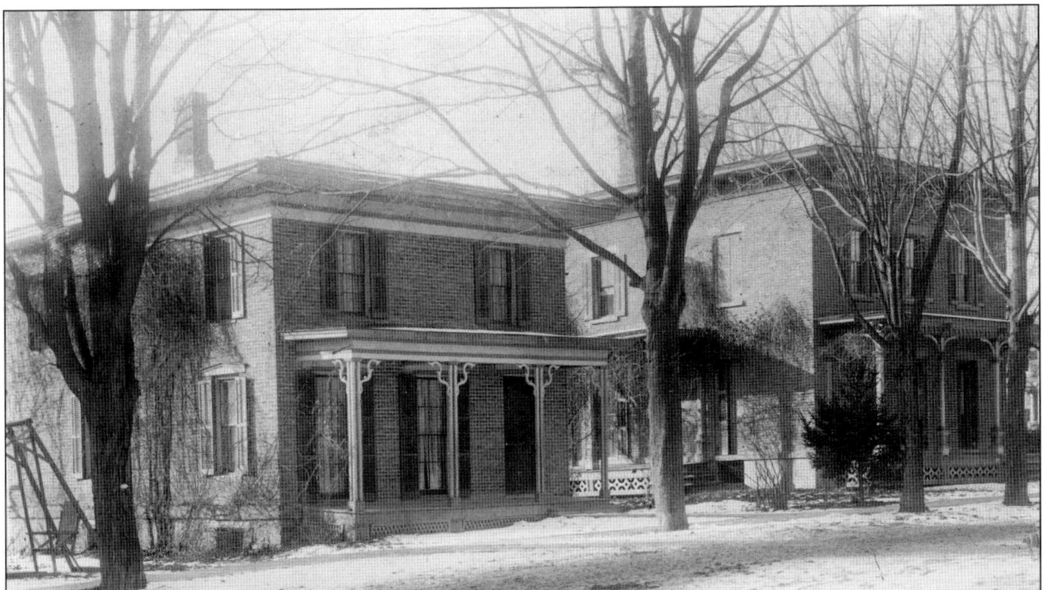

This brick house, located at 8 Mechanic Street, was built in the early 1800s by George Ainsworth. He operated a store out of the home. In 1862, the Methodist Church bought it, and it was used as a church until 1867. At that time, a fire at a next-door foundry damaged it. It is once again restored to a residence, with the Culpepper Mercantile store operating out of the first floor.

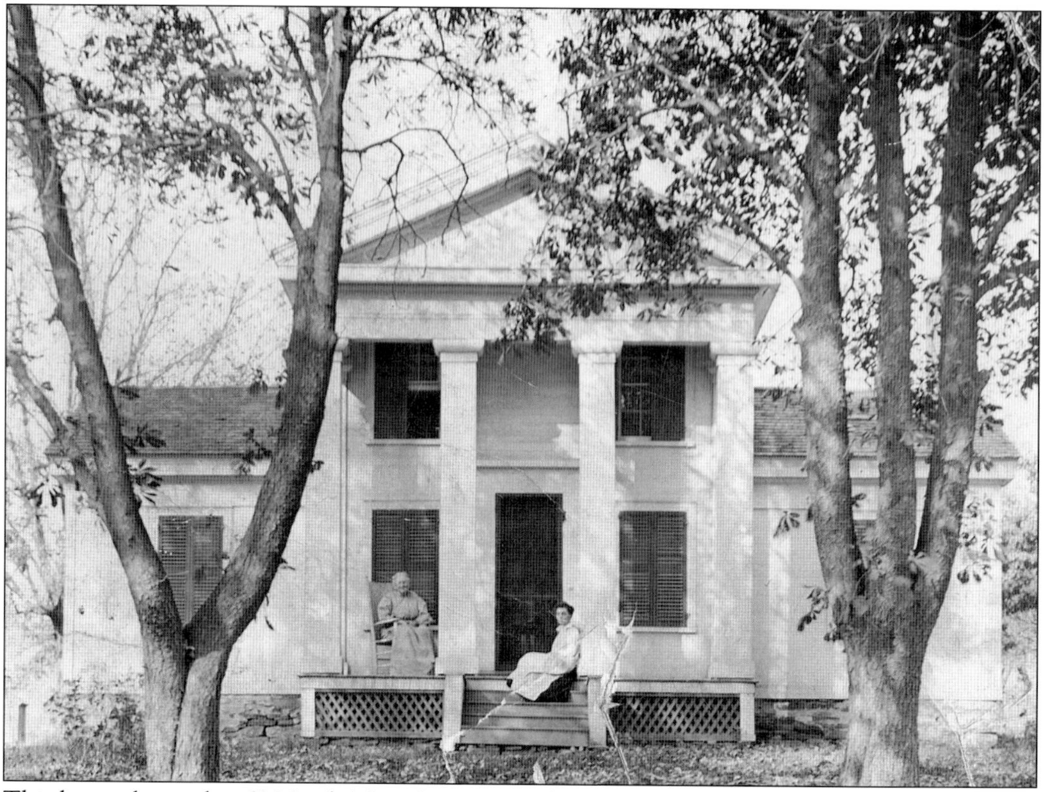

This home, located at 68 North Main Street, was the homestead of Holland Clark Horton, who was born in 1872 and died in 1938. An inscription on the wall of the cellar forever acknowledges his original ownership of the home. Horton is buried at the Prattsburgh Rural Cemetery.

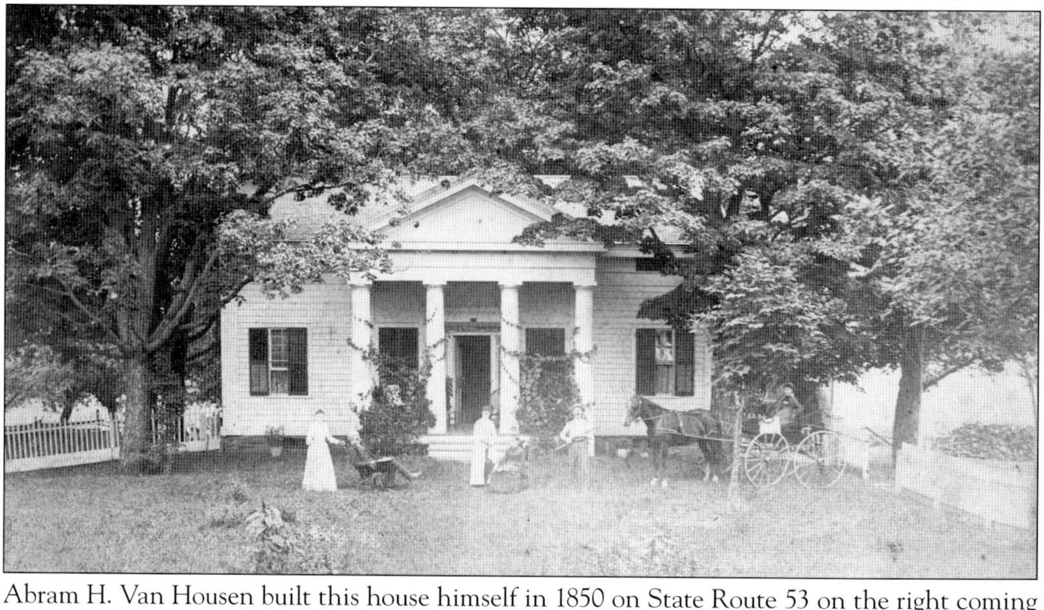

Abram H. Van Housen built this house himself in 1850 on State Route 53 on the right coming into Prattsburgh. Over the course of time, this house has been many things, like a beauty shop and a Kubota dealership.

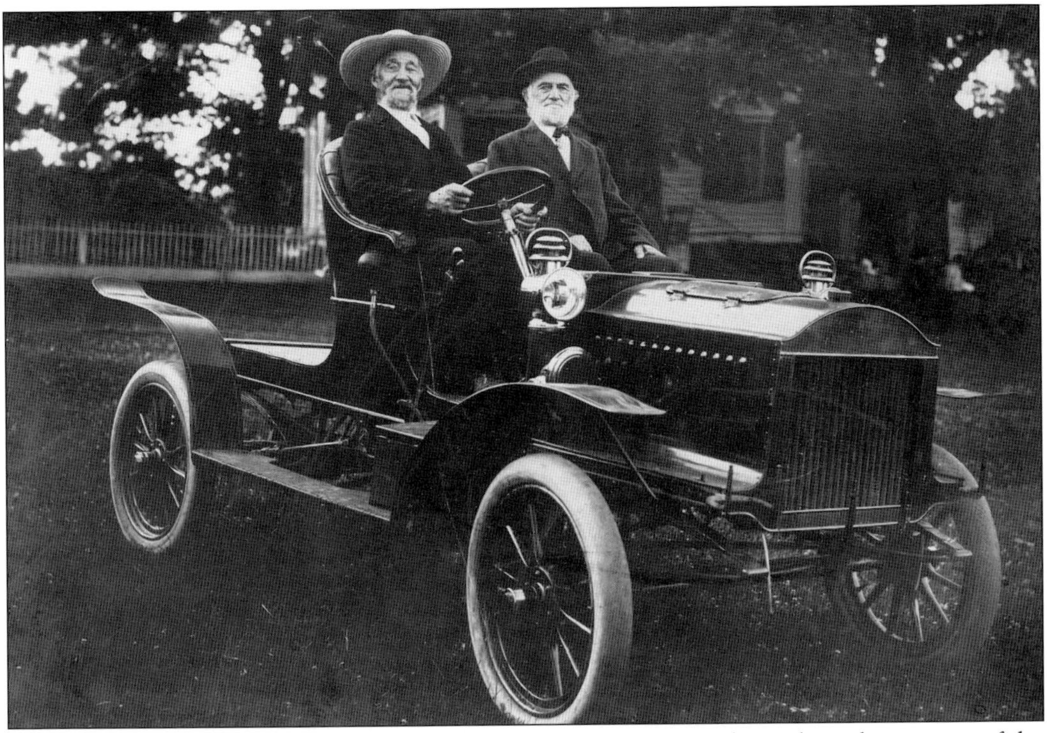

Abram Van Housen was one of the directors of the railroad. He is shown here driving one of the first automobiles in Prattsburgh.

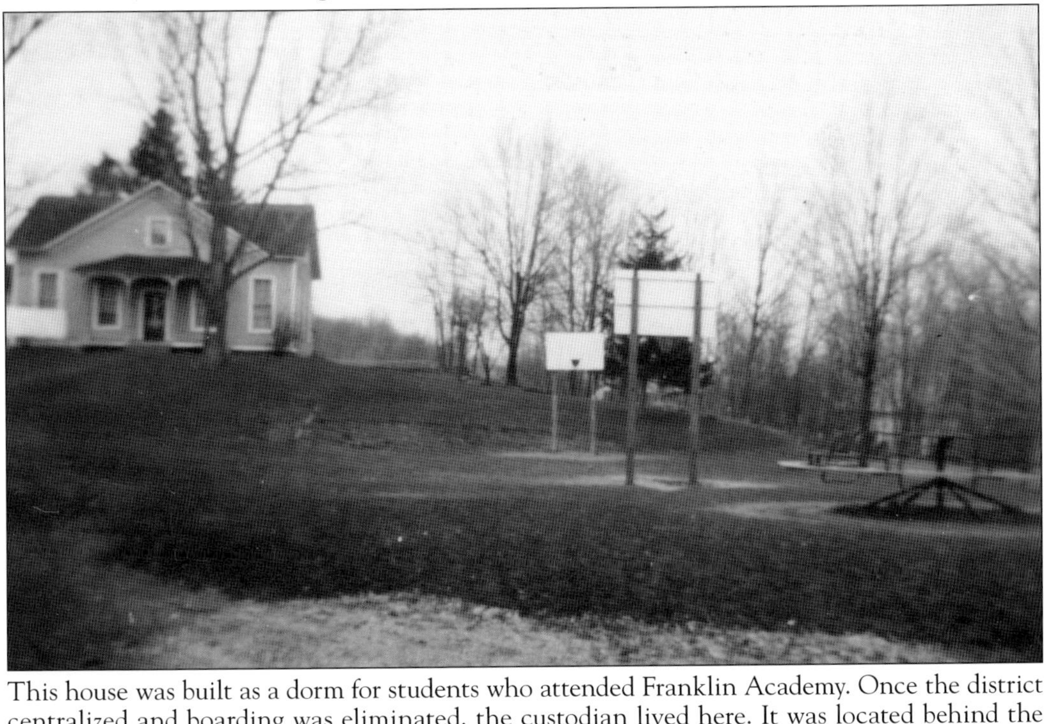

This house was built as a dorm for students who attended Franklin Academy. Once the district centralized and boarding was eliminated, the custodian lived here. It was located behind the school but was torn down to make room for the addition to school in 1958.

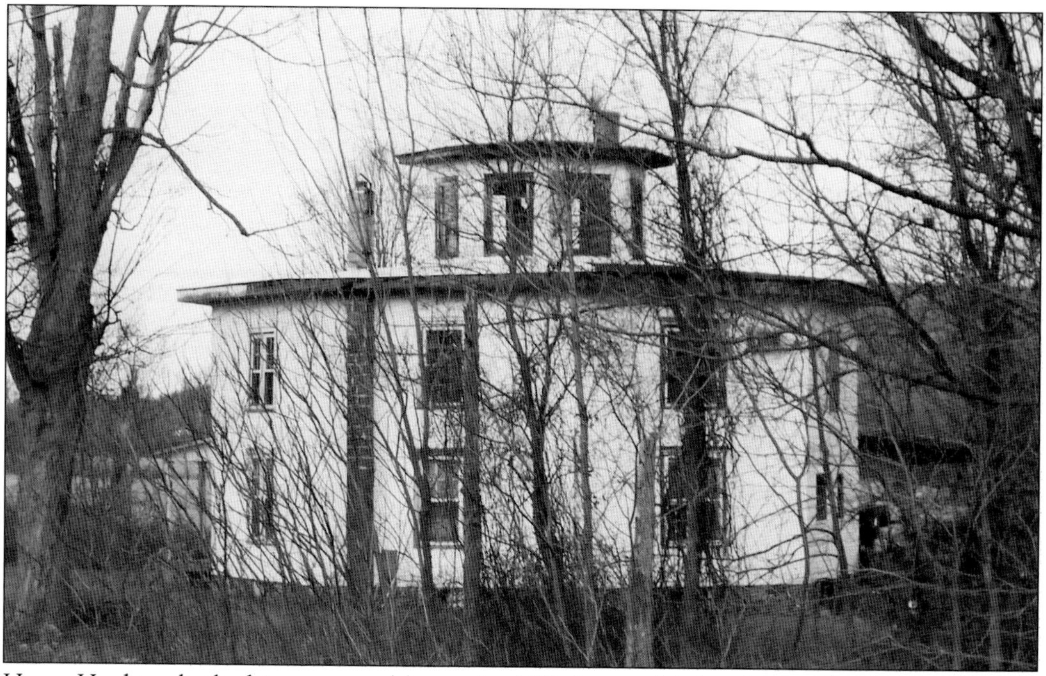

Harry Hopkins built this octagonal house in 1852. Located 1.5 miles south of town on State Route 53, the home also shared space with a sawmill and a gristmill. Local legend has it that the house was a stop on the Underground Railroad during the Civil War. The railroad ran close to the back of the house. Hopkins built the town clock at the Presbyterian church largely by hand at his sawmill on the same site.

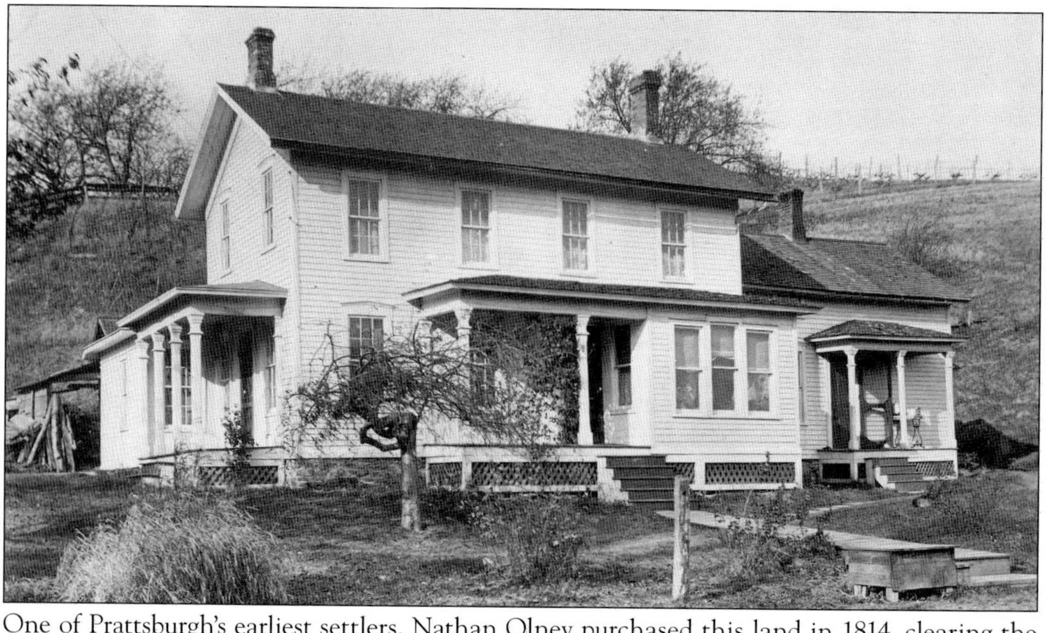

One of Prattsburgh's earliest settlers, Nathan Olney purchased this land in 1814, clearing the way for a good-sized farm. Olney donated part of the land to the school district, where the Block Schoolhouse still stands today. Nathan Olney was the great-grandfather of Henry "Cad" Olney, the town's postmaster in the 1930s and 1940s.

Two

Churches and Cemeteries

Religion was very important to the early settlers. Prattsburgh namesake Capt. Joel Pratt stipulated in the sale of land that $15 per every 100 acres be placed into a fund to support a minister in town. Through this effort, Prattsburgh was able to obtain the Reverend John Niles, a prominent minister, to provide religious services even before the town was officially established. This early church was known as the Congregational Church and laid the foundation for a strong community commitment to religion. As the population grew, so too did the variety of religious denominations and subsequently the churches to serve them. Prattsburgh continues to support several church congregations within its borders.

As in any community, there is a need to establish a final resting place for deceased loved ones. Some of the cemeteries were small family plots, and others grew from the affiliated churches. Prattsburgh currently has 13 cemeteries, including eight small family burial plots.

In 1954, the care and upkeep of the cemeteries became the responsibility of the Prattsburgh Town Board, thus ensuring that these places be properly maintained long after the loved ones of the deceased have also passed away. Walking through these cemeteries helps acquaint visitors with those who came before and paved the way for all that is enjoyed today.

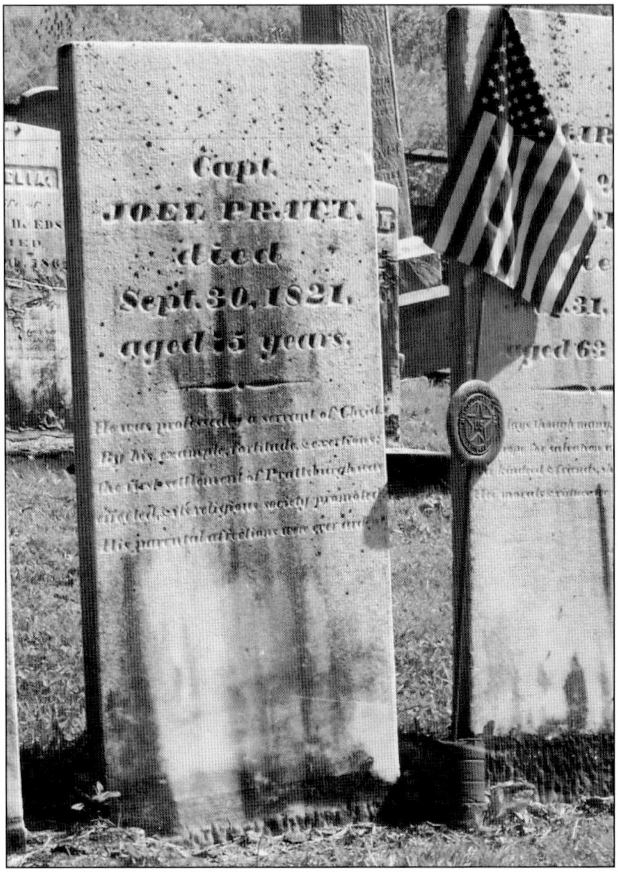

Capt. Joel Pratt deserves all the credit for helping to establish a religious society in Prattsburgh. Pratt died in 1821 at the age of 75. Captain Pratt is laid to rest in Pioneer Cemetery beside his wife, Mary, and son Harvey on land he donated for that purpose.

Capt. Joel Pratt donated an acre of land to be used for burials when his son Harvey died. This land, known as the Pioneer Cemetery, was utilized between 1806 and 1860. In 1860, four additional acres were purchased, and lots sold for $4 each. The cemetery was eventually turned over to the Rural Cemetery Association.

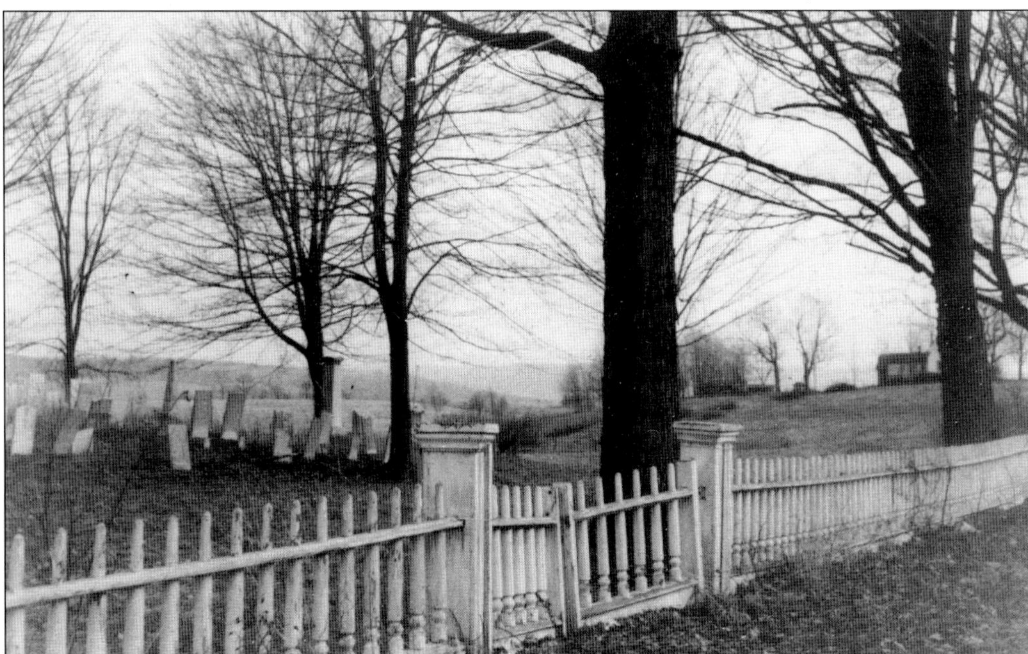

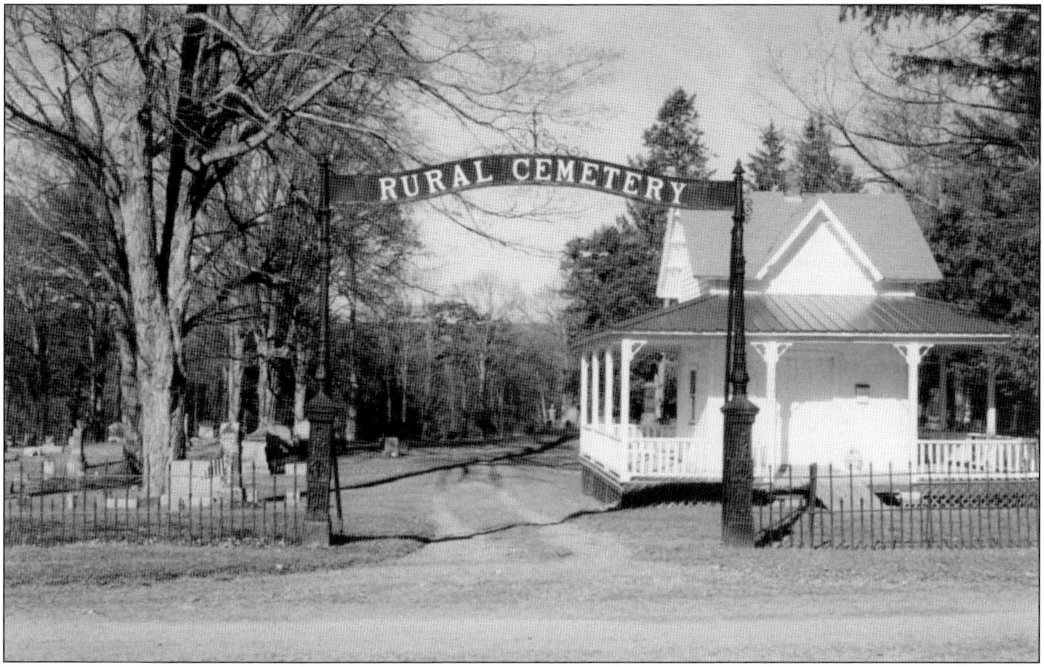

The Prattsburgh Rural Cemetery, located on County Route 75, was established by the Rural Cemetery Association to accommodate the growing need for more burial space. The Rural Cemetery Association maintained it until the town took it over in 1954. The iron gate and arch were purchased in 1914 for $149. In 1947, a plot of land was donated to the Frances T. Flaherty American Legion Post for the burial of veterans and their spouses.

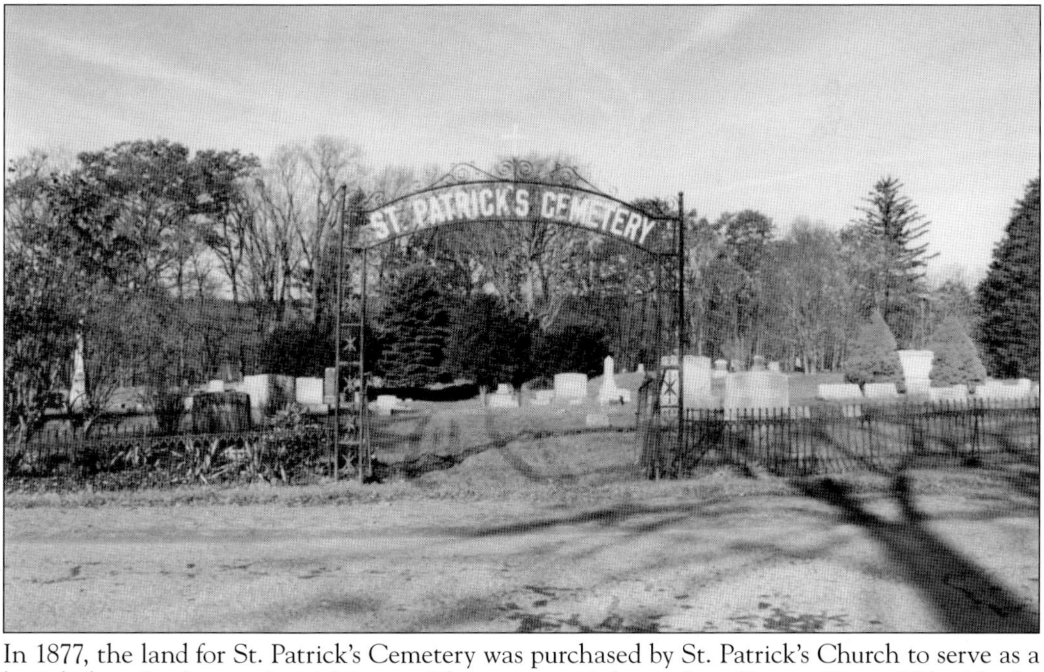

In 1877, the land for St. Patrick's Cemetery was purchased by St. Patrick's Church to serve as a burial place for deceased parishioners. The cemetery is located on County Route 75 beside the Rural Cemetery.

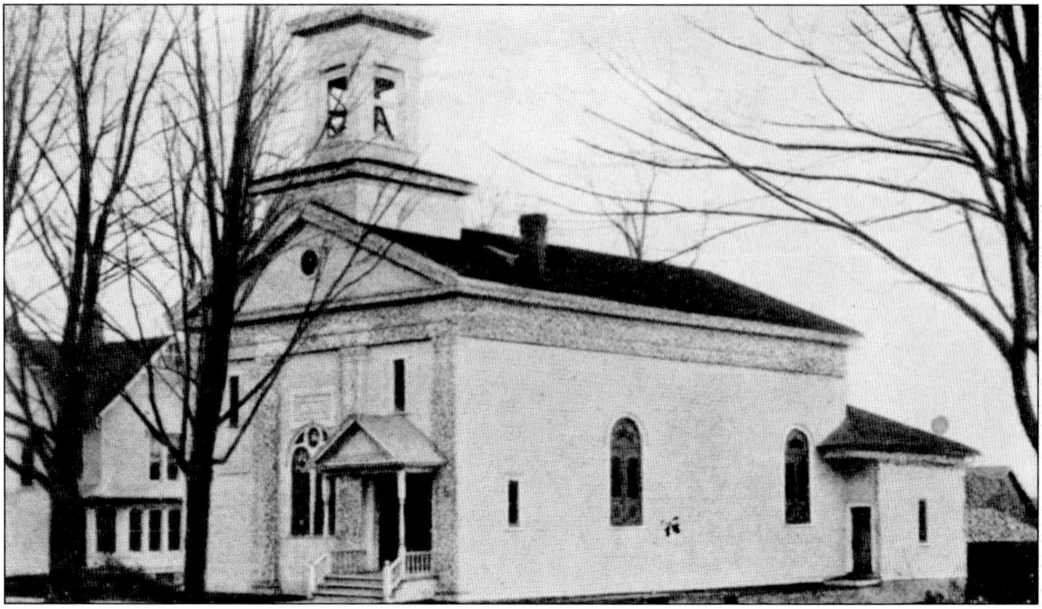

The Old Baptist Church of Prattsburgh was organized on West Hill and was mainly composed of members formerly belonging to the Baptist Church of Wheeler. In 1822, a log cabin meetinghouse was built and sheltered a devoted congregation for 11 years until it was destroyed by fire. A few years after, a new building was erected; the membership divided into four parts, with one part coming to the village of Prattsburgh. This church, known as the Prattsburgh Baptist Church, is the only Baptist church that remains of the four. It was organized in 1842, and the present house of worship, shown here, was built in 1845. Through the years, the church has seen many renovations, and the membership has varied.

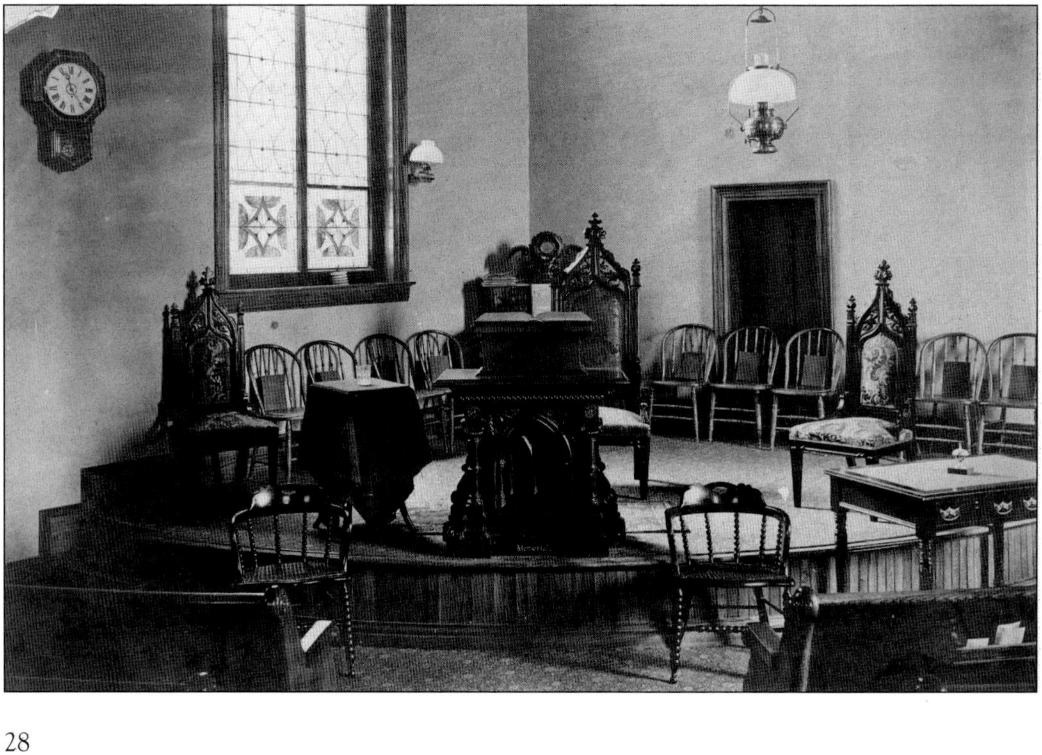

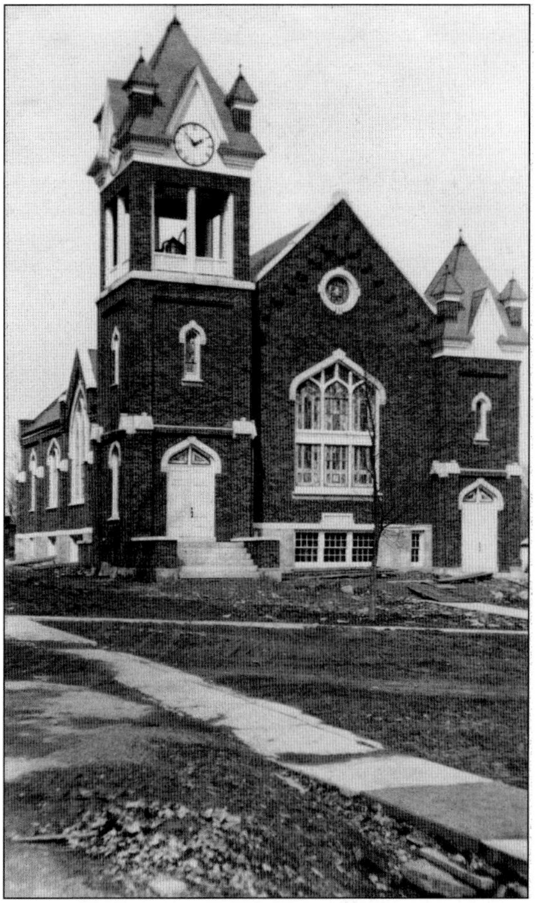

The Presbyterian Church grew out of the Congregational Church that was originally located on the southeast corner of the public square. A new Presbyterian church was built next to Franklin Academy. In February 1923, the church was destroyed by fire, along with portions of the school. The church that now stands was built in 1924 and dedicated on April 19, 1925. Through the years, many distinguished ministers have served the church, the most important being Rev. James H. Hotchkin. He was the first, serving over 20 years and inspiring Narcissa Prentiss and Rev. Henry Spaulding to journey west with Narcissa's husband, Dr. Whitman. Today, the church still houses a strong, dedicated congregation. The inscription on the Memorial Window is perhaps most appropriate to express thanks to those who have served so well: "To All the Saints Who From Their Labors Rest."

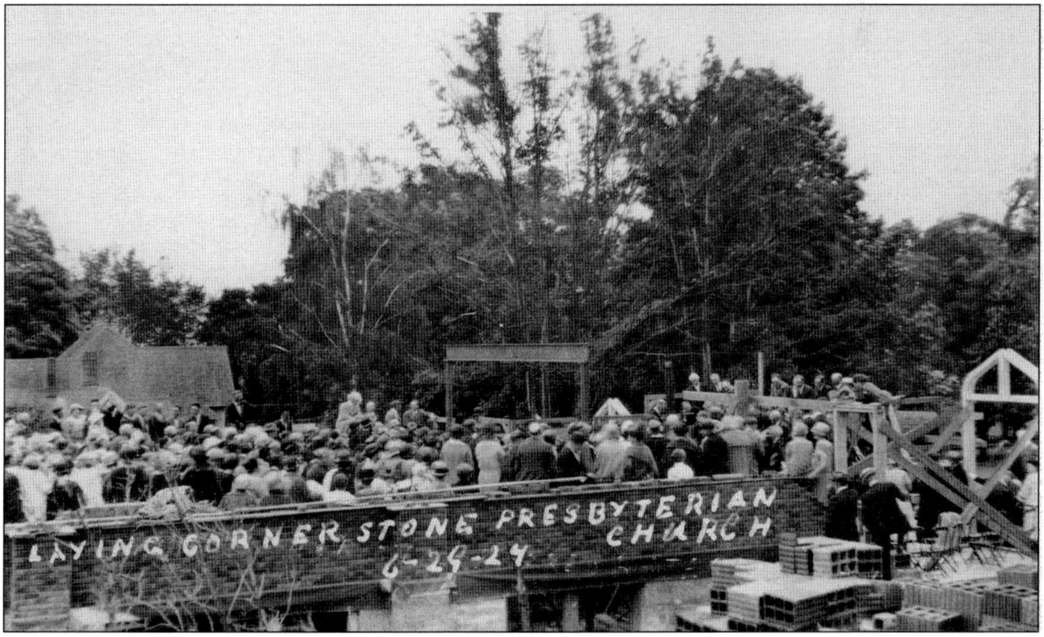

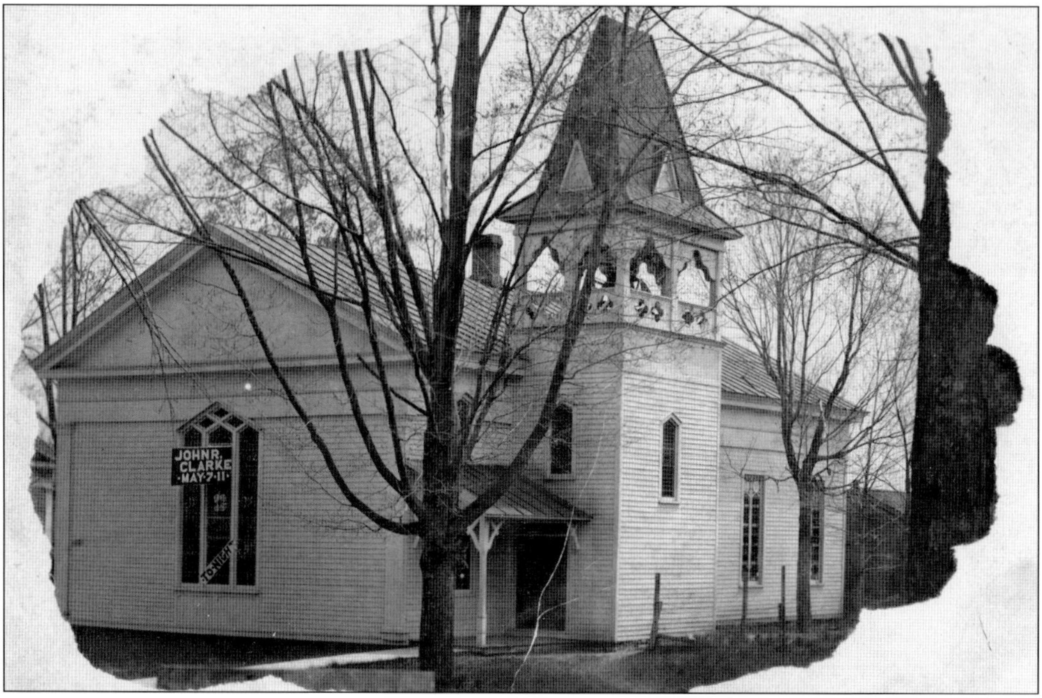

The first Methodist church in Prattsburgh was erected on Chapel Street in 1829. The Methodist Society worshipped there until 1840. A new church was built on Mechanic Street but, after standing only five years, was destroyed by fire in 1853. For several years, meetings were held in a brick store on Mechanic Street. In 1868, a lot was purchased on Porter Street, and the present church building was erected. In 1890, the front of the church was cut loose, moved forward, and enlarged to form a prayer room and vestry. Between 1913 and 1917, a kitchen and dining room were added in the basement. Today, the Methodist Church contributes greatly to Prattsburgh, hosting an annual turkey dinner as well as the monthly Bluegrass/Country Music Jams.

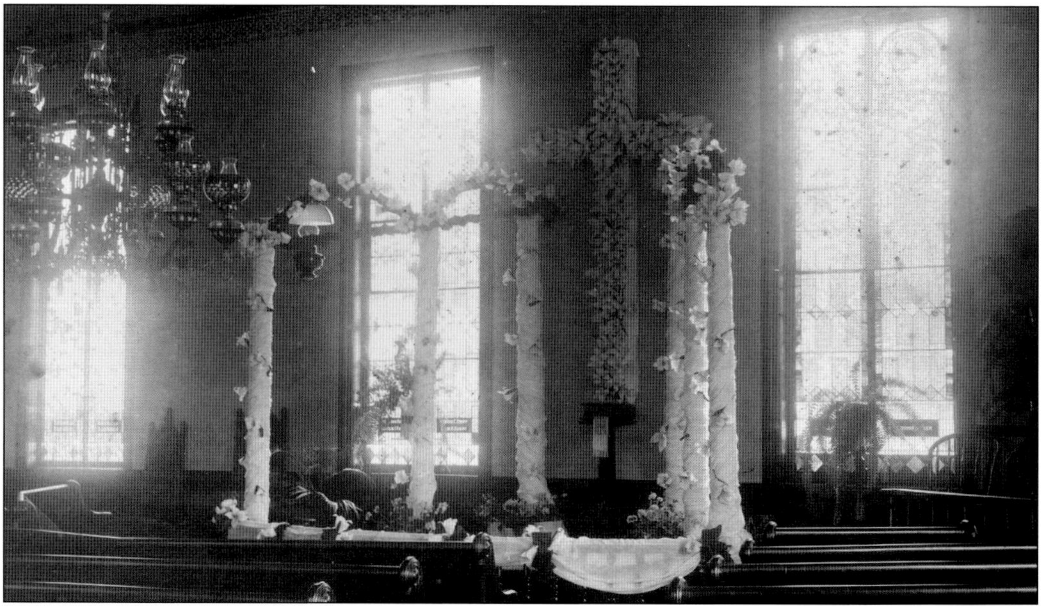

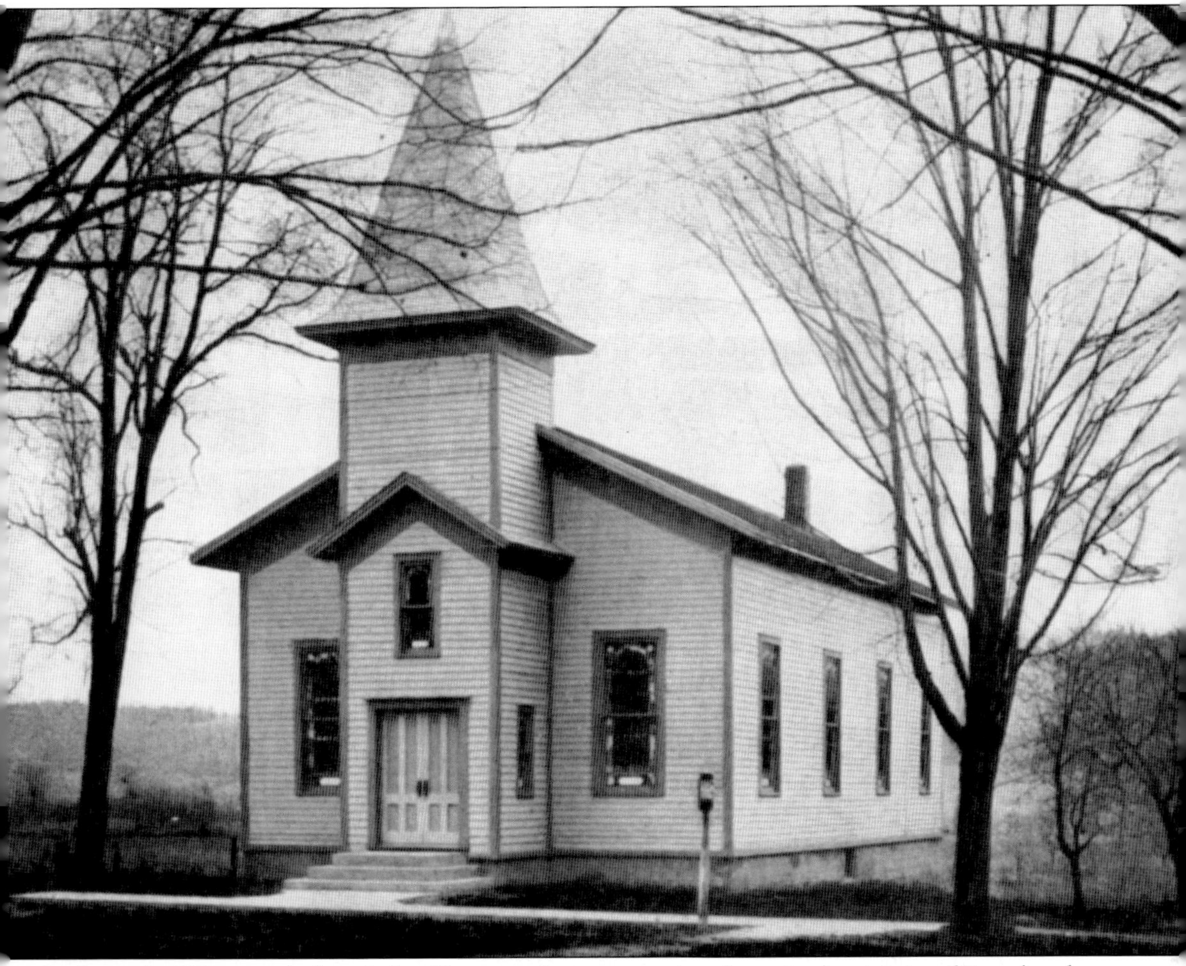

In the early 1850s, people from Ireland began to locate on various farms in the vicinity of Prattsburgh village, and during the next 15 years, the Irish population increased. They were mostly Catholic, and their church affiliations were first in Bath and later Hammondsport. In the early 1860s, they purchased a lot on North Main Street, and in 1866, the church was built. By the mid-1920s, the membership consisted mostly of Polish Catholics, Irish Catholics, and members of Italian descent. In 1949, the church was improved with a basement and heating furnace. Several years ago, St. Patrick's became part of a church cluster called Our Lady of the Lakes with churches from Penn Yan, Dundee, Stanley, Rushville, and Naples. Today, St. Patrick's has a large membership, many being from families that have been members of the church for a number of decades.

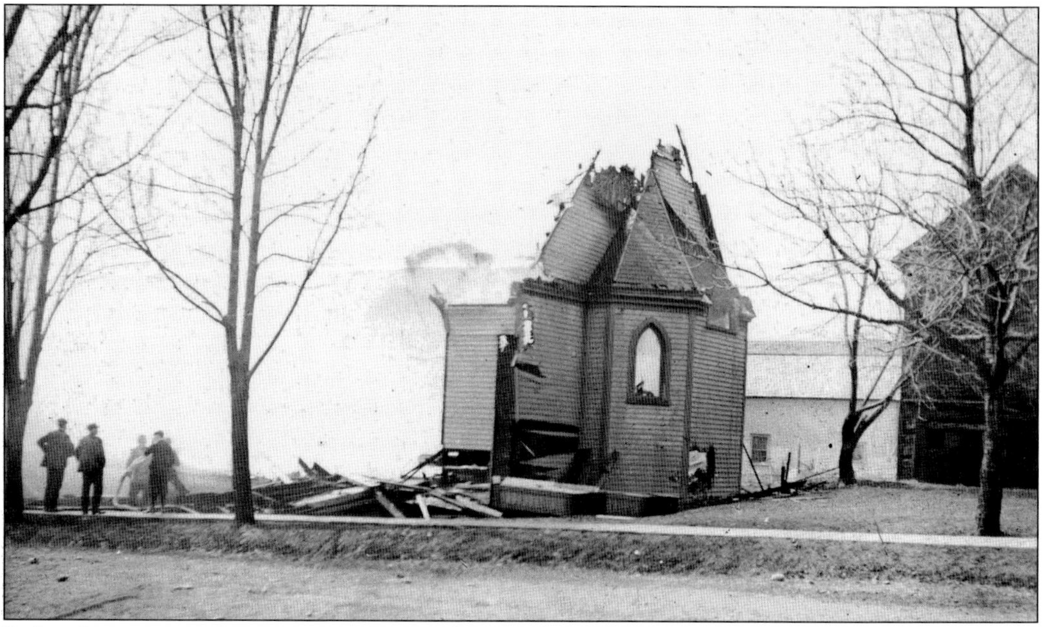

Before locating on Porter Street, the Methodist church stood on Mechanic Street. Since these buildings were constructed of wood, they were susceptible to fires. Many of the wood structures in Prattsburgh suffered the same fate, leaving only memories intact.

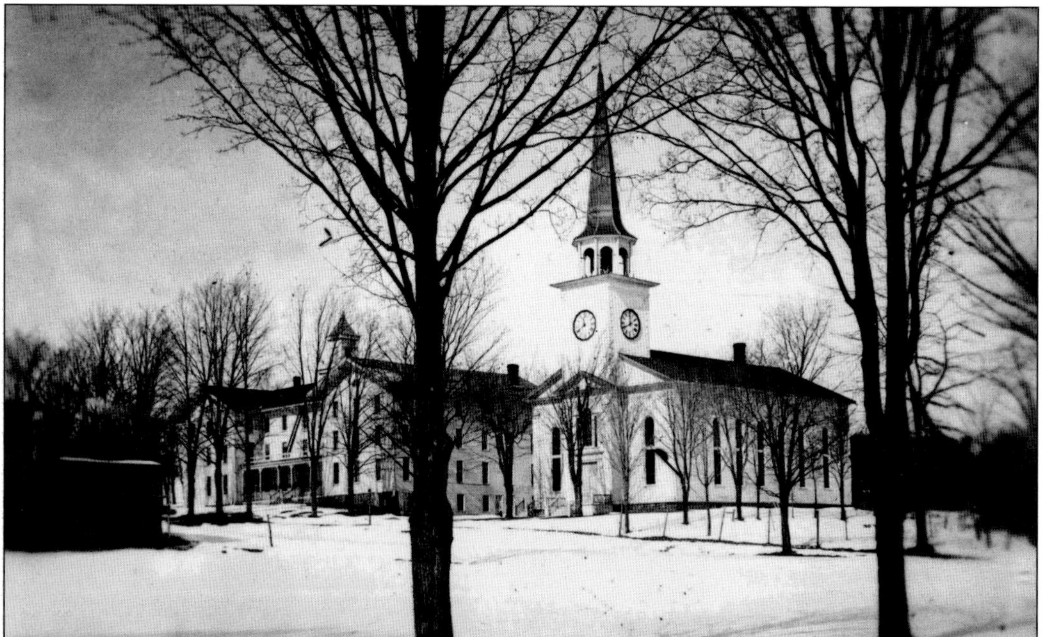

H.A. Hopkins made a cherry wood town clock for the original Presbyterian church. Because it did not have sufficient protection from the weather, the clock got wet, warped, and cracked. In 1852, Hopkins built a replacement that beat once every two seconds and was guaranteed to last 20 years. It ticked for almost 70 years, until the church burned down. In 1923, Wallace W. Cole donated a new clock to the village that still keeps time today by chiming on the hour as the day goes on.

Three

MAIN STREET AND BUSINESSES

To serve a thriving community, Prattsburgh became host to many businesses and industries. The little town once boasted a sash and blind factory, a tannery, a pottery shop, glove and mitten factory, four blacksmith shops, and a boot and shoe shop. In addition to providing valuable employment, these industries spurred on the creation of secondary businesses, such as restaurants, hotels, millinery shops, and grocery stores, which sprung up along Main Street and beyond.

Some of these industries continue to serve the town, but by and large, there is little evidence of this bustling commercial community in present-day Prattsburgh.

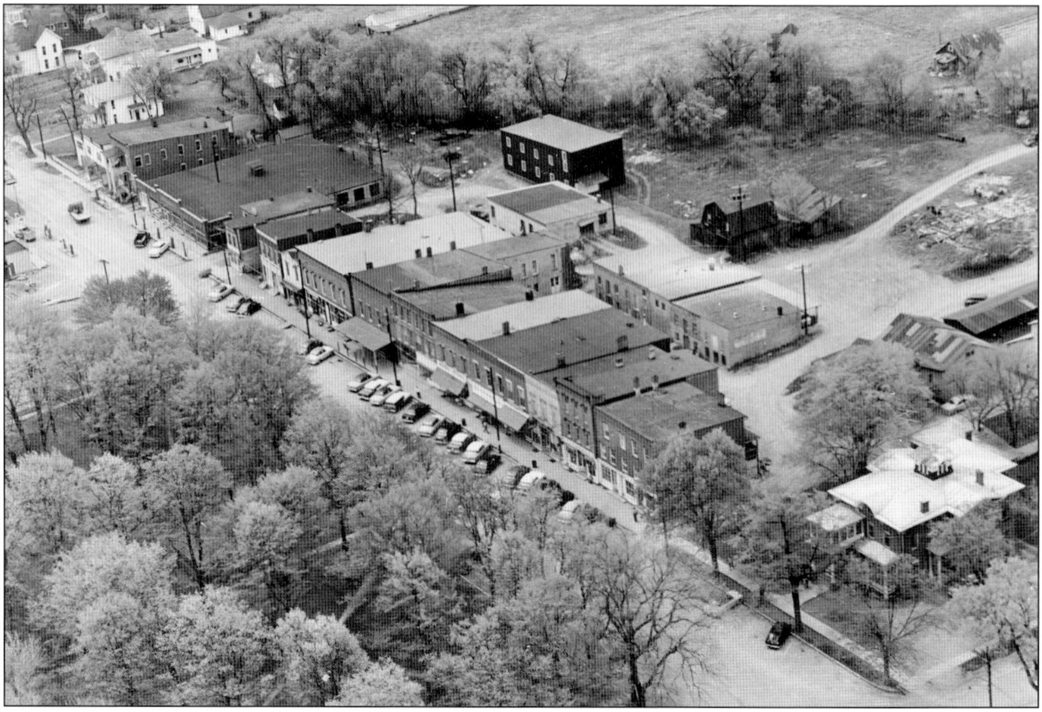

Prattsburgh is located at the northeast corner of Steuben County and boasts a population around 2,000. It is about 12 miles from Bath, the county seat. This aerial view from the 1950s shows Main Street or State Route 53 looking south. While some of these buildings still remain, many have been torn down to make way for new construction.

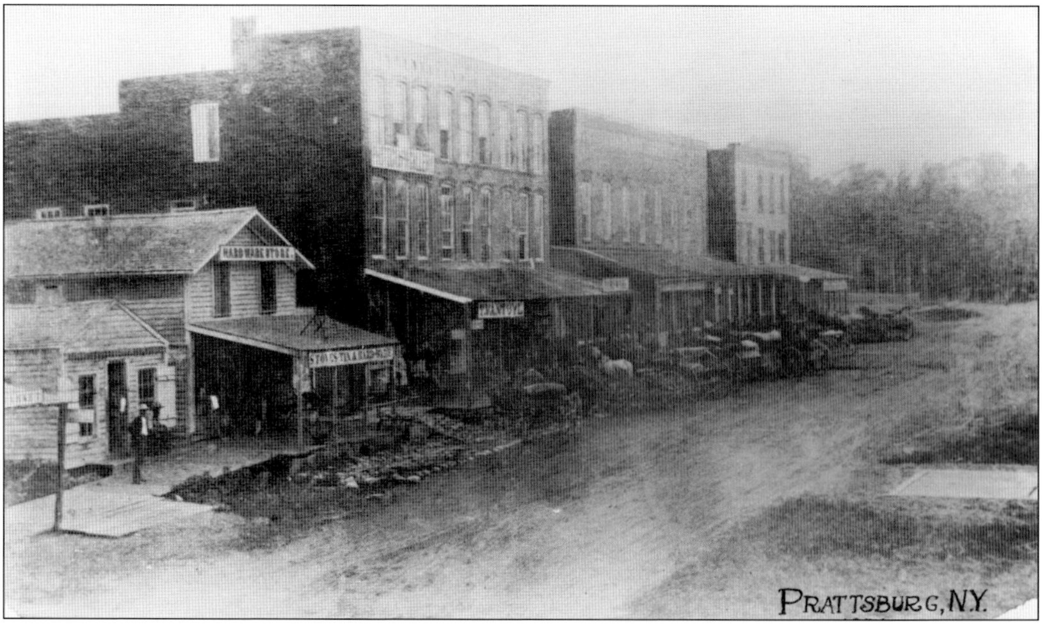

The first known picture of Main Street in 1874 shows among other things a hardware store, a mercantile, and the opera house. Horse and buggy was the mode of transportation of the day, and raised wooden sidewalks kept residents out of the mud.

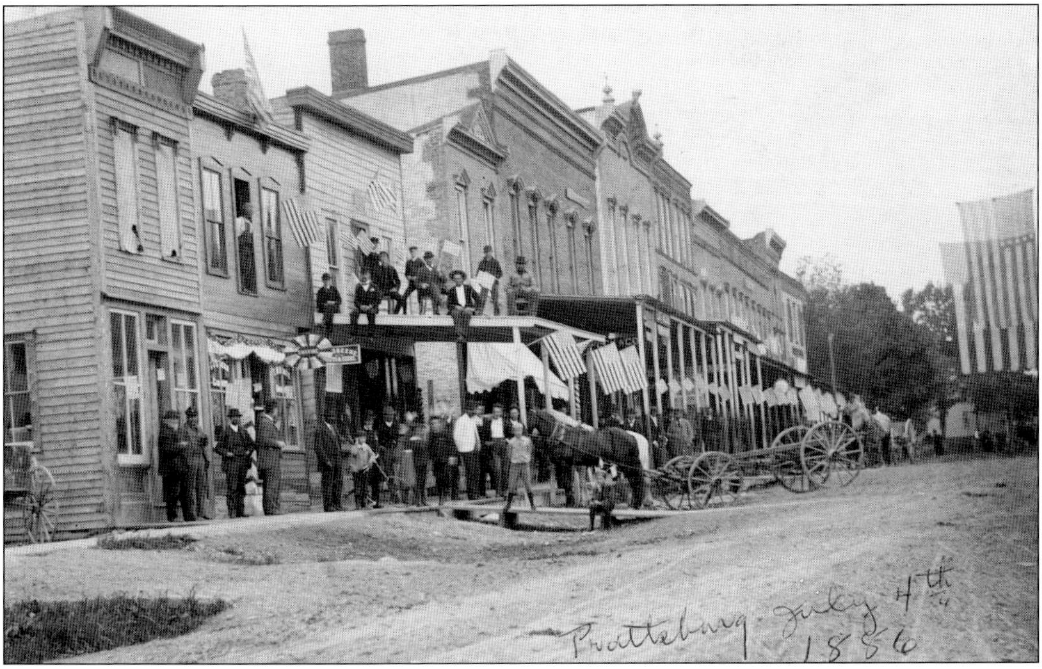

Main Street was the center of activity in Prattsburgh, especially for holidays and special events. The town prided itself on celebrating Independence Day, as shown here at the festivities of July 4, 1886. While many of the buildings are gone or renovated, that same spirit exists today.

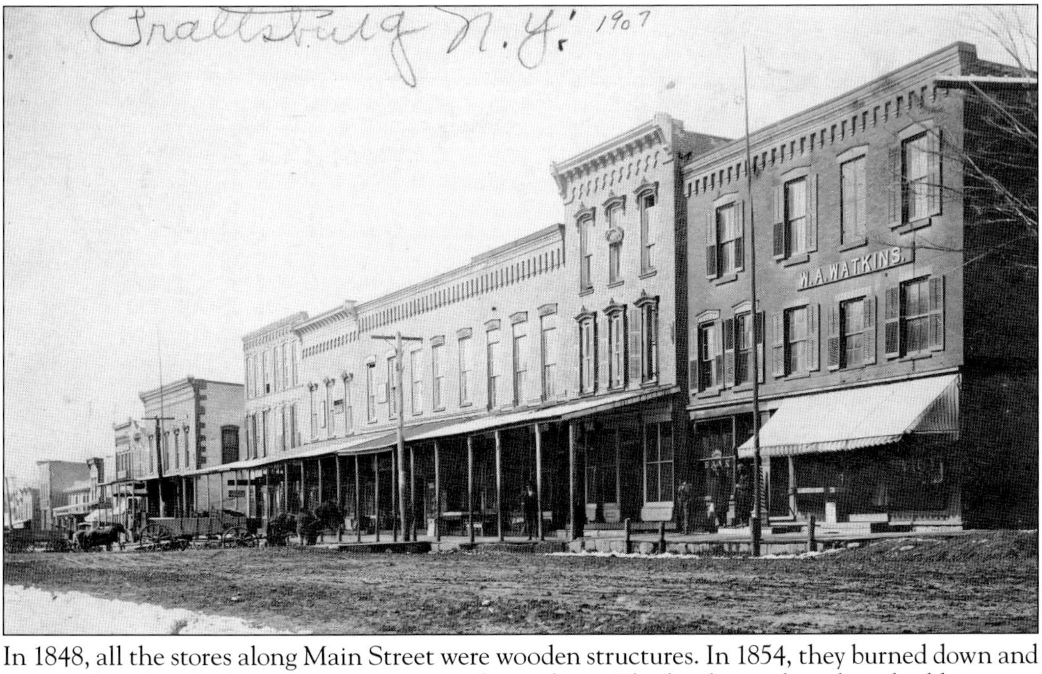

In 1848, all the stores along Main Street were wooden structures. In 1854, they burned down and were replaced with the current structures, shown here. The bricks used in the rebuilding were made at Hopkins farm on Bean Station Road from clay obtained along Five Mile Creek. Those structures still standing look much the same as they did at that time.

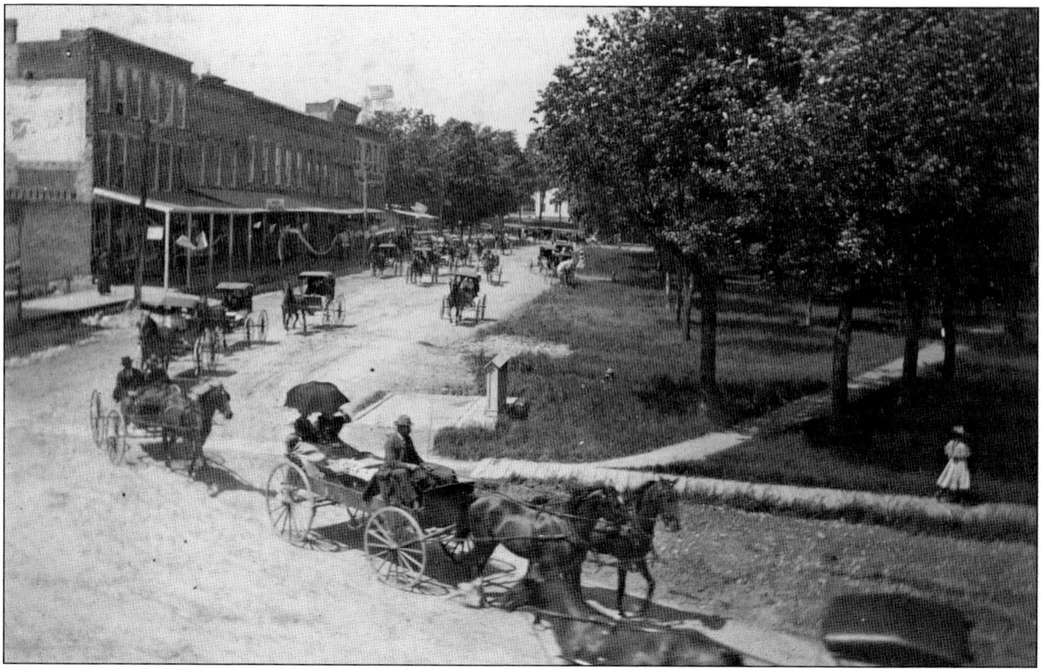

This view of Main Street looking north shows the hustle and bustle that existed "downtown." One could shop for essentials, take in a play at the opera house, or enjoy a leisurely stroll through the park.

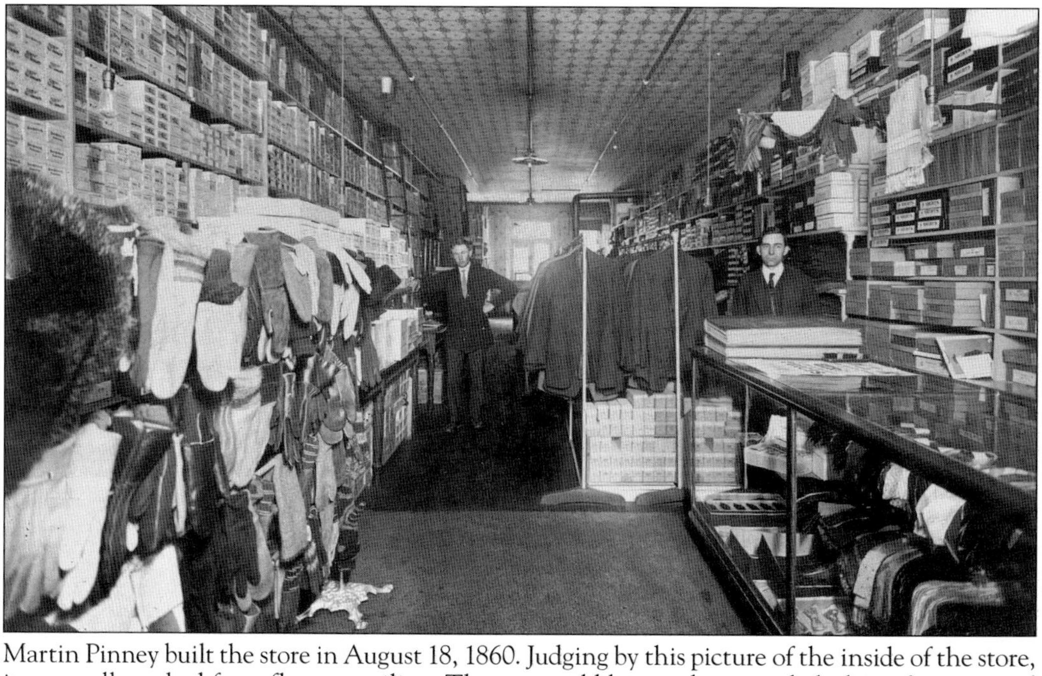

Martin Pinney built the store in August 18, 1860. Judging by this picture of the inside of the store, it was well stocked from floor to ceiling. The store sold boots, shoes, and clothing for men and boys. The Conine family owned it from 1889 to 1994, beginning with G.T. Conine. It was taken over by Leon H. Conine and finally by Leon's daughter Betty Hall. The Robbin's Nest restaurant is now located in this building.

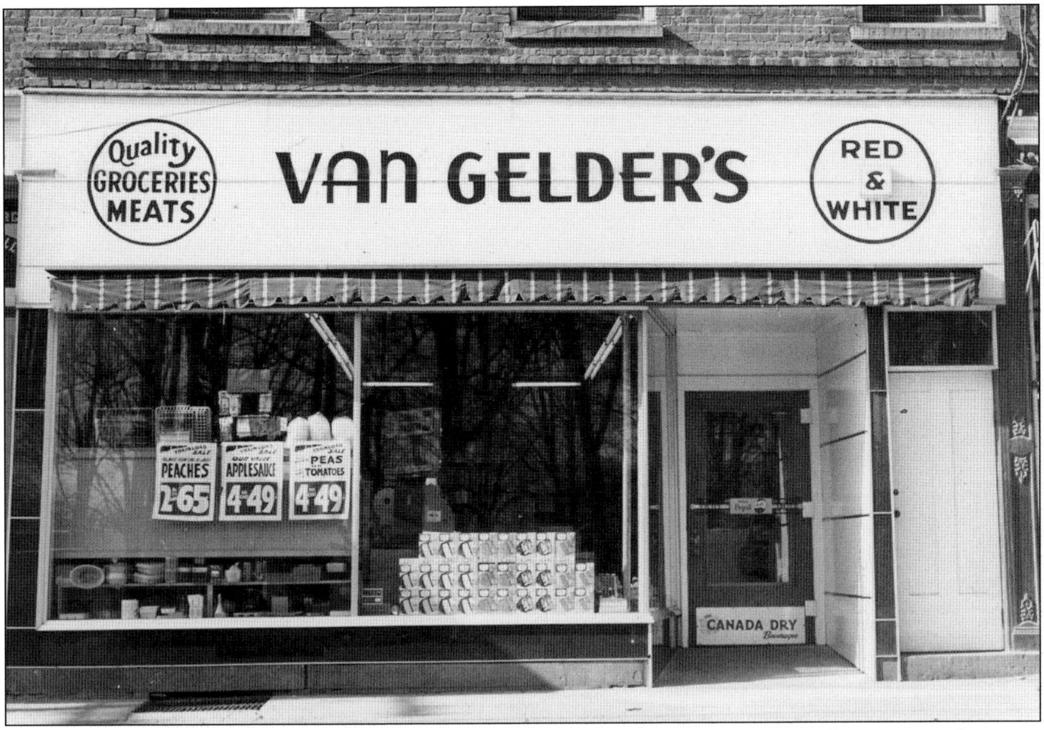

The Red & White store was built before 1860 to serve the community. Martin Pinney ran the store in 1896, followed by Art Putnam and later James Drumm. In 1940, Dewitt Van Gelder ran the store, as shown here. Upstairs over the store were club rooms and the Grange. In addition to household grocery staples, the store offered an ample supply of candy bars for the younger crowd.

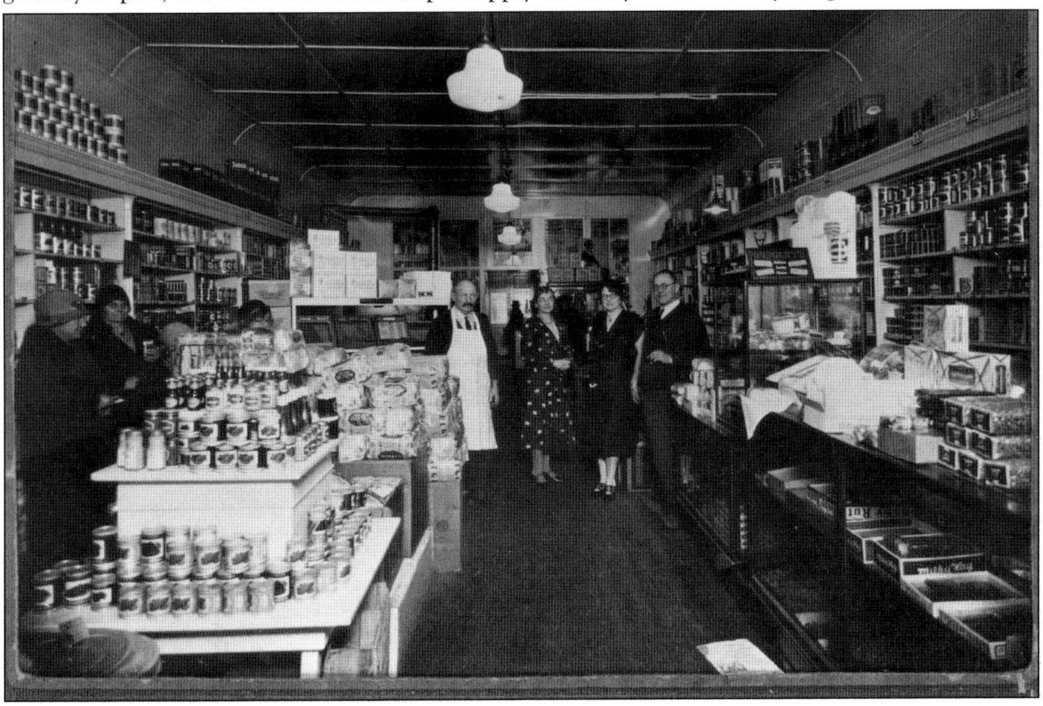

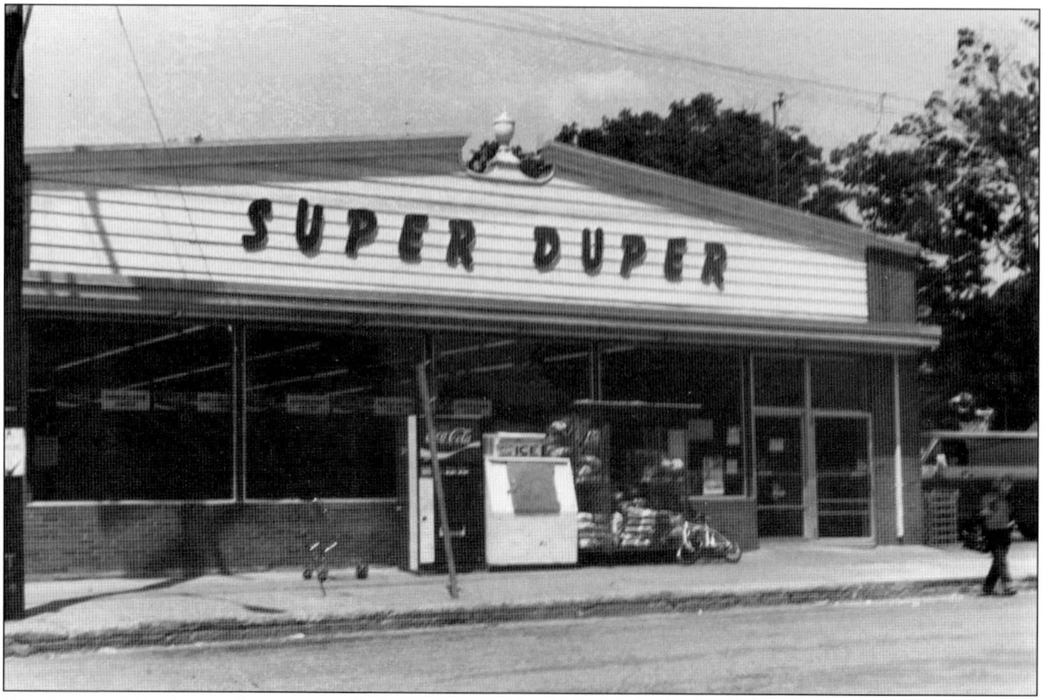

Shirley and Barbara Shaver purchased the Red & White store in 1963 and ran it until 1965. At that time, they purchased the old post office building and had it torn down, replacing it with a new building to house the Super Duper store. Today, the building houses the Prattsburgh Market Place and is the only grocery store left in town.

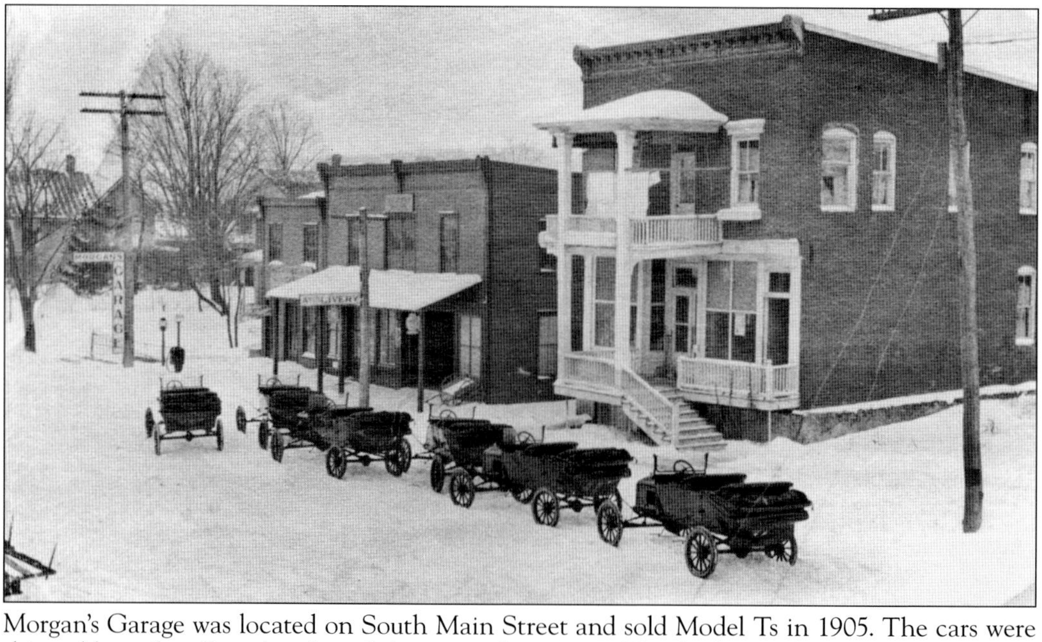

Morgan's Garage was located on South Main Street and sold Model Ts in 1905. The cars were shipped by rail to Prattsburgh and driven to the garage. The fenders and running boards were attached at the garage. Unaccustomed to driving, some of the customers did not want the fenders so that they could see where the wheels were going.

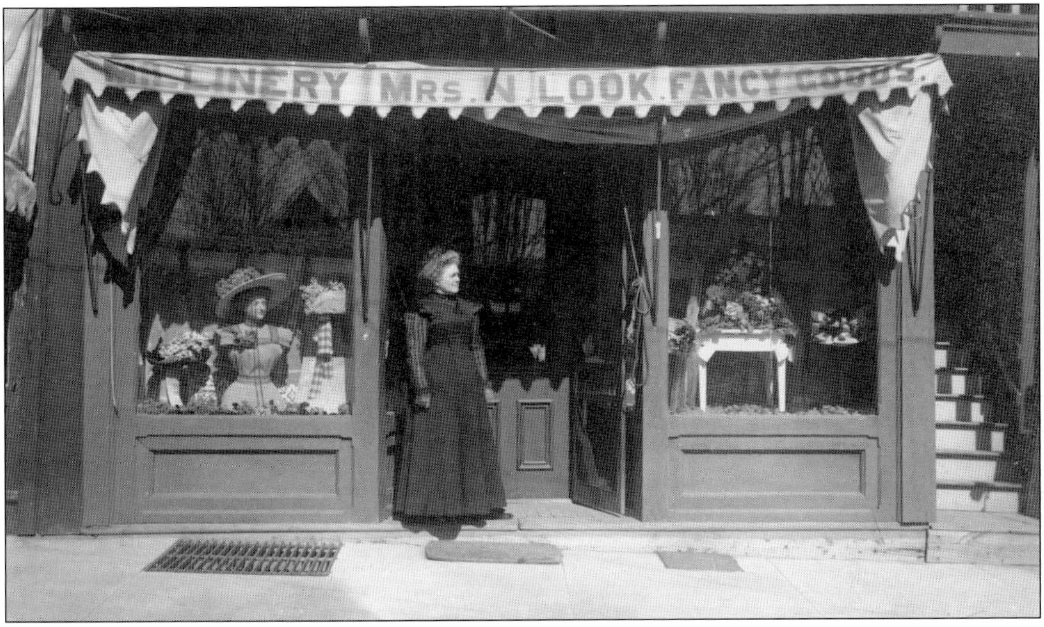

In 1901, wearing hats was quite fashionable. These were some of many stores that sprung up along Main Street to serve the fashion needs of the local women. It was common for the proprietors to travel to New York City for the hat and dress patterns featured in their stores, providing customers with access to the latest fashion trends.

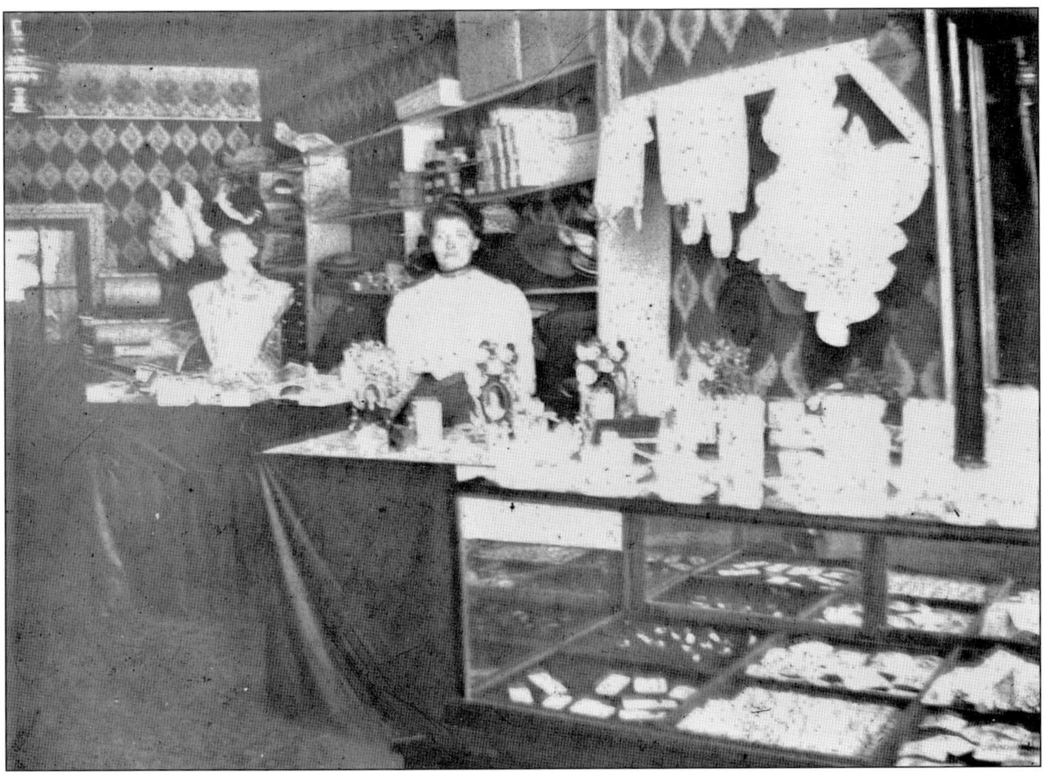

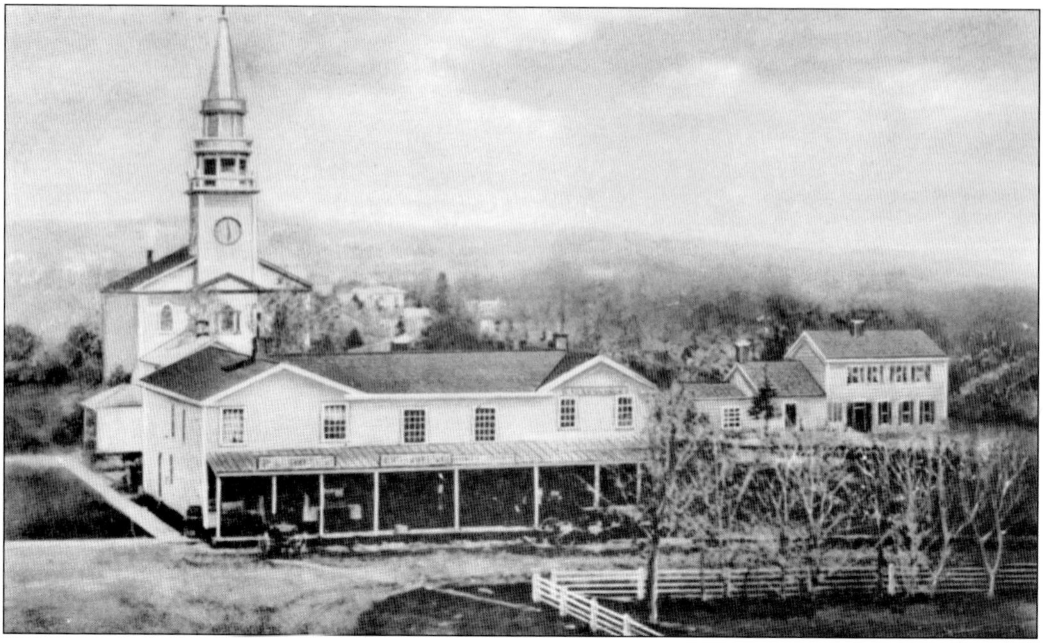

The Old Kremlin Block, located at the four corners of Main and Chapel Streets, housed several businesses and meeting rooms until it burned in 1869. It was rebuilt with stones in 1870 by Paul C. Howe.

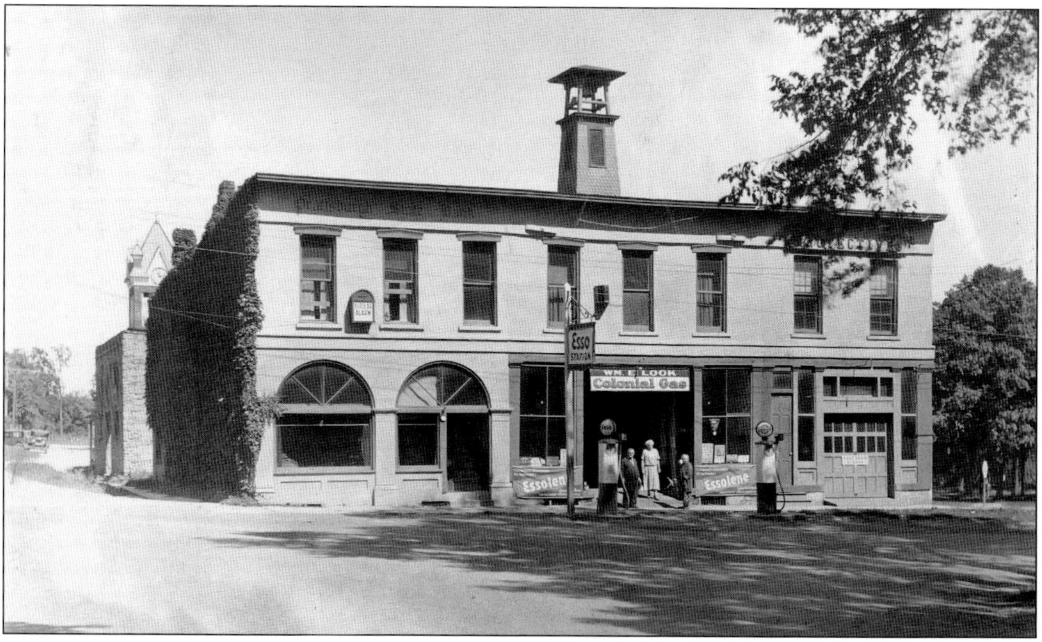

The Stone Building was constructed to replace the Old Kremlin Block and was a multipurpose structure. In the rear, it housed the *Prattsburgh News* from 1872 to 1894 and the post office in 1904. The west side of the building housed the McLean Bank, which was succeeded by the Prattsburgh State Bank. The firehouse was located in the east side of the building, and the Village Bus Company was in the center. There was also a wagon shop run by J.H. Frost and a paint shop run by H.J. Pinneo located upstairs.

This view of the backside of the Stone Building shows the J.H. Frost wagon shop and Henry J. Pinneo paint shop. The tower that looms above the building contains the fire siren that called out the Prattsburgh Protectives when fire erupted.

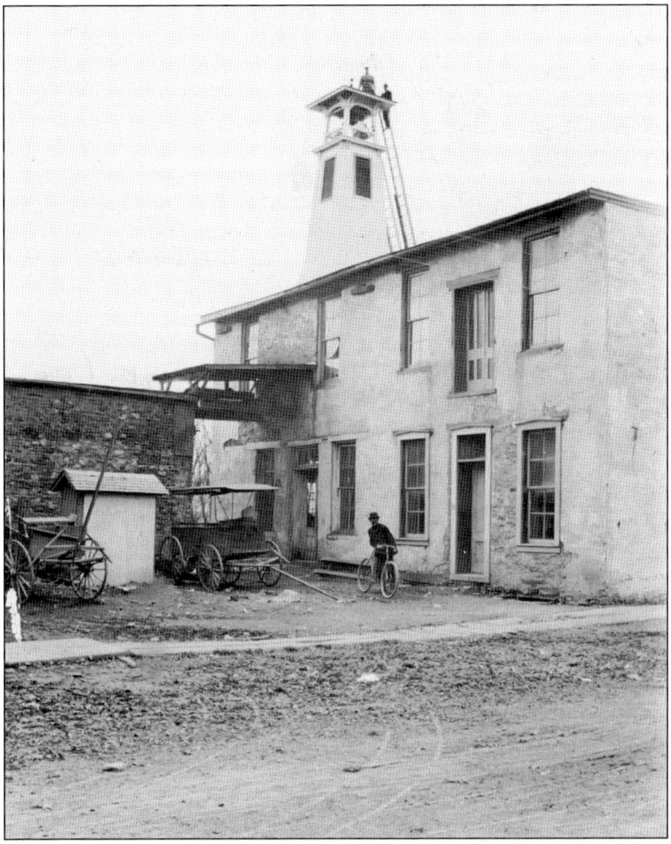

George Avery operated a foundry located on this site on Mechanic Street; it burned about 1869. This 1874 home by Sanford Foster was constructed with bricks made at the brickyard on Five Mile Creek. Lynn and Cloyes McConnell purchased it to be used as a funeral home in September 1954. It is currently the Bottoni-Wood Funeral Home.

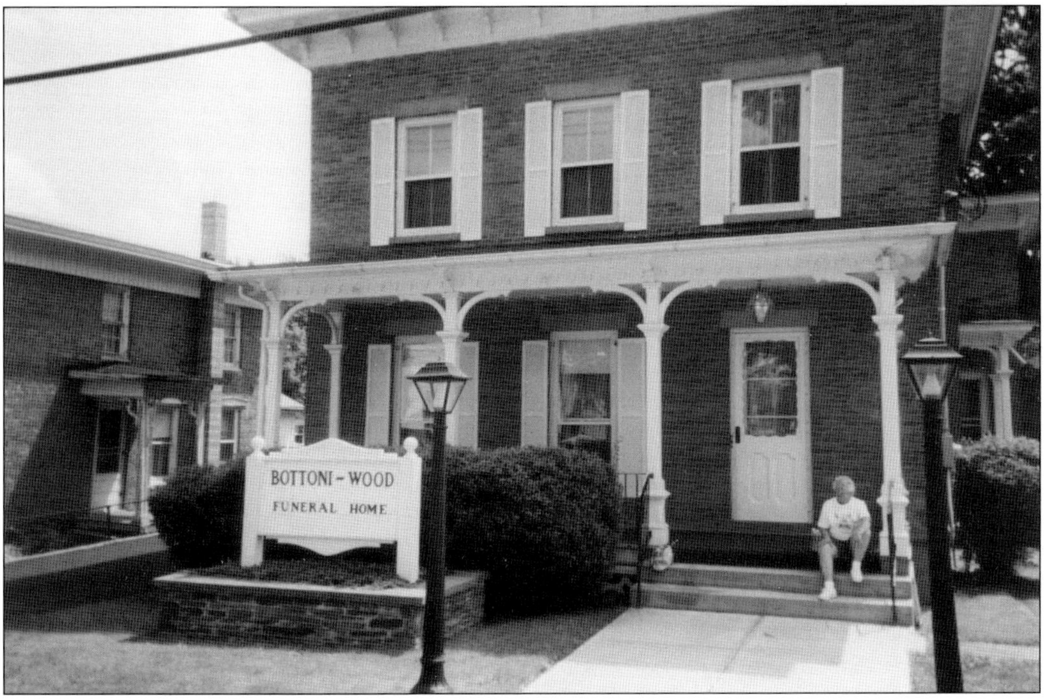

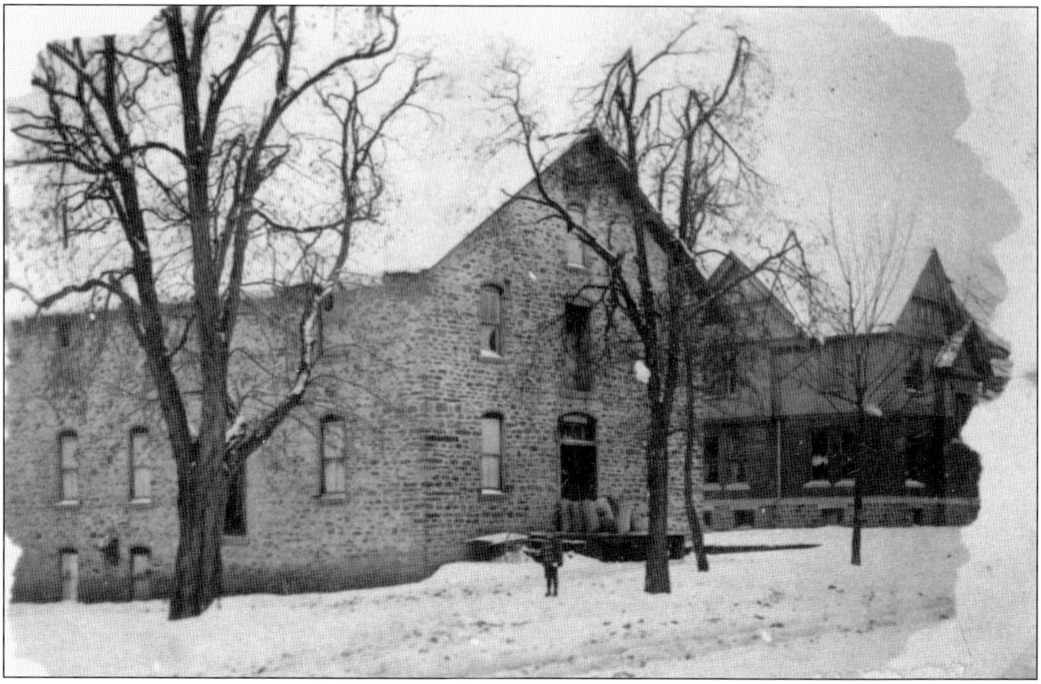

The Stone Mill was built by brothers Ralph and Henry Hopkins on Mechanic Street in 1887. This was the fifth gristmill built in Prattsburgh. Over the years, it was operated by S.B. Merritt and George Draper. Later, in the 1940s, it was run by Fred Hopfinger. It has been turned into five apartments but is currently empty for renovations.

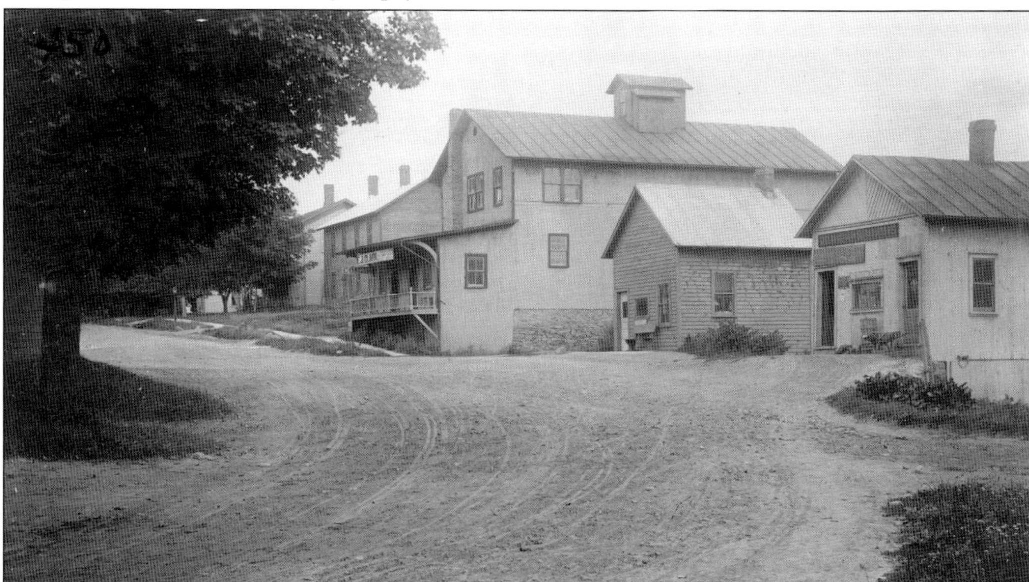

Charlie and Spencer Clark owned this feed mill on Mechanic Street across from the railroad station. It was a valuable commodity to the local community, and farmers could bring in their grain for milling and have it shipped out on the railroad. The building burned and is now the site of the home at 59 Mechanic Street, which once housed the Italian laborers who laid the railroad tracks.

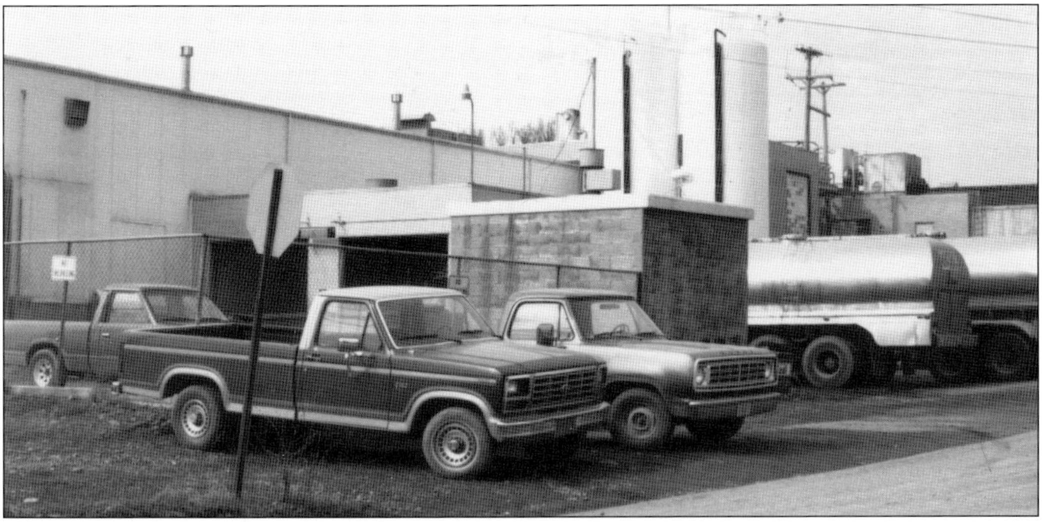

The Prattsburgh Milk Plant, or Creamery, was built in the spring of 1895 as a place for local dairy farmers to deliver their milk. They pasteurized the milk for bottling and made butter and other dairy products, such as powdered milk, shown below being bagged by James Crean. The Patterson Milk Company bought the building in 1925, improving and adding on until it became a large factory. In 1946, a new boiler with the latest in automatic stokes was installed. It was later owned by a milk company in Jamaica, New York, but was eventually closed in 1993.

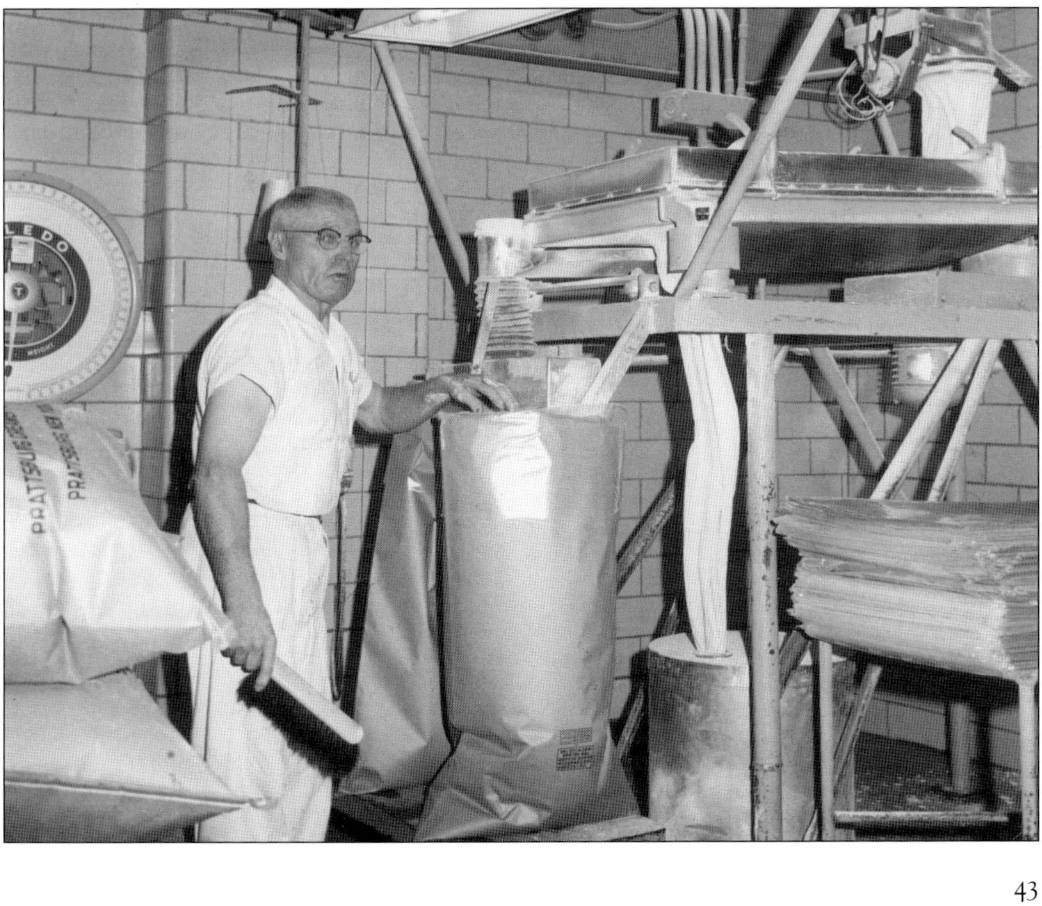

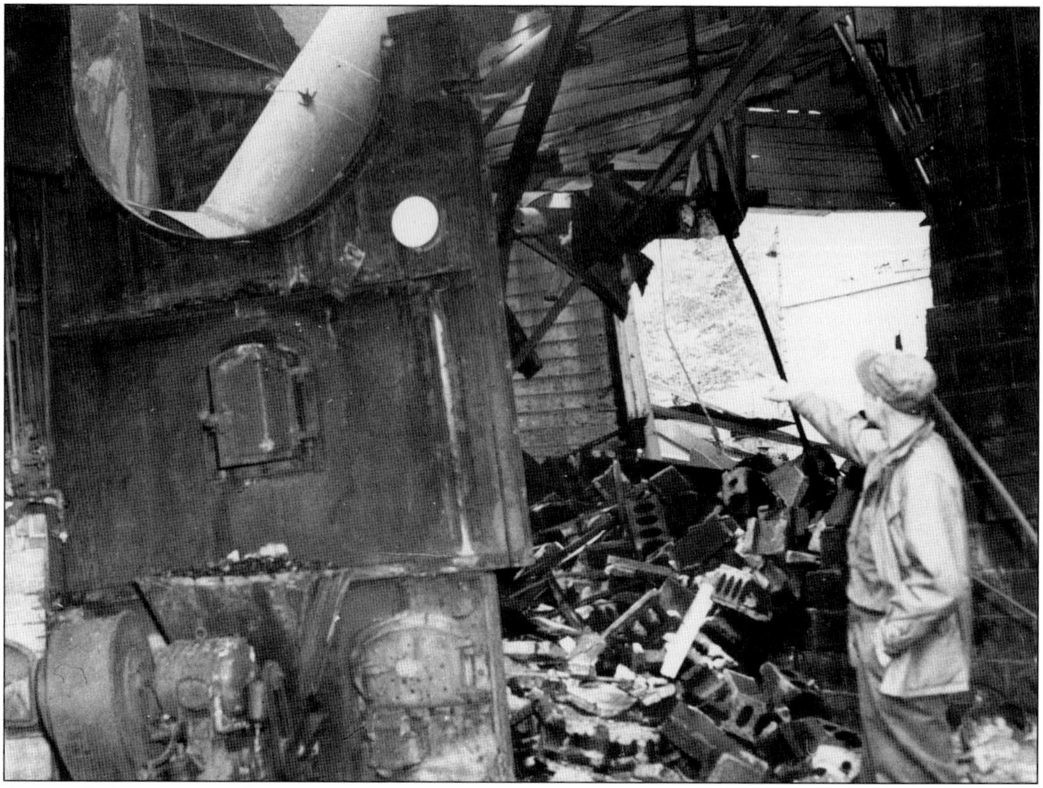

At 11:15 a.m. on a Sunday in May 1956, the boiler exploded at the Prattsburgh Milk Plant, blowing out walls and collapsing a large section of the roof. One person died in the explosion, and two were injured from the steam. Only a small fire resulted from the blast, but the estimated property damage exceeded $75,000. This 10-year-old boiler was due to be replaced within a short time.

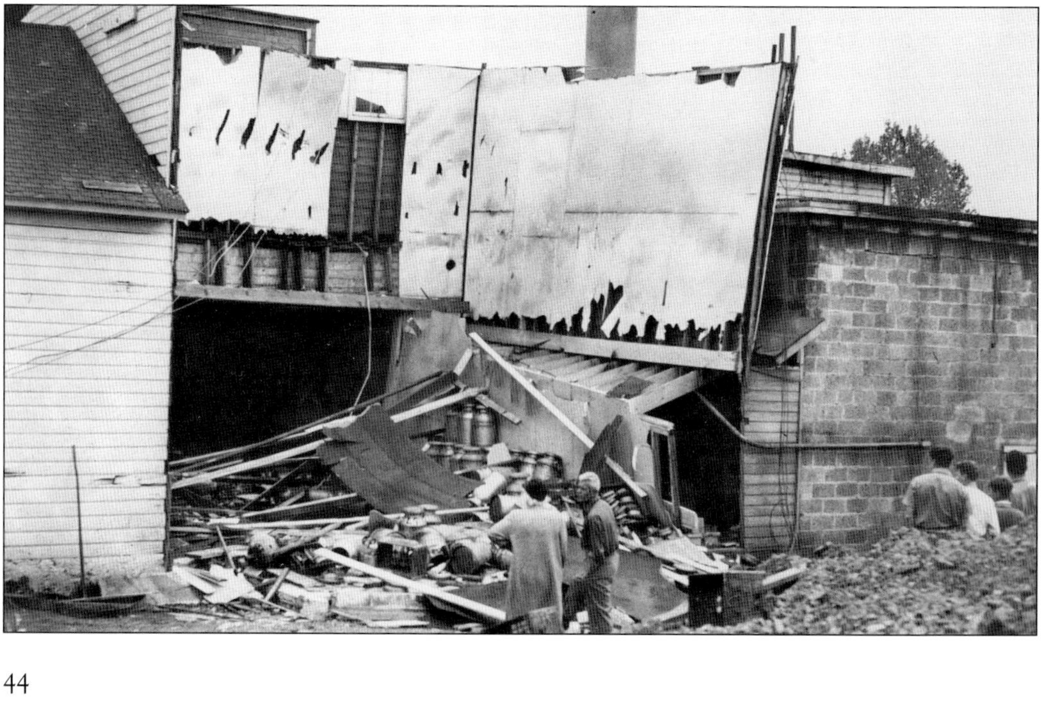

Built in 1893 by William G. Dean on South Main Street, this building was occupied by P.C. Howe and Sons Printing, publishers of the *Prattsburgh News*. There was a bicycle shop in the basement run by Frank Mahan, and the second floor housed community halls, including Dean's Hall. It later served as a private dwelling, a gas station, and machine shop and was eventually torn down. In 1894, P.C. Howe and Sons Printing moved from the Stone Building to the Dean Building and published the *Prattsburgh News* until 1920. As this picture shows, printing a newspaper at that time was a very manual task.

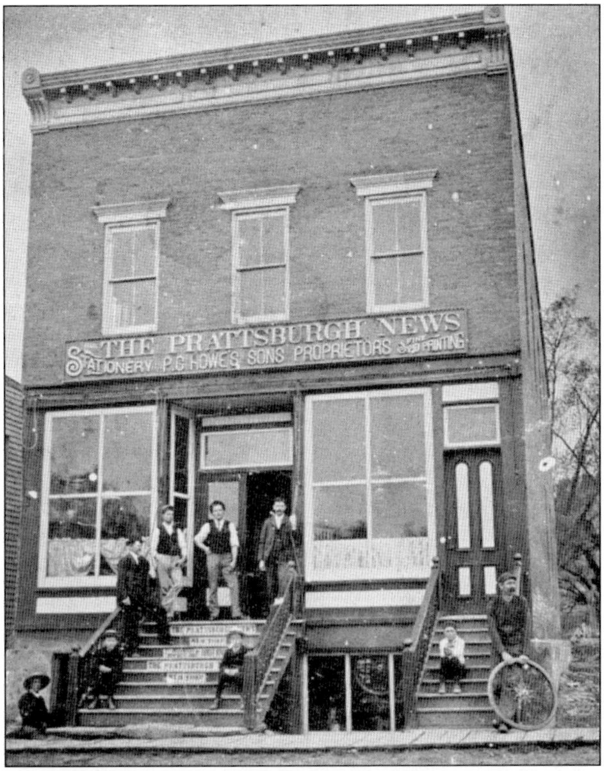

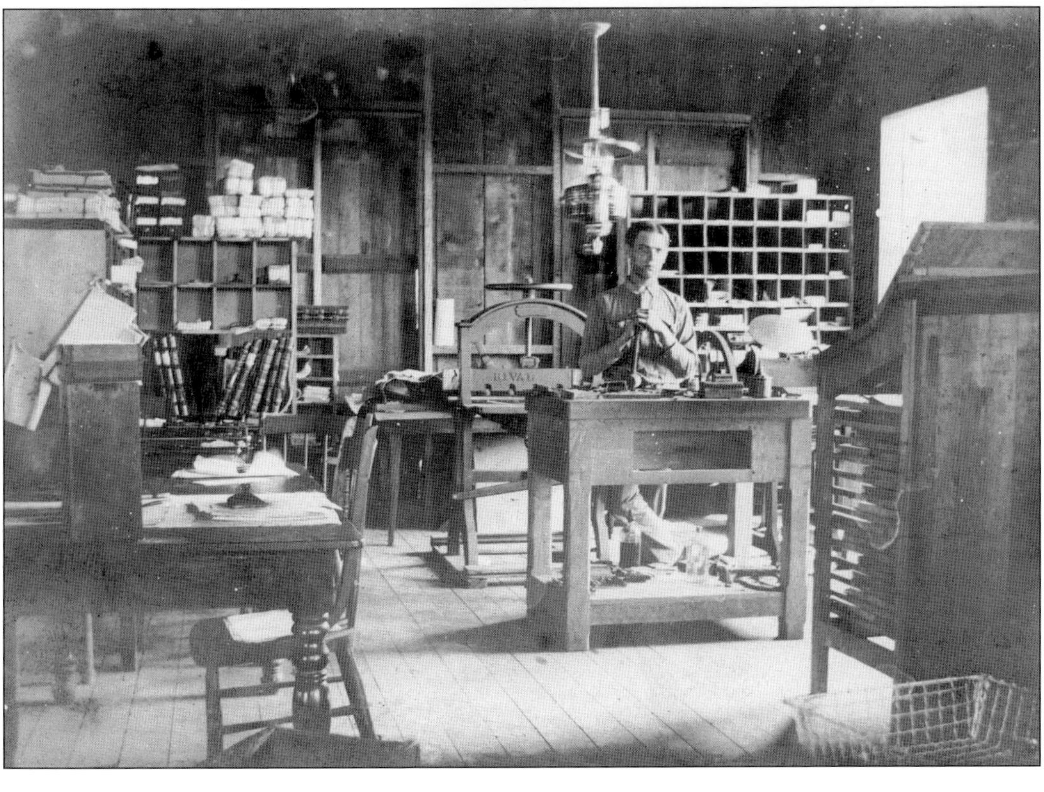

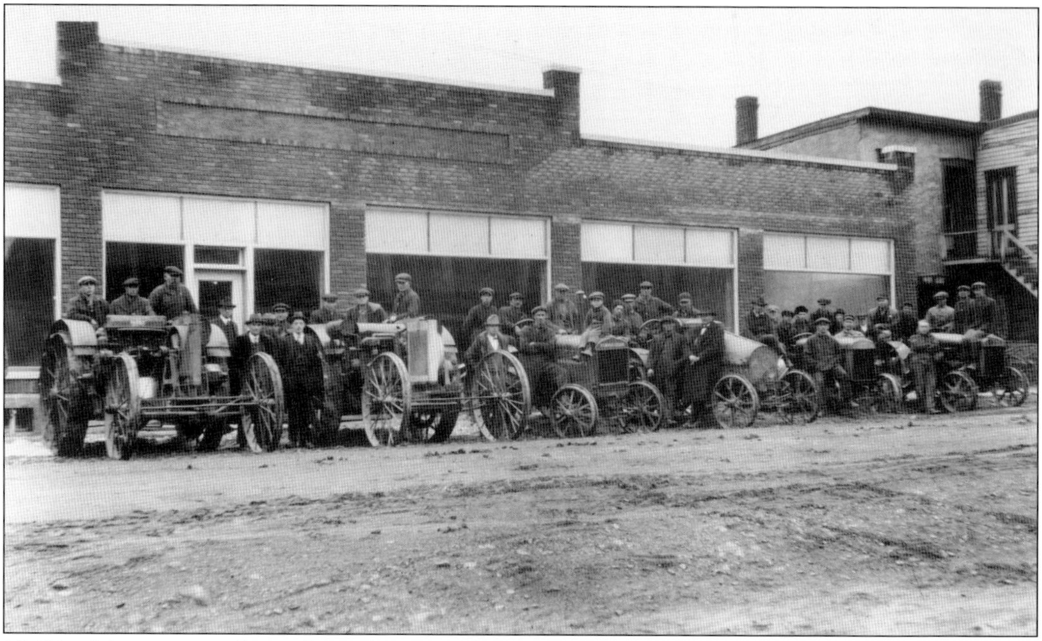

H. Clay Morgan tore down the Relyea Hotel in 1923 in order to build his Ford garage. In 1946, it was sold to E.V. DeZetter, who used it for many businesses. The garage was next sold to J. Ward McConnell Jr. for the building of farm machinery. Later, it was replaced by Air Flo Manufacturing Company, Inc., which continues to operate at the site.

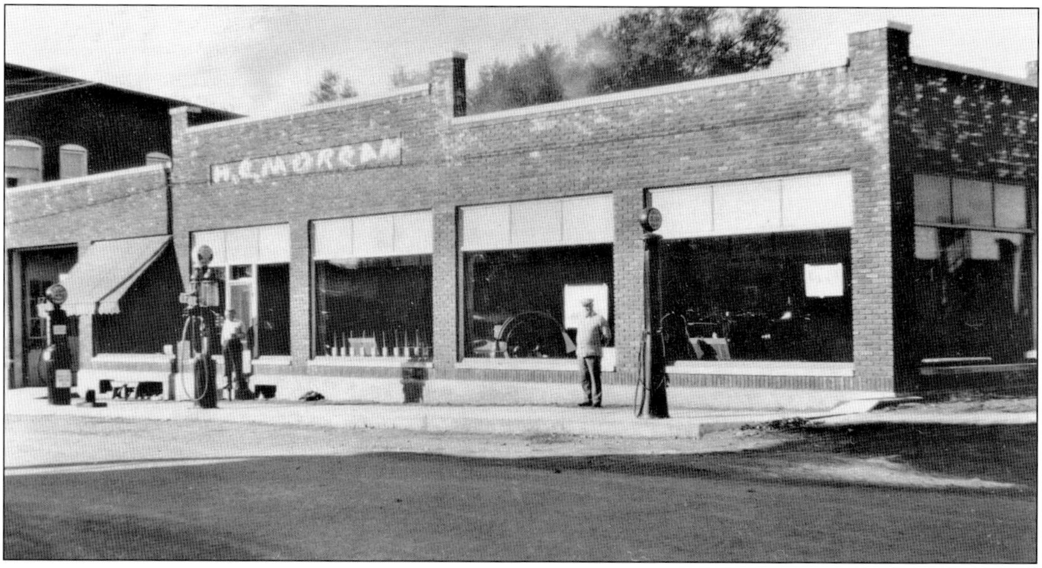

Air Flo Manufacturing Company, Inc., operated by the Musso brothers, purchased this building from J. Ward McConnell for its business. Makers of dump boxes and spreaders for road maintenance, Air Flo is one of the largest employers in Prattsburgh. In 1979, the company built another facility on North Main Street to be used for the painting and storage of the boxes. The building looks much the same now as it did then except for the large windows being replaced by brick.

The first telephone was set up by Gamaliel Conine in 1896 from his home to store. It became popular and led to the creation of the Prattsburgh Home Telephone Company, which was purchased by the New York Telephone Company after several owners. The company was sold to Herman and Ann Wagner in 1946. Prattsburgh subscribers were the first to receive dial service beginning in 1948. All remaining exchanges were converted to dial service by 1960. At this time, the name was changed to Empire Telephone Company. Direct distant dialing (long distance) was offered in 1968. Empire Telephone currently has six exchanges and covers over 320 square miles of service territory. The company employs a large number of people and is very active in the community.

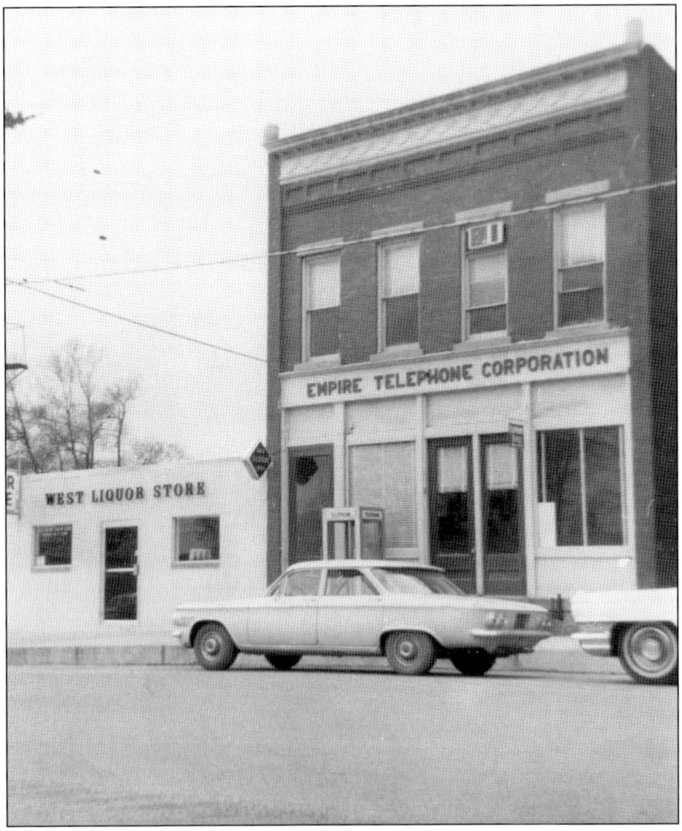

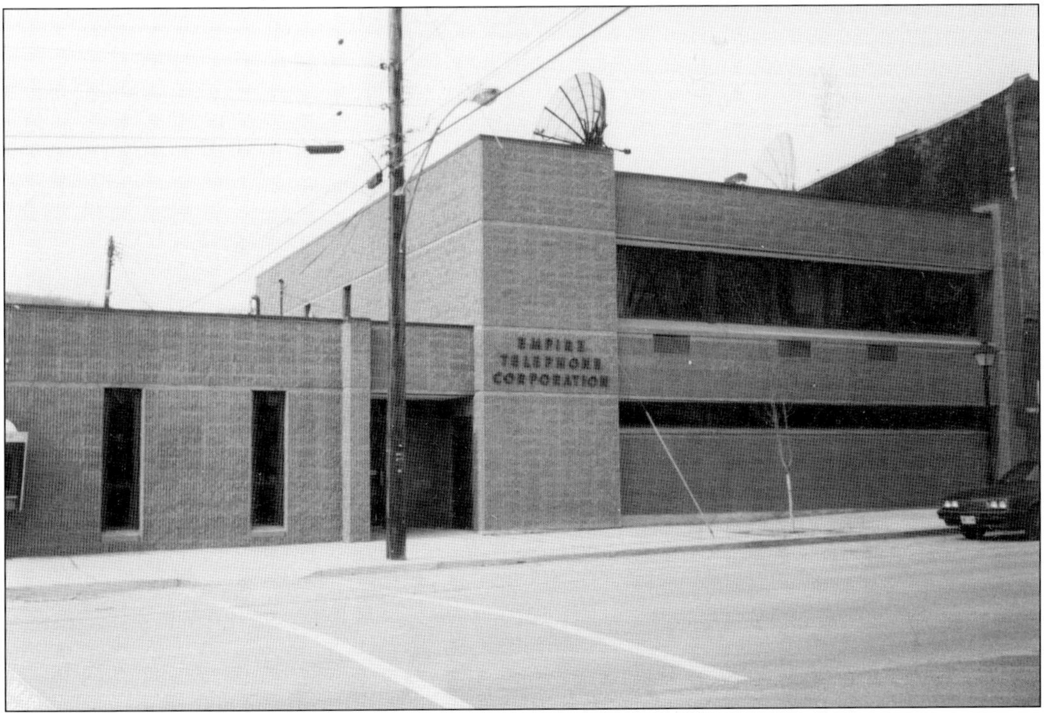

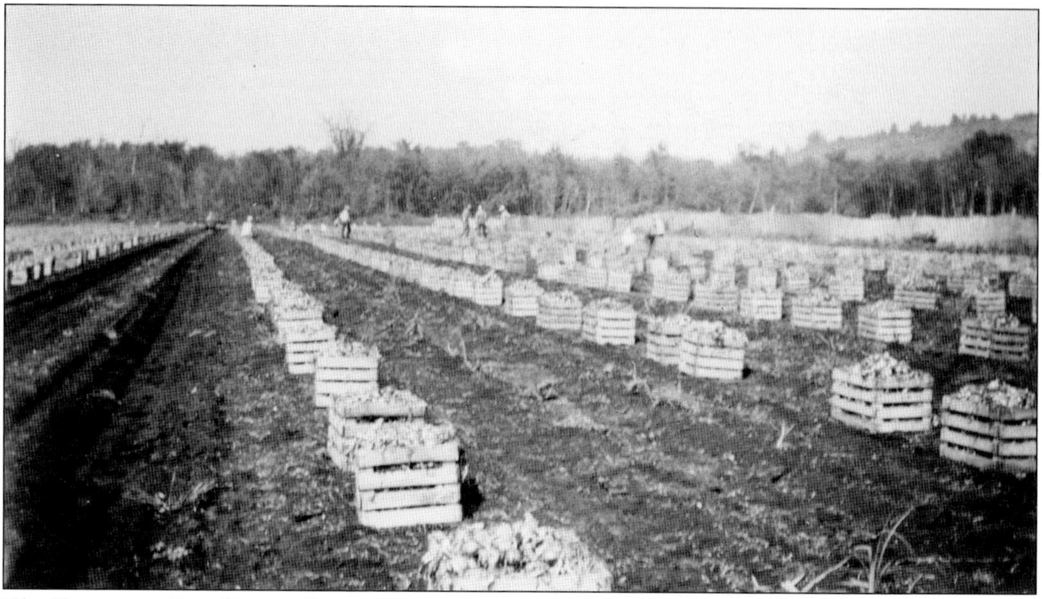

The "big swamp" on County Route 77 was cleared and drained in 1936, creating about 700 acres of rich, fertile soil. The land, known as "the muck," was worked by several farmers and used to grow onions, lettuce, cabbage, carrots, and potatoes, which were all shipped by railroad at first. Today, the muck is owned mostly by Squires Onion Farm and continues to be a prosperous business. In the beginning, most of the labor was done by hand, but today, large machines are used to harvest the crops. The large muck land is located in both Prattsburgh and Wheeler.

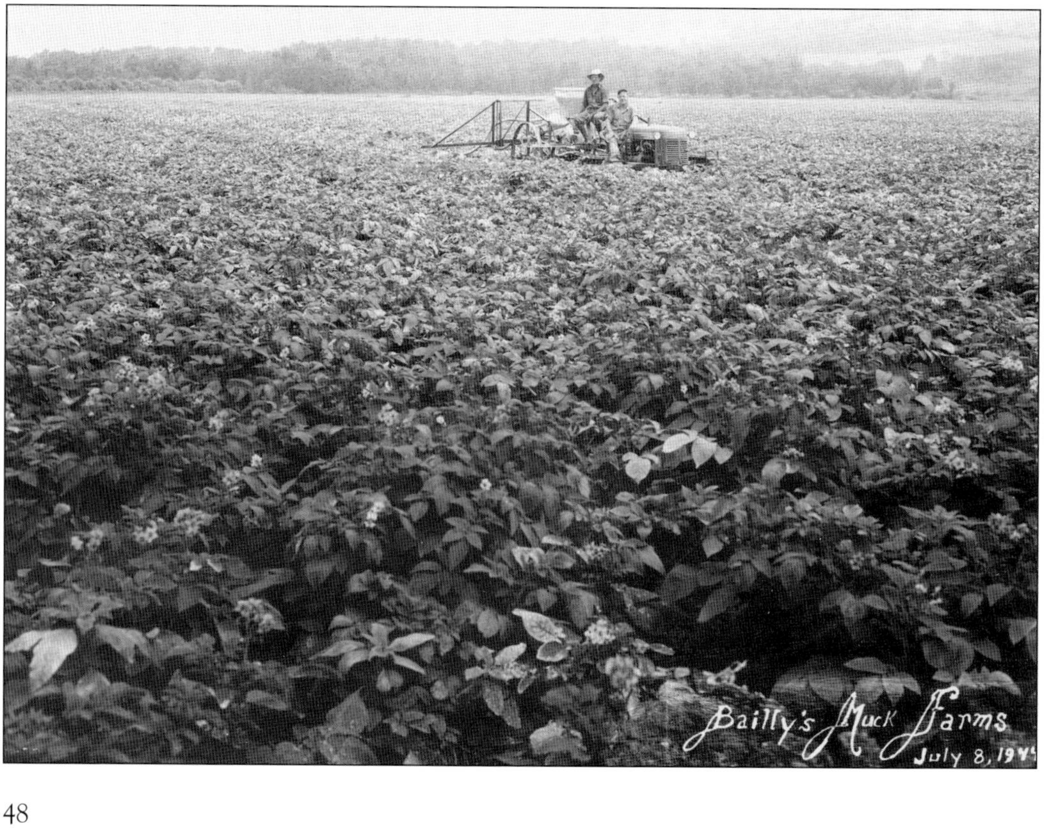

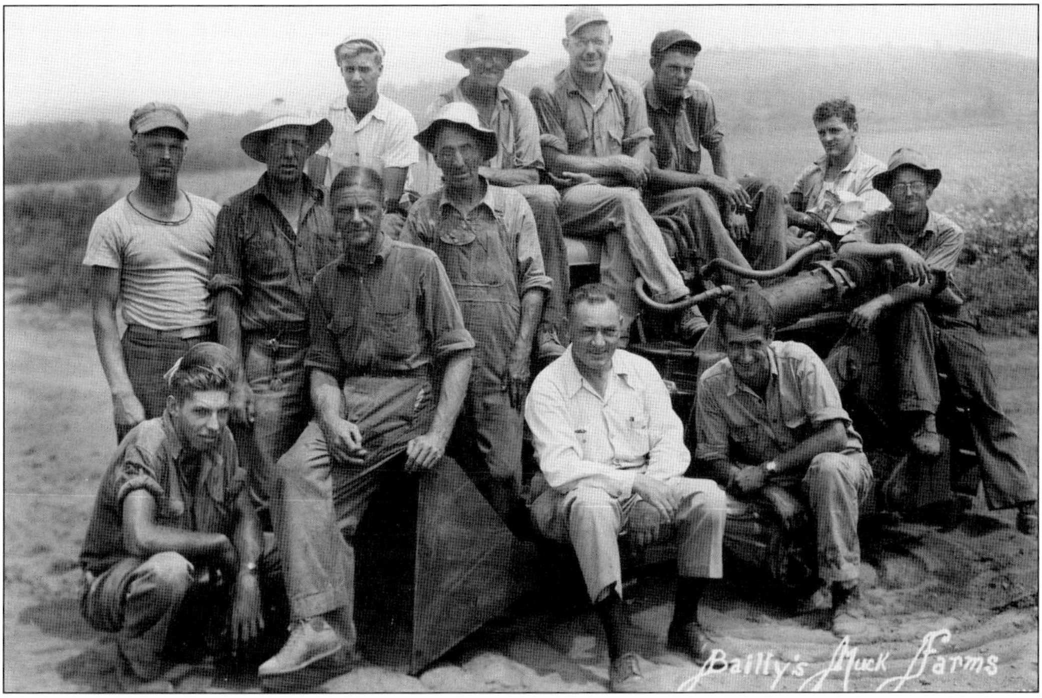

Agriculture provided many economic opportunities in Prattsburgh. On July 8, 1944, this hardworking crew at Bailly's Muck Farms took a well-deserved break to pose for this picture. The men harvested the onions, potatoes, and other crops by hand, filling the large crates that were placed along the crop rows.

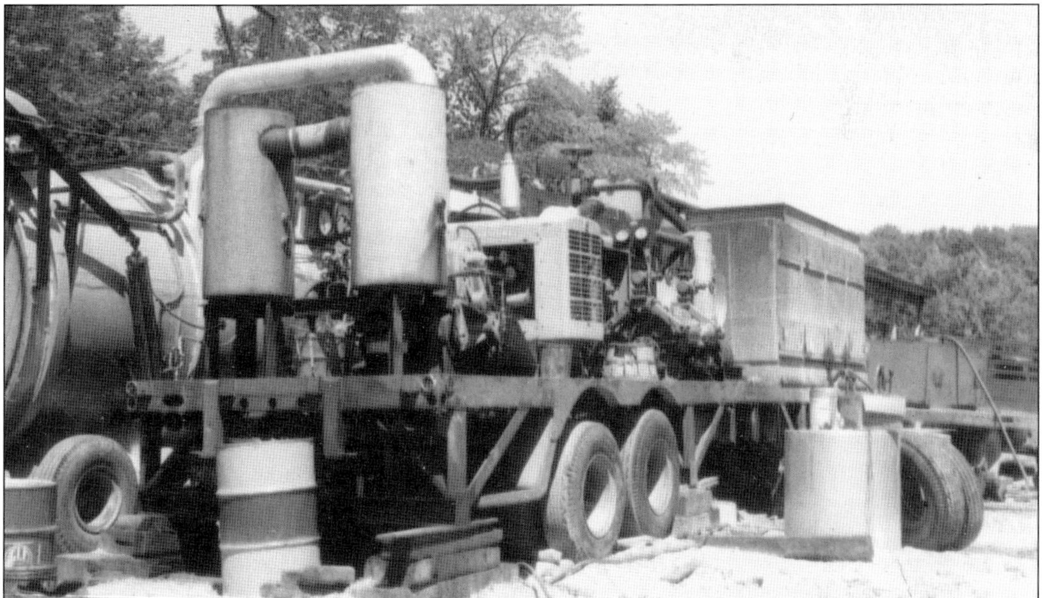

When lettuce was a major crop on the muck, there was a need to cool it once it was picked. Large machinery was installed to accommodate this task quickly and efficiently so that it could be loaded on trucks for transport to the rail yard.

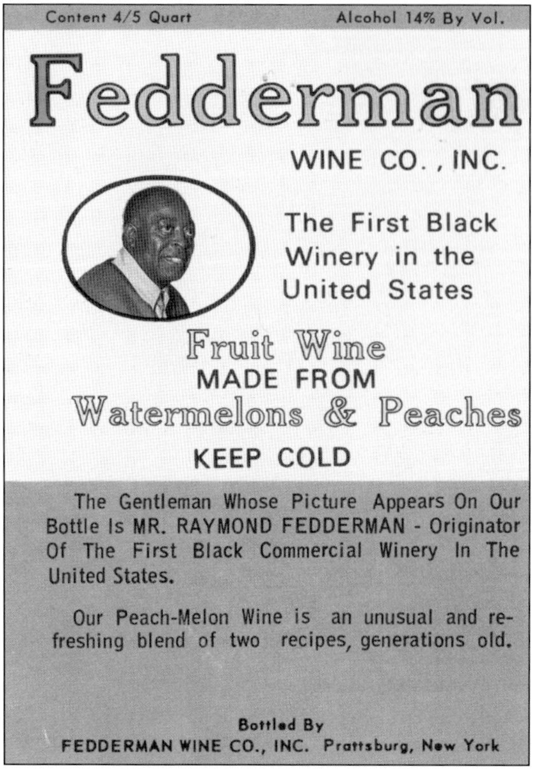

Fedderman Wine Company was the first black-owned winery in the United States. The winery, located on Route 53 South, produced both red and white wines. Founder Raymond Fedderman was a former migrant farm worker who was encouraged to start the winery by prominent local winemaker Greyton Taylor and son Walter Taylor. Although many wineries exist in the area today, Fedderman's is no longer among them.

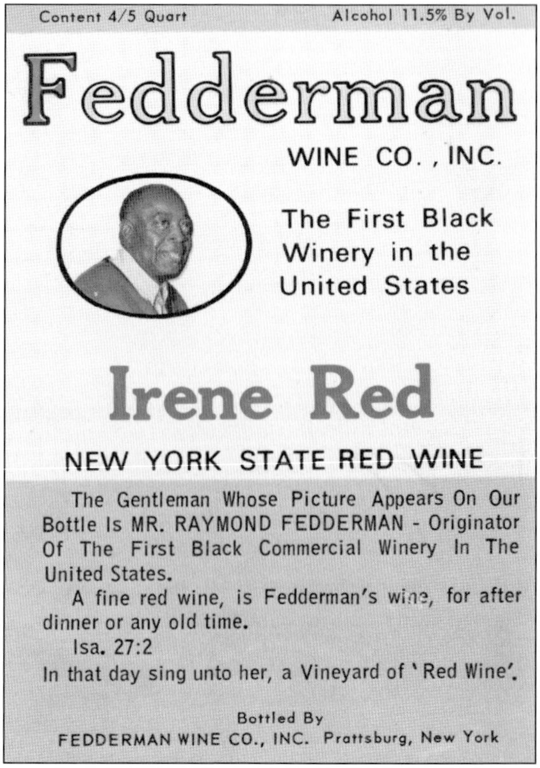

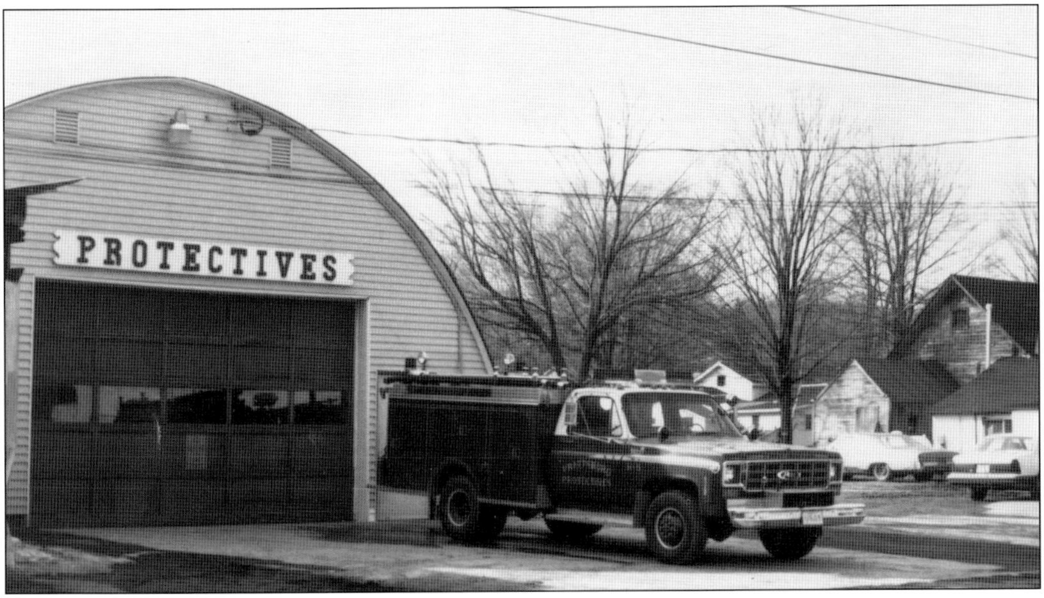

The Prattsburgh Protectives volunteer firefighters were organized in 1882 with 28 charter members. The fires were extinguished by use of a "pumper," which was operated by two men at each end and water was carried by buckets. Wells were established in two different positions, one in the Village Park and one behind the stores. The firehouse was in the Stone Building (formerly the Kremlin Block). In 2005, a new firehouse was built, and they were able to move in on January 13, 2006. Membership currently totals 68 active members, eight honorary, and nine junior firefighters. A far cry from 1882, the Prattsburgh Protectives now own five trucks—a 1990 Freightliner pumper, a 1996 Freightliner tanker, a 1996 GMC Brush Truck, a 2000 Freightliner Rescue Truck, and a 2010 Pierce Pumper. Instead of the two wells, there are now 67 fire hydrants located throughout the town.

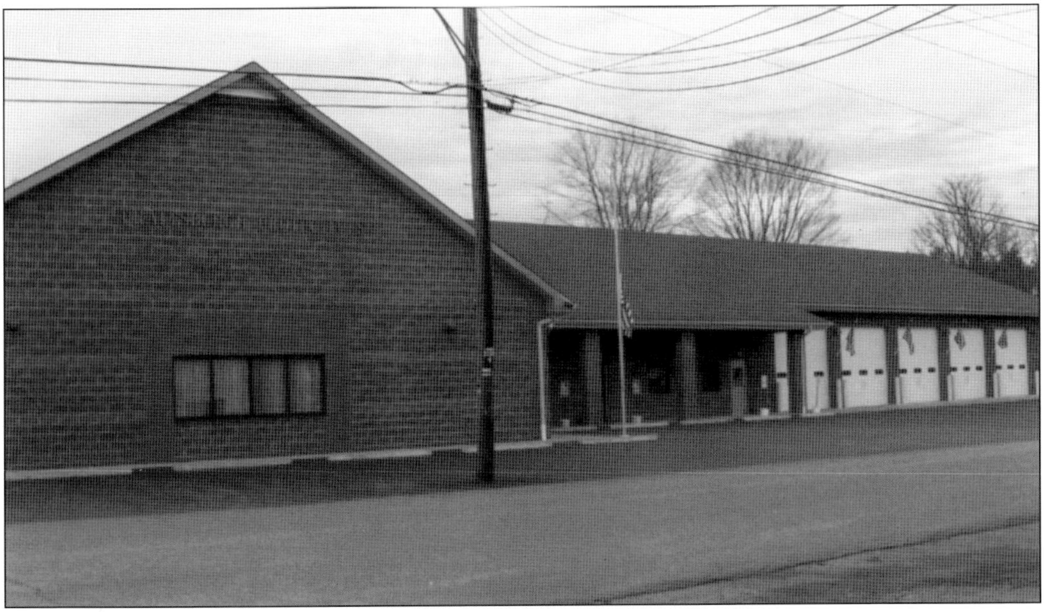

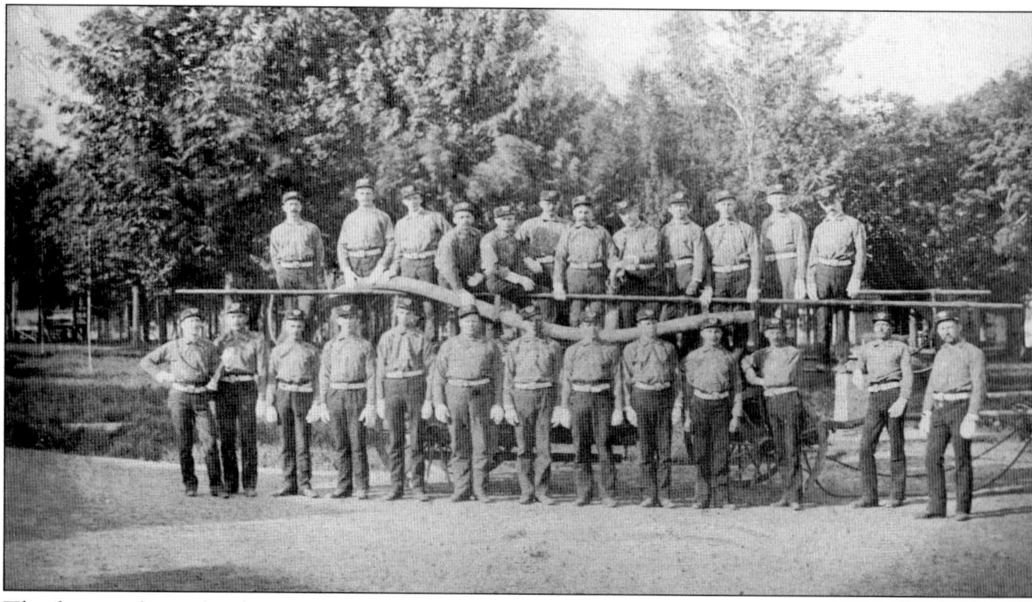

The first uniforms for the Prattsburgh Protectives were purchased in November 1883 and consisted of a cream-colored shirt and wide belt. A fine of $1 was imposed on anyone who wore his uniform on any other occasion except company activities, parades, or drills. In July 1892, the Fire Protective Company became a member of the County Firemen's Association. These brave men voluntarily provided a valuable service to the community, a service that proudly continues to this day.

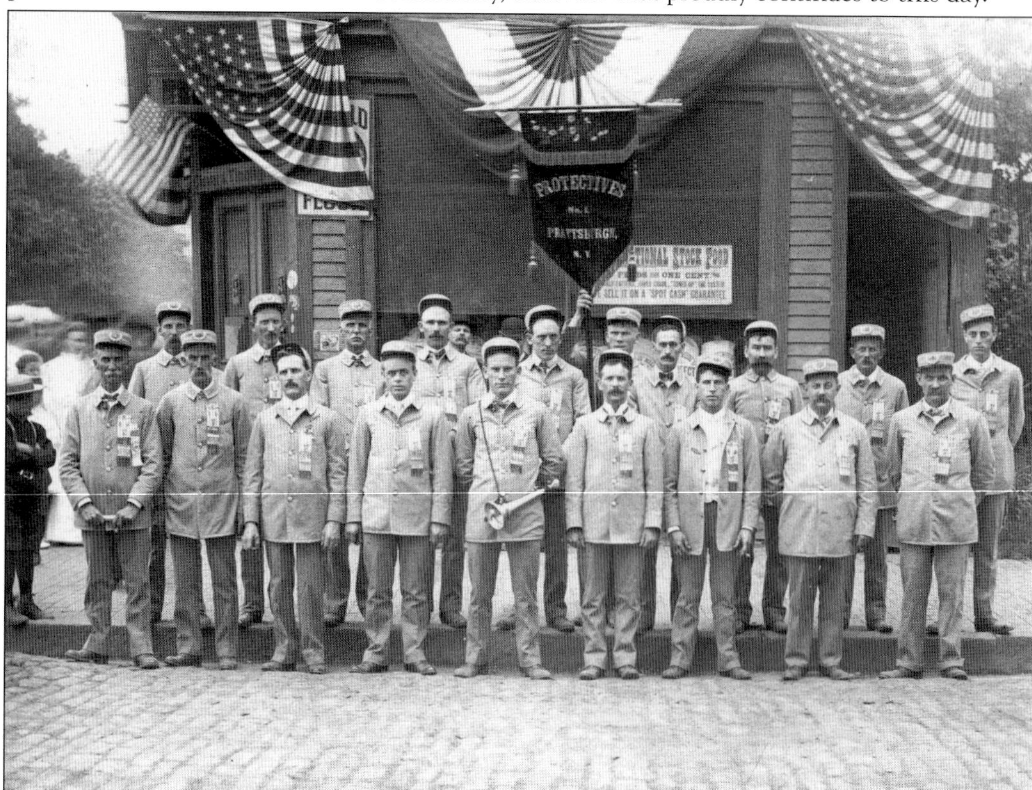

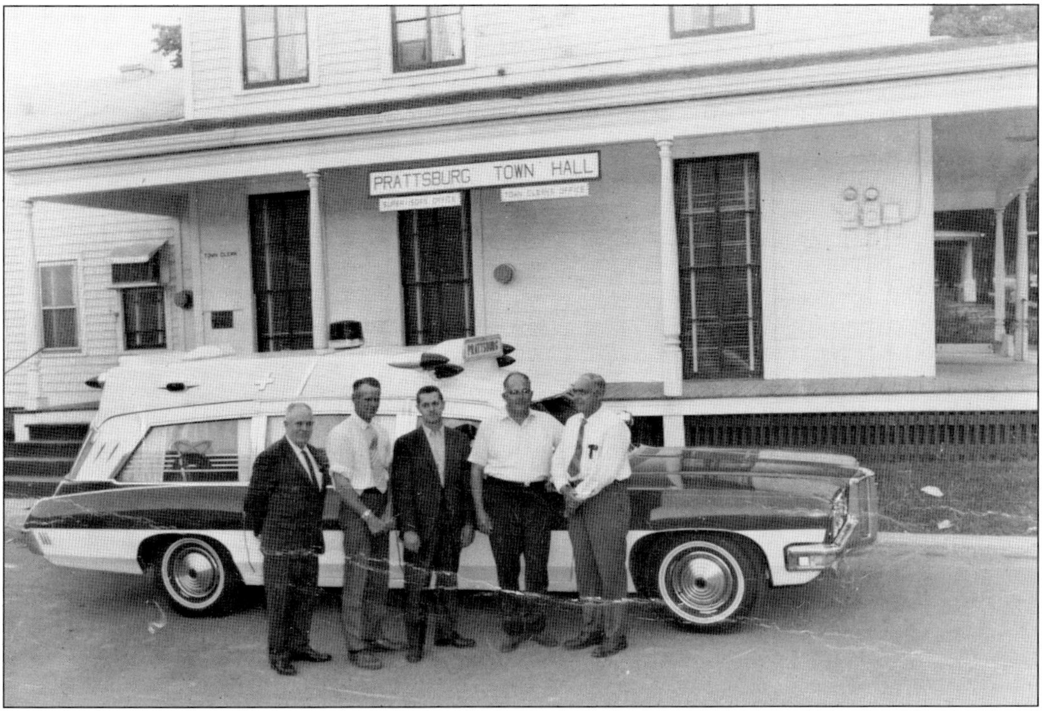

The Prattsburgh Ambulance Corps was run by the Town of Prattsburgh and dispatched by the town clerk. In May 2004, the town decided to turn over the Prattsburgh Ambulance Corps to the fire department, and the agreement was finalized January 2, 2005. Town fathers Walton Pulver, Robert Babcock, Paul Graves, Charles Moesch, and Stanley McDougal are shown here in front of a newly purchased ambulance.

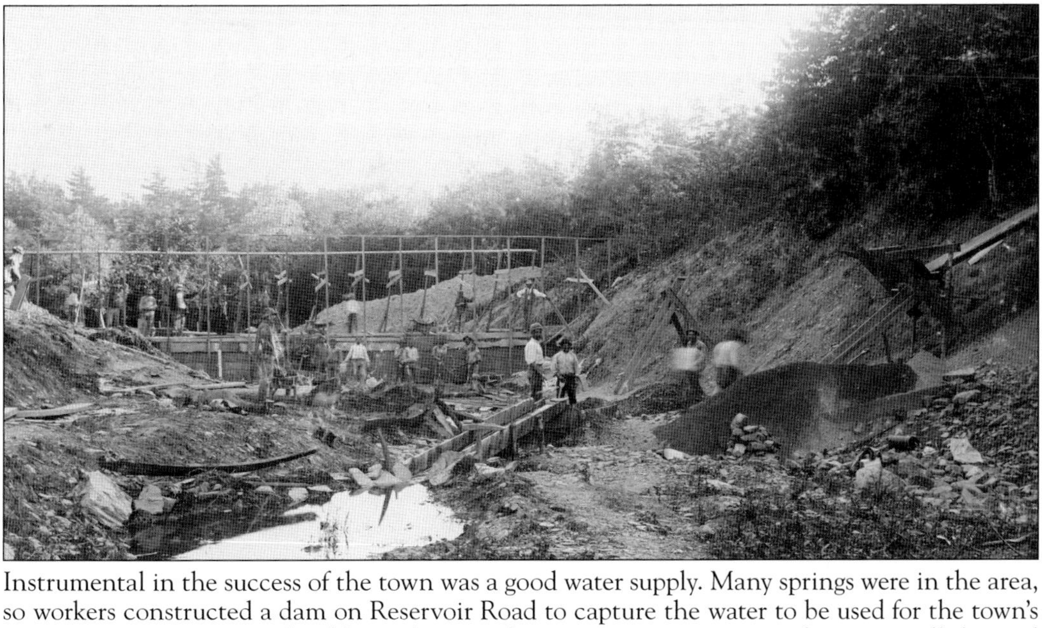

Instrumental in the success of the town was a good water supply. Many springs were in the area, so workers constructed a dam on Reservoir Road to capture the water to be used for the town's water source. Due to state health regulations, the town now gets its water from two wells located on County Route 75.

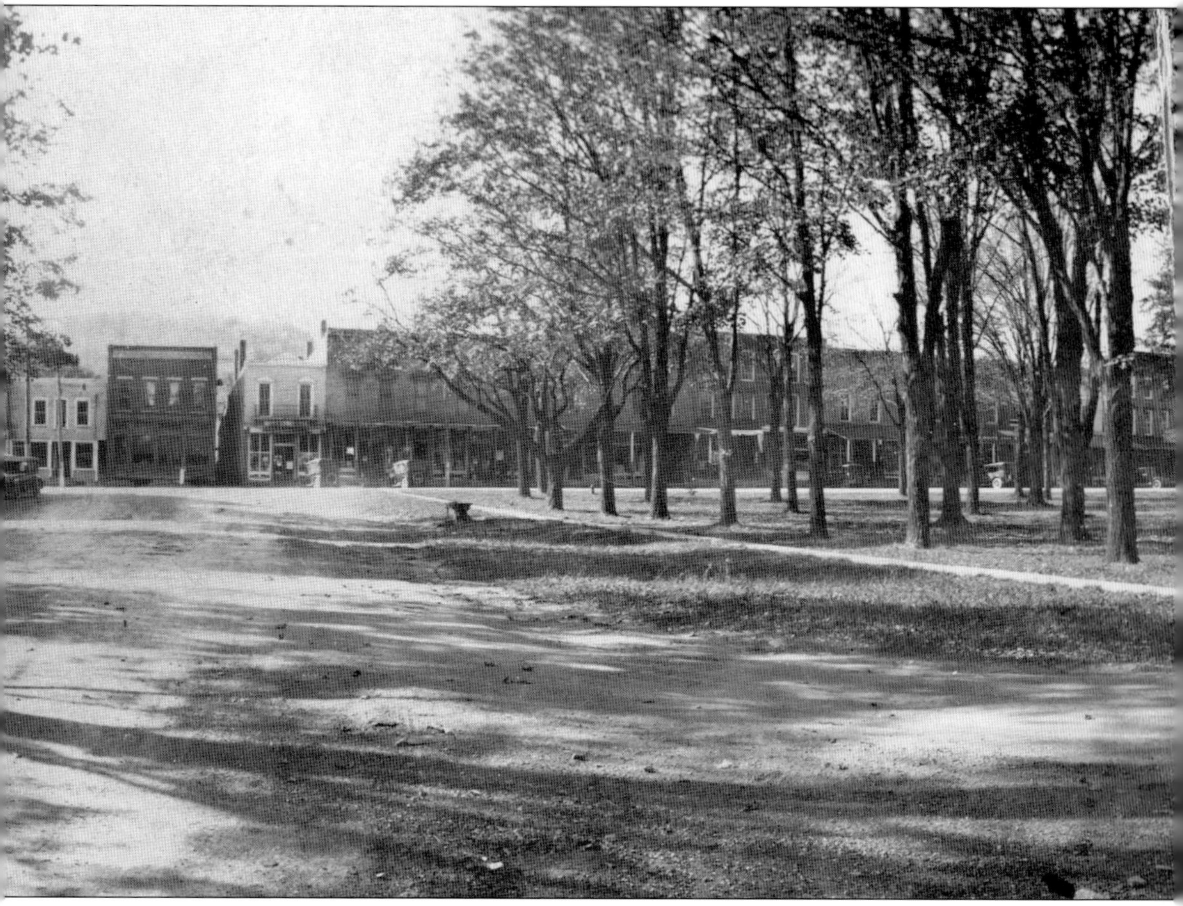

The Village Park is one of the town's greatest assets. It was deeded to the Prattsburgh Religious Society by Robert Porter, who stipulated that the land be forever free from permanent buildings so that all could enjoy recreation there. The park was graded and the first trees planted in 1848. The park was enclosed with a rail fence until 1876. Martin Pinney acquired the rails, which were

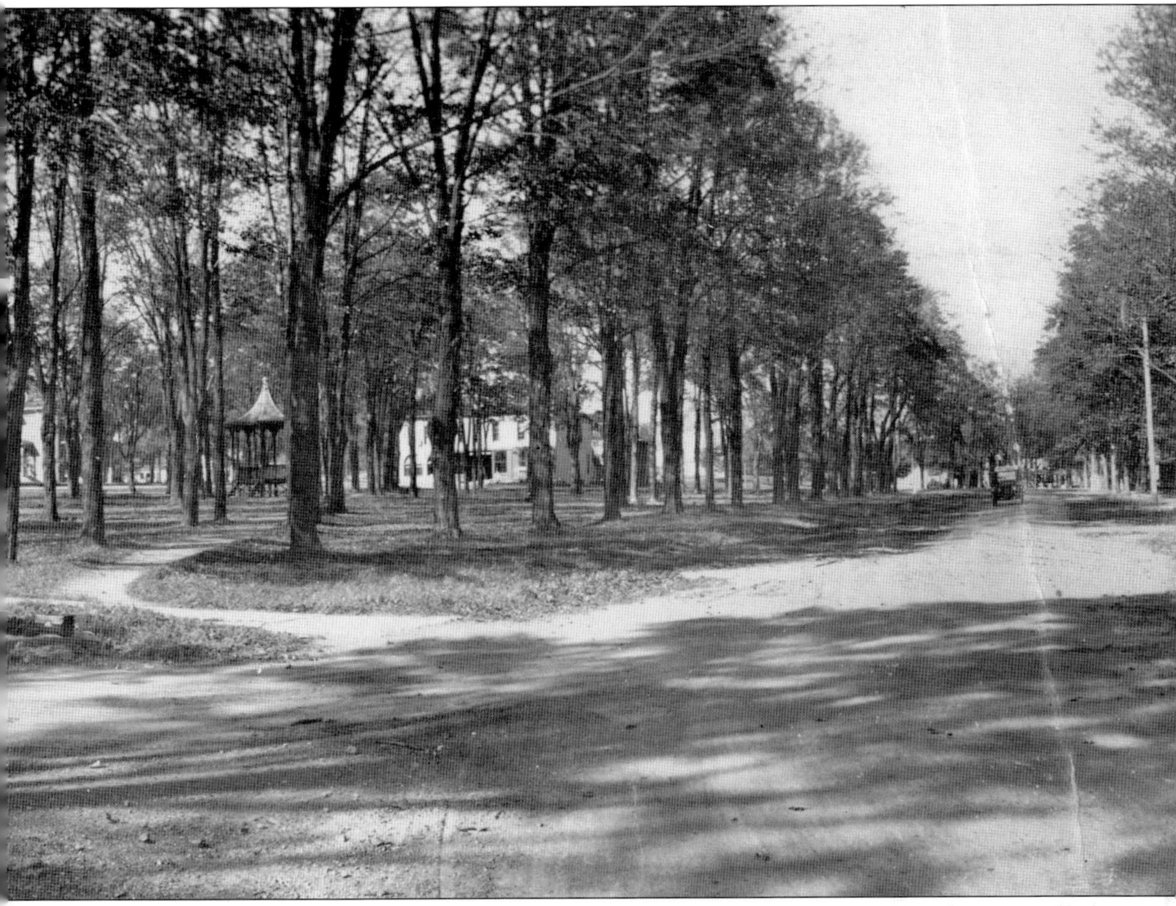

turned by a lathe into spindles for a picket fence for his own use. The fence was later installed in front of the Pioneer Cemetery. In the middle, there was a small pond, which was thought to have been used by the Prattsburgh Protectives as a source of water for firefighting.

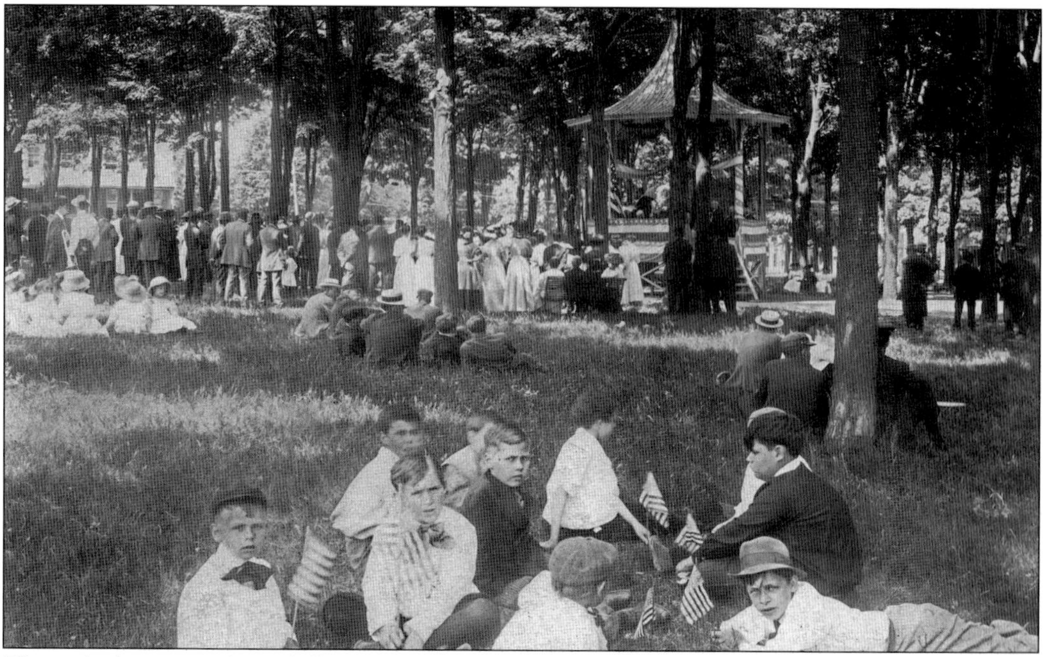

Through the years, three different gazebos have been built in the park. The first one was built in 1877 and had eight sides and a curved, pointed roof. This was torn down in 1938, and a new bandstand without a roof was built. In 1949, a cement floor was installed and a roof was added. This bandstand allowed for many hours of musical enjoyment by providing a place for bands to perform. This bandstand was eventually torn down, and in 1976, Warren Johnson designed and built the present gazebo as a project for the nation's bicentennial celebration. The current one closely resembles the first gazebo but now includes an honor roll of the town's veterans.

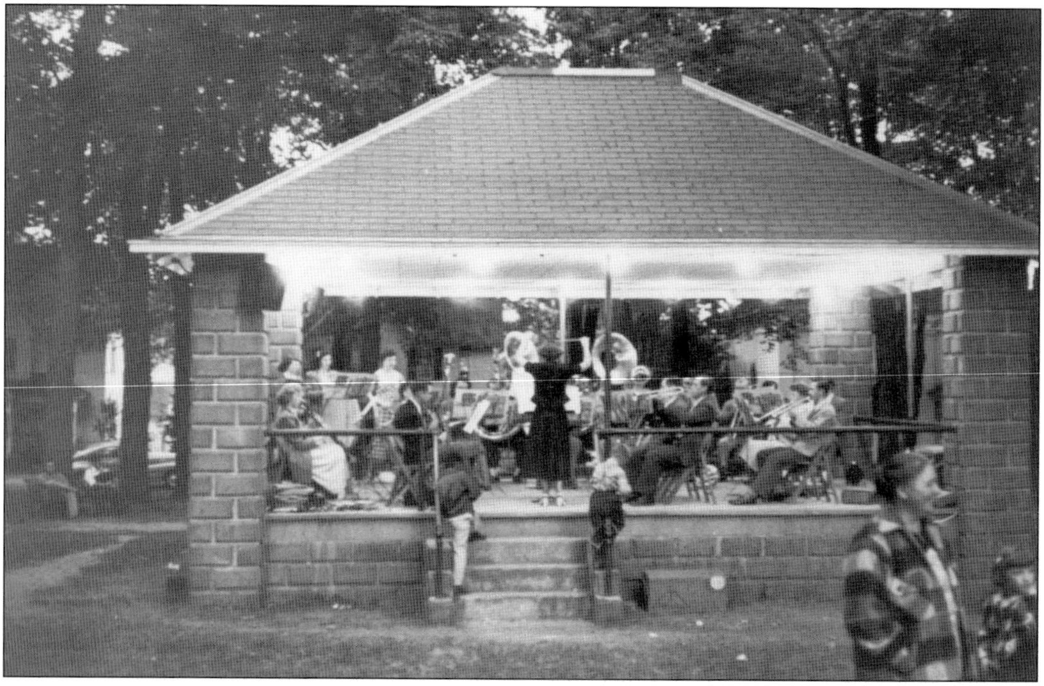

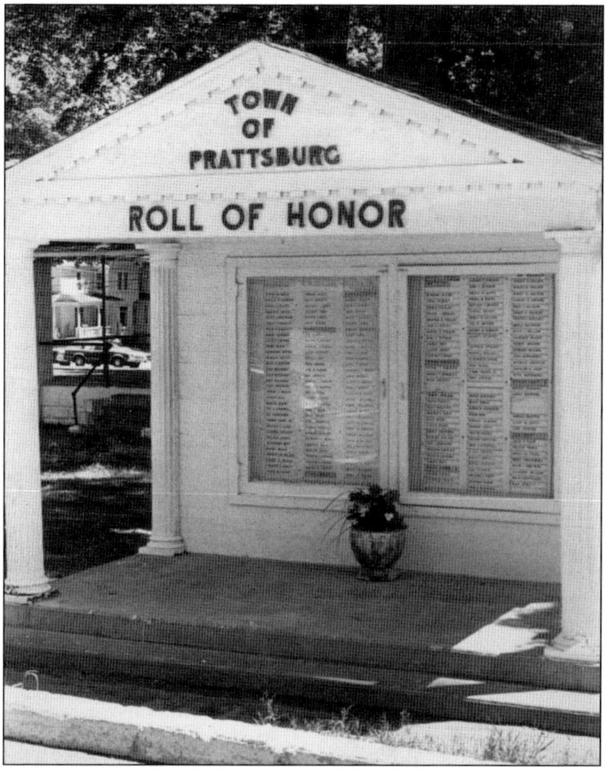

The Roll of Honor was built to honor the Prattsburgh veterans. It was eventually torn down and replaced by a flagpole and landscaping. The Roll of Honor was then placed in the center of the current gazebo to allow for new names to be added as needed. Memorial Day services led by the Francis J. Flaherty American Legion Post are held every year at the park by the flagpole to honor those who served. A loyal citizen of Prattsburgh, Ralph "Stub" Wetmore always raised the flag on Memorial Day.

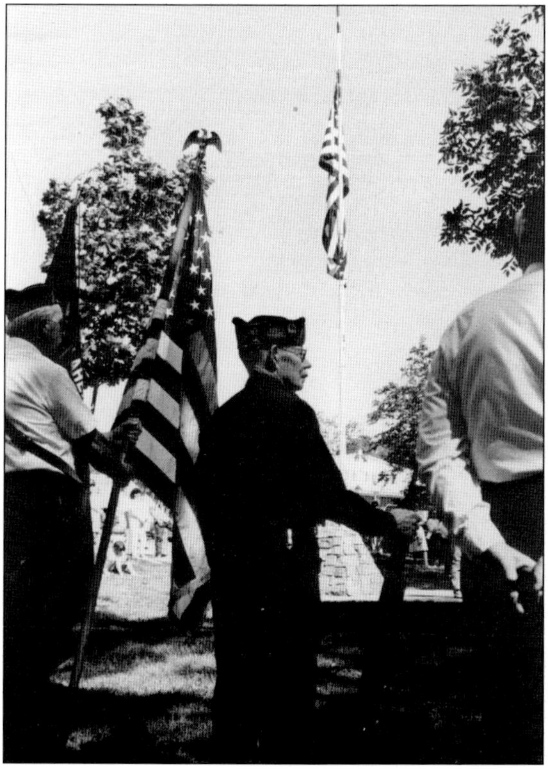

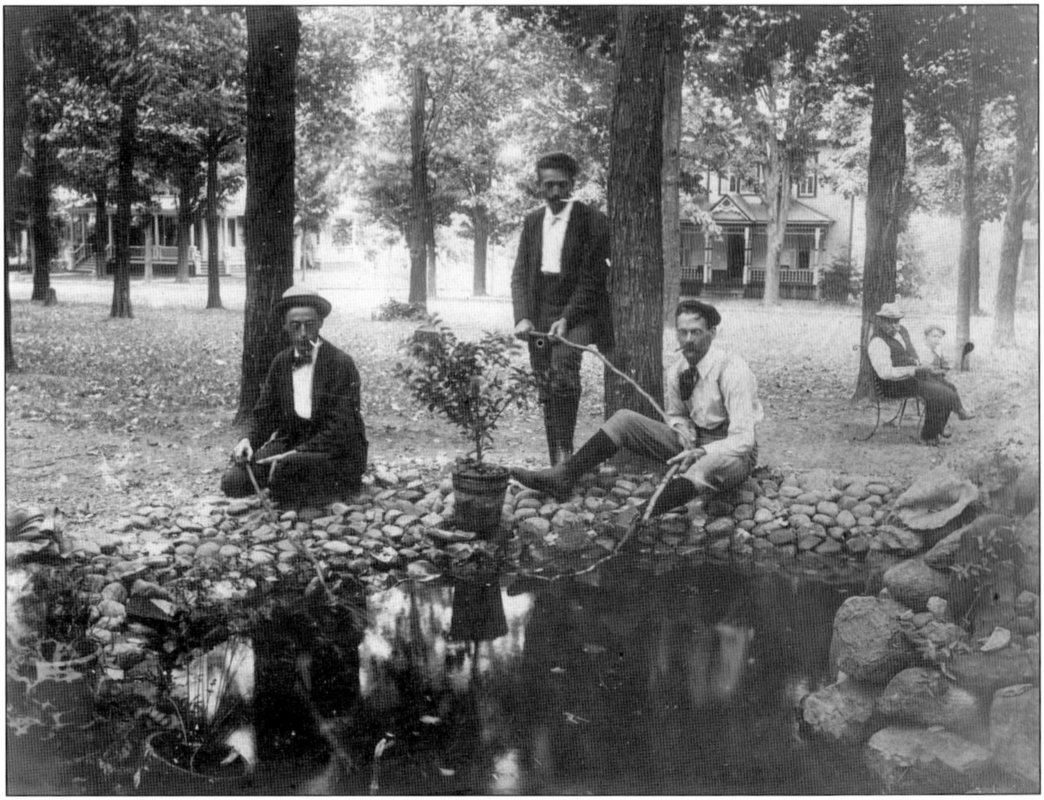

True to its original covenant, the park in the center of town remains a public space free of permanent buildings. Past residents have used the park for many activities, including Memorial Day and Fourth of July celebrations, annual festivals, and leisurely recreation. The park continues to provide much enjoyment for the town's residents, hosting Music in the Park concerts, the annual Summerfest, the winter Festival of Trees, and the occasional wedding.

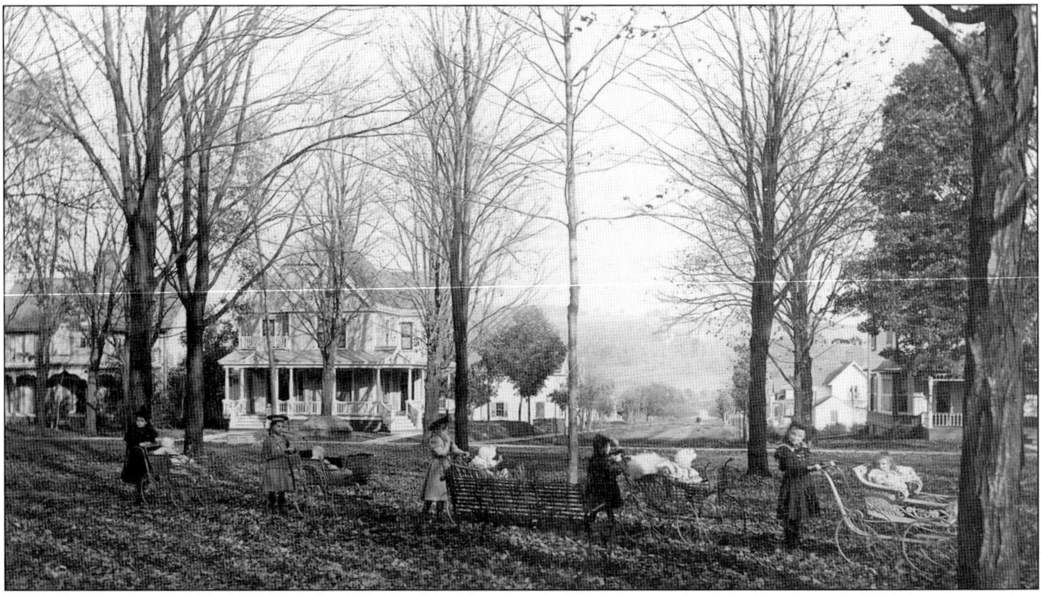

Four

Prattsburgh in the Past

Like other towns across early America, Prattsburgh was a thriving place in its heyday. The town was self-sufficient, with businesses providing residents with food, clothing, and blacksmith services to name a few. The construction of the railroad enabled goods to be transported in and out of the town and also brought visitors to the area.

Prattsburgh had the fortune of having good flowing creeks running through the town. This allowed for several lumber and grain mills, which derived their power from the water, to spring up along the creeks. These mills provided essential lumber, flour, and animal feed to the town.

Residents also found time to enjoy the many cultural and recreational activities available. There were several venues for plays that featured such performances as *The Cantata of Queen Esther*, *H.M.S. Pinafore*, and *Regards of the Bachelor.* Regular weekly dances were held at the Park Hotel and Dean Hall. Memorial Day and Fourth of July celebrations always featured a parade of gaily decorated buggies, and later cars, that would roll down Main Street. The town once boasted three hotels to accommodate the many visitors coming in on the stagecoach and railroad.

Currently, there is little evidence of this bustling community in present-day Prattsburgh.

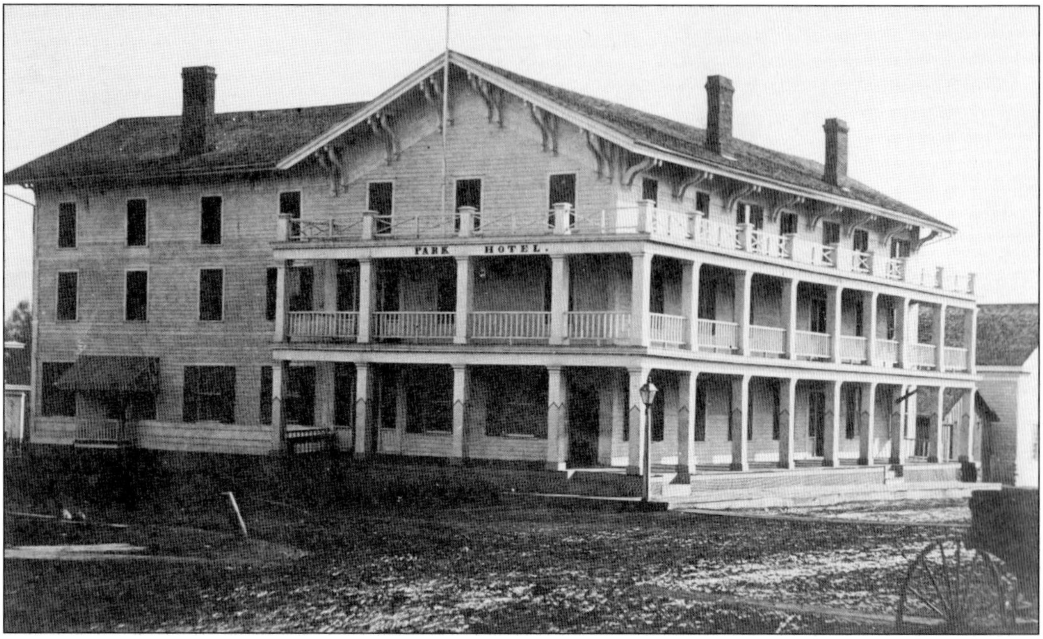

The Park Hotel was built in 1852 and operated as a hotel and restaurant until 1946. It had three stories and 44 rooms. The third floor was a magnificent floating ballroom, where dances, patent medicine shows, and theatrical presentations were held. The hotel closed briefly during the Prohibition era when alcohol could no longer be served. The contents of the hotel were auctioned off, and the hotel was razed in 1955 to be replaced by a garage and filling station in 1962. With the destruction of the Park Hotel, a part of the history of Prattsburgh had come to a close.

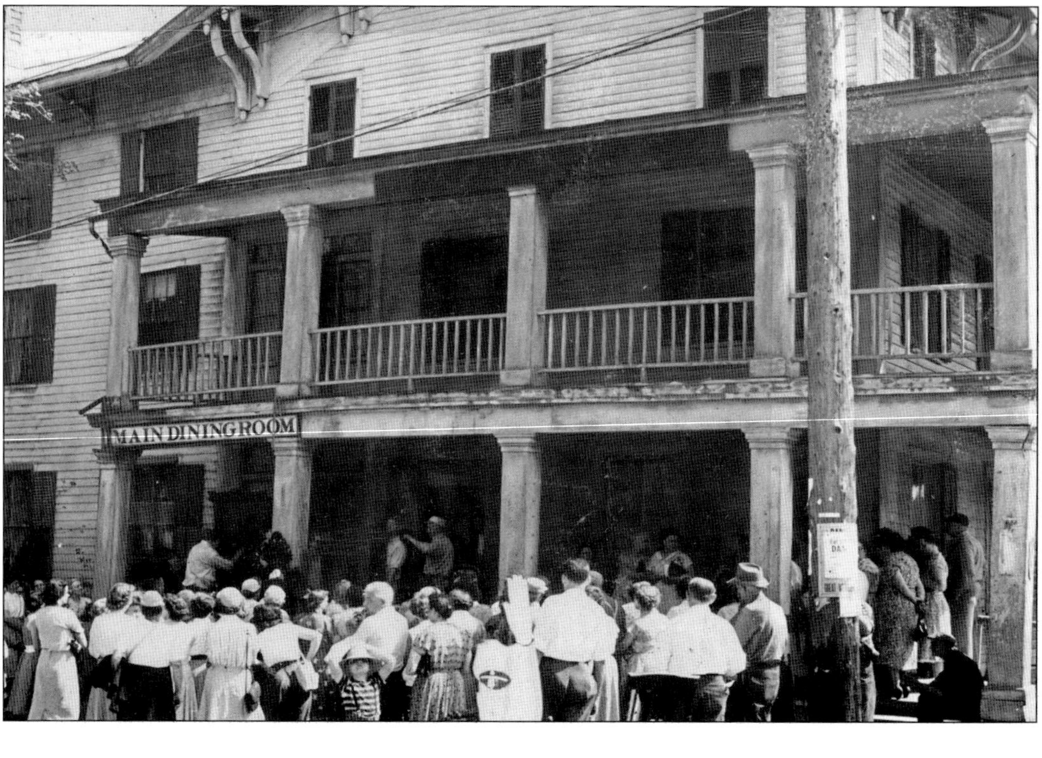

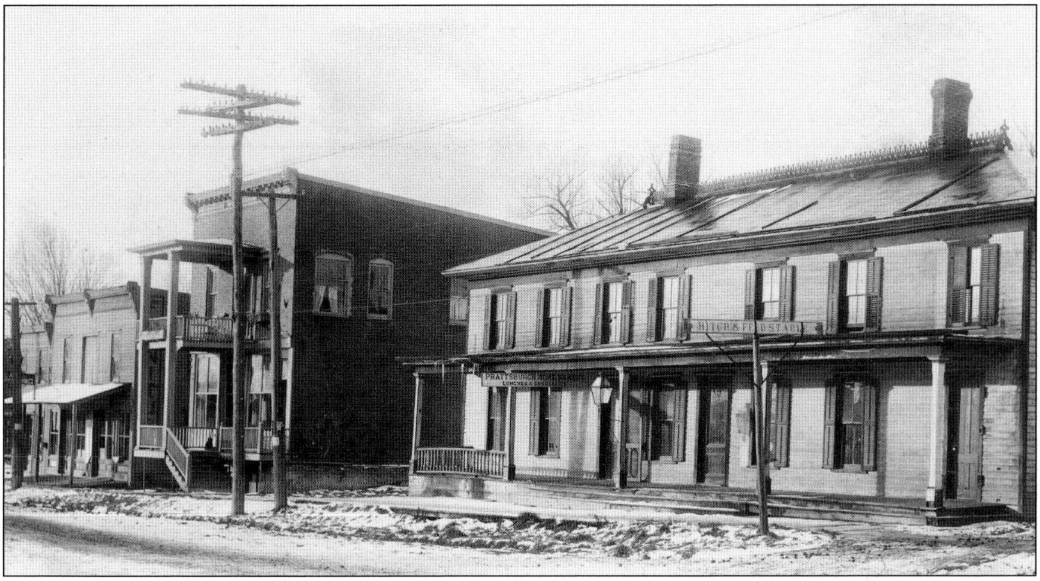

The Relyea Hotel was located on South Main Street at the site of the first school building in Prattsburgh. That building was dismantled by Frank Relyea, who constructed a home there in 1839. In 1915, it was converted into a hotel to accommodate travelers when the Park Hotel closed briefly during the Prohibition era. It was torn down in 1923.

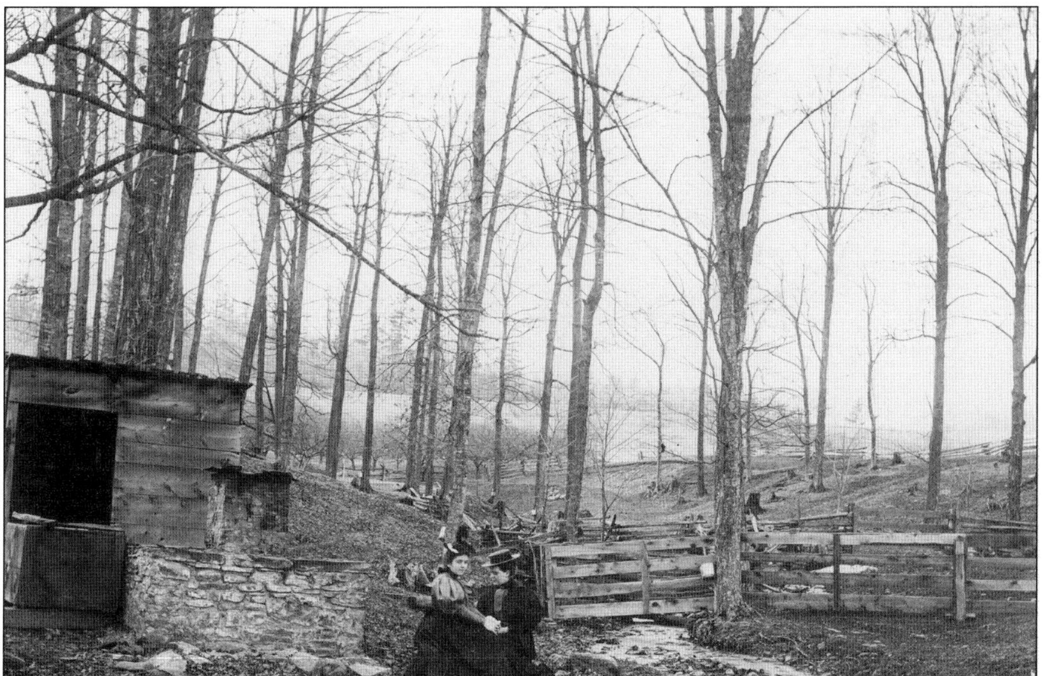

The prevalence of maple trees in this heavily forested area made for good maple syrup production. This sugar bush was located behind Capt. Joel Pratt's home on what is now State Route 53.

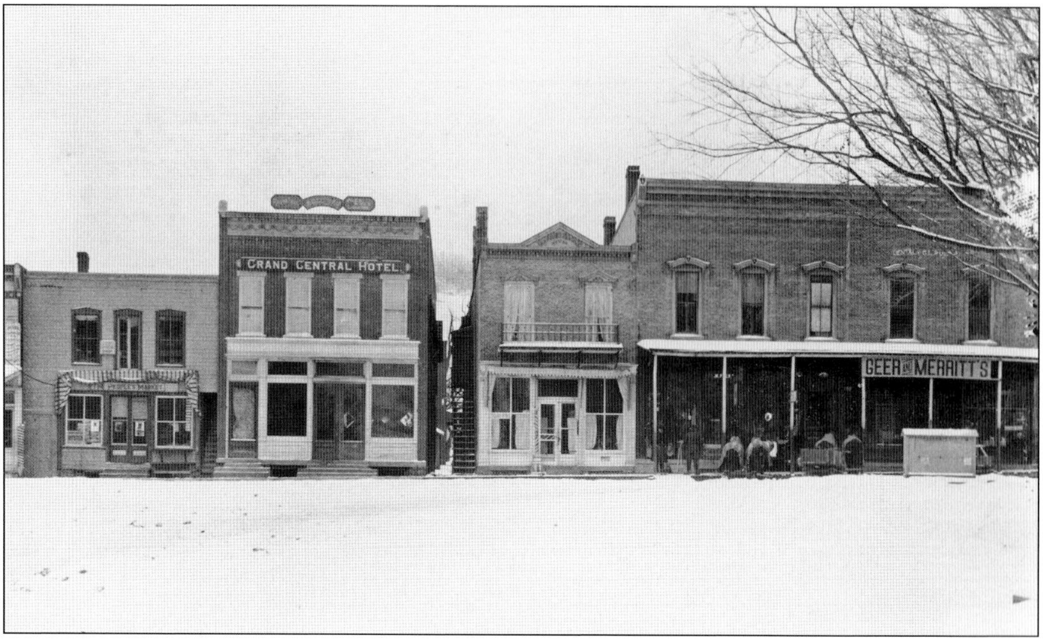

The Grand Central (second from left) was built in 1869. It was a saloon occupied by Michael Curran. After many years, the wooden front was removed and used as part of a residence on Mechanic Street. Curran replaced the front with bricks. This structure was used by the Prattsburgh Phone Company, which tore it down and constructed a new building in 1961.

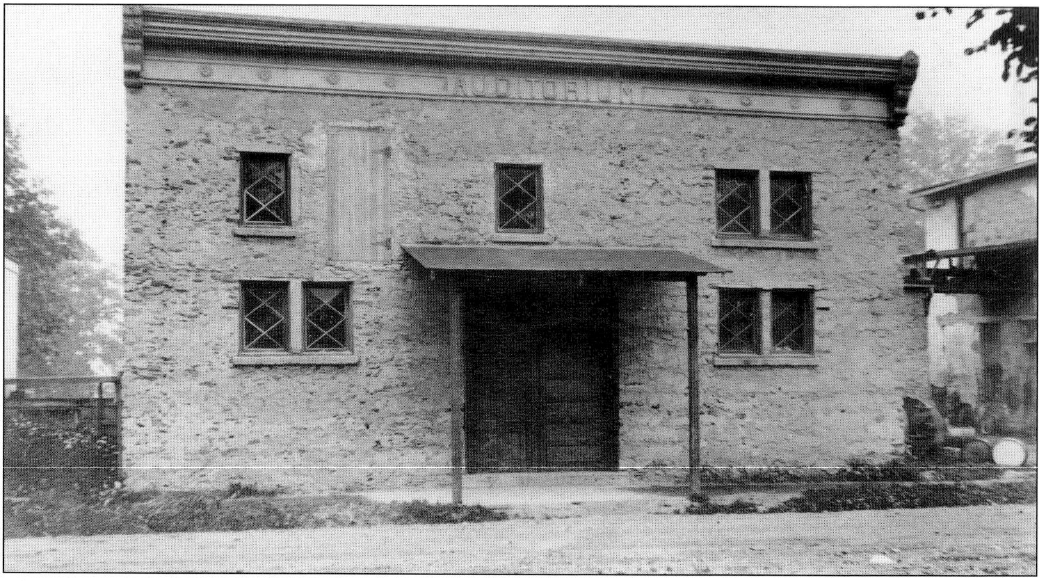

The auditorium was built in 1906 by William A. McConnell and was used for many forms of entertainment. Silent moving pictures were shown here by Wallace W. Cole, assisted by Harold Lee, who later managed the Babcock Theatre in Bath. From 1924 to 1936, this building was also used by Franklin Academy for school-related activities until the school constructed its own auditorium. It burned in 1932, and the stone was removed from the walls for use in road building. The cellar was filled in and graveled over for a parking lot.

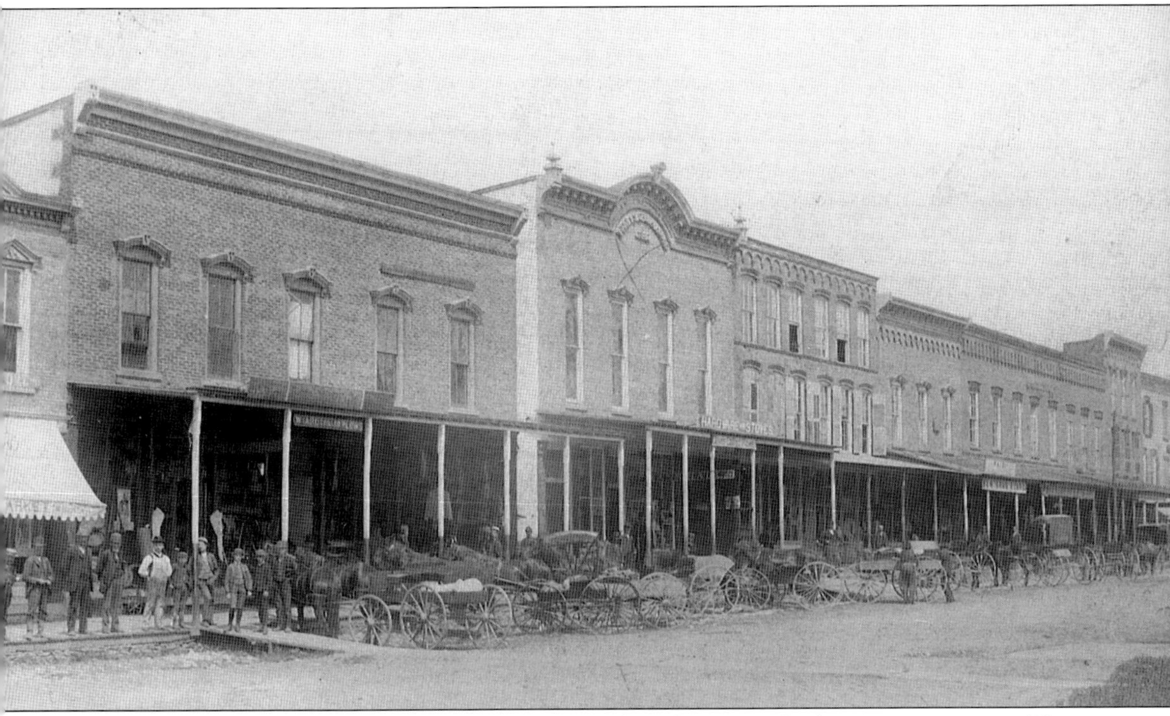

Martin Pinney built the opera house in 1882 to be used for dances and other entertainment. The building extended over the alleyway creating a good size second floor for use of showing movies, holding parties, and organization meetings. In 1898, the building caught fire in the basement and was entirely burned. It was rebuilt in 1900 by George W. Peck, and the first floor was occupied by a dry good store in 1901. It was later used as a drugstore, known as the Wheeler Brothers, until 1951.

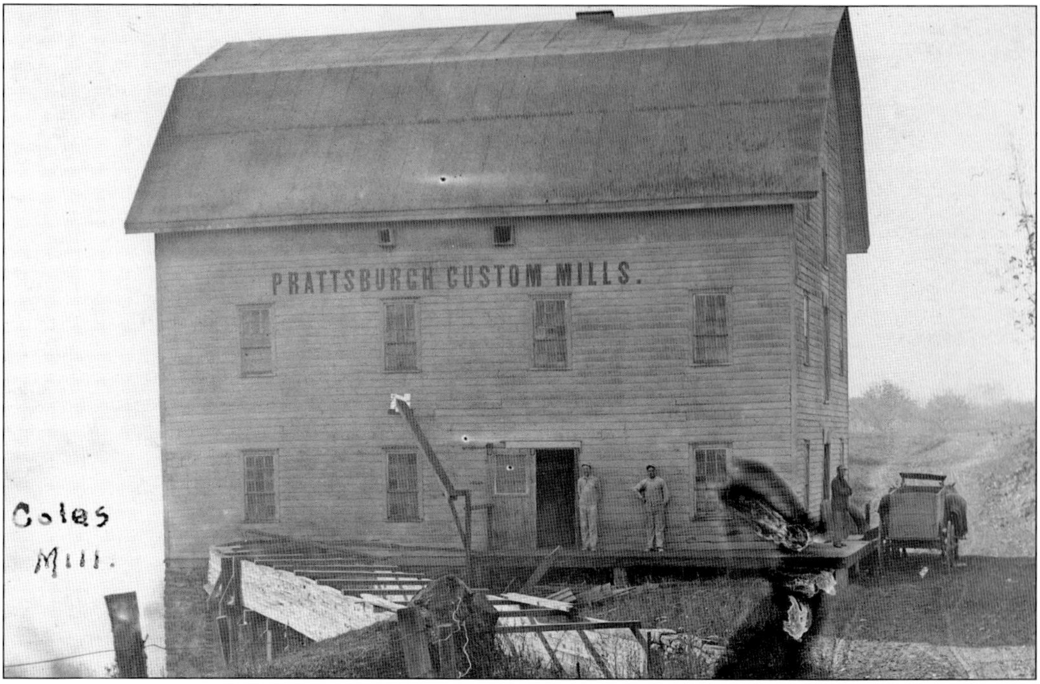

Built by Charles G. Higby 1850, this flour mill on County Route 74, or Mill Street as it was known then, made flour by stone grinding. The mill was equipped with four runs of stone. On the first run, the shuck was taken off the grain. Next it was ground a little finer and middlings taken off, and finally, the next two produced the fine bread flour. The mill ran for 78 years with different owners. It was destroyed by fire in 1928 and never rebuilt.

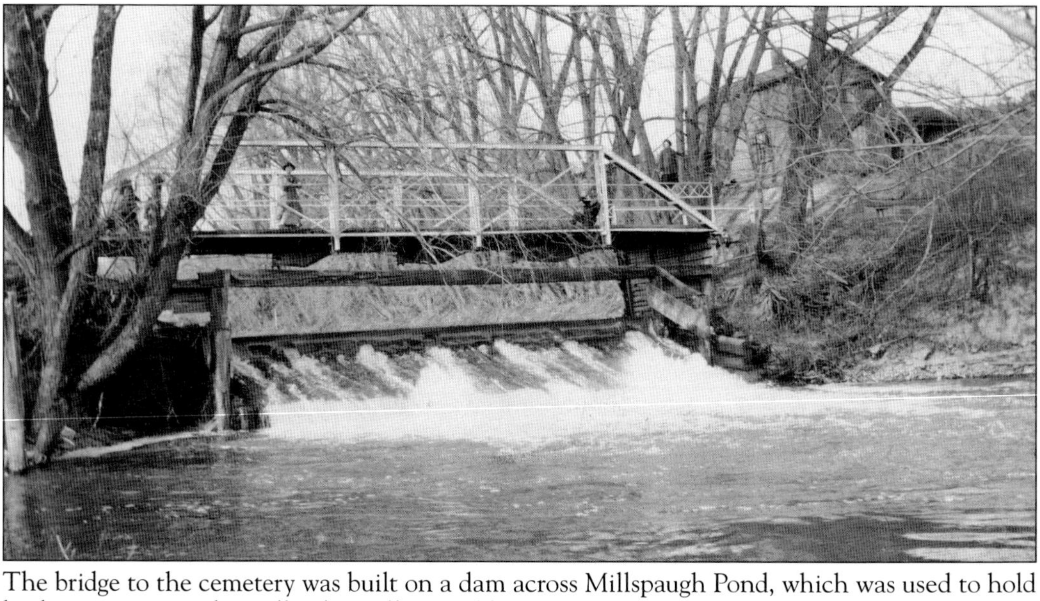

The bridge to the cemetery was built on a dam across Millspaugh Pond, which was used to hold back water to run the mill. The miller would take a tenth of the grain for his fee (called toll). The grain was ground between millstones by a covered cylinder that revolved slowly and sifted through a cloth. It was said to be the best flour anywhere. This mill was known for a long time as the Cole Mill.

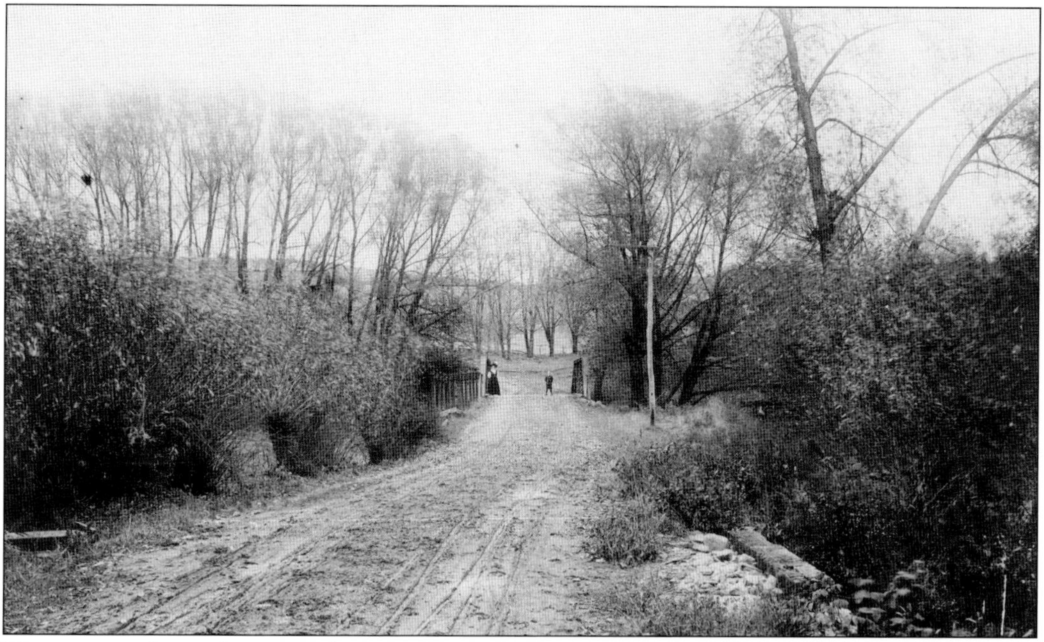

This picture shows the view of the top of the dam on County Road 75, heading toward the cemetery. In these early days, the dirt roads bore the scars of the wagon wheels and made travel in wet weather difficult.

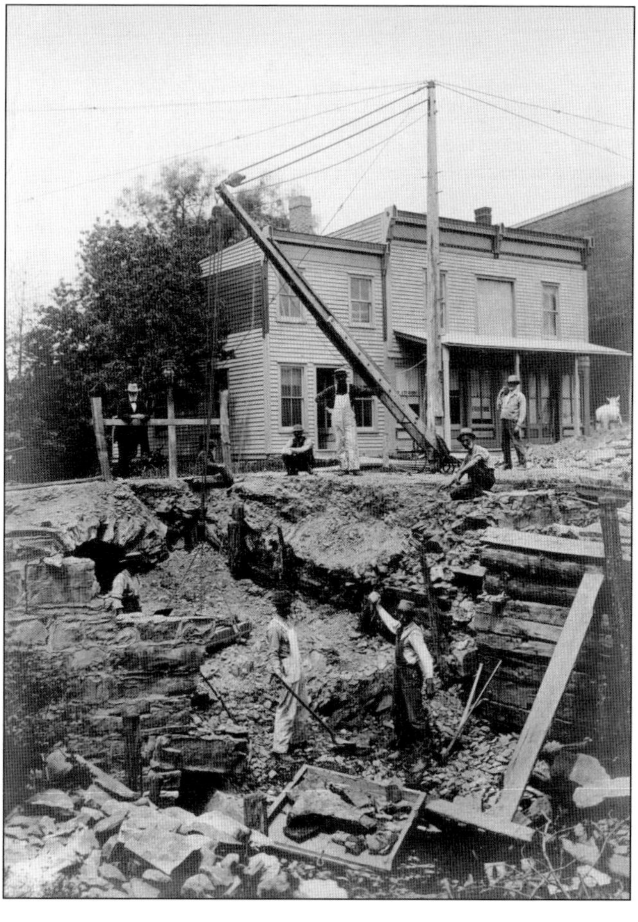

Creeks provided a valuable resource for the town, except when the flow of water became destructive. As seen here, there was much devastation when the bridge on South Main Street washed out in a flood on July 5, 1902.

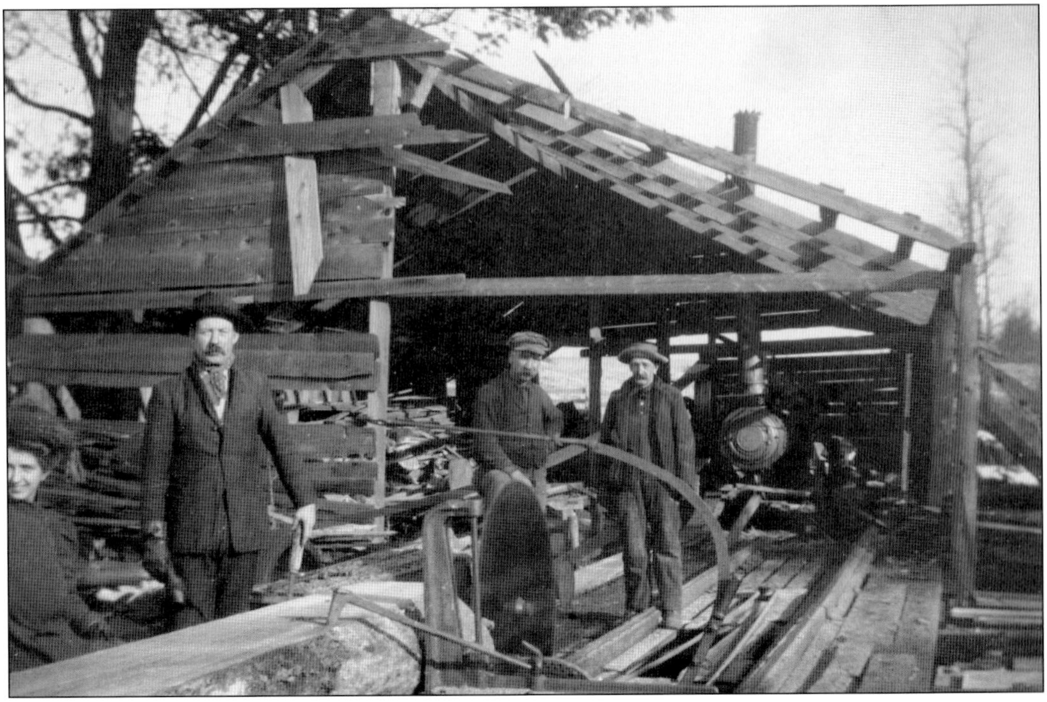

Sawmills were a critical part of the development of Prattsburgh. The lumber used to build the homes and businesses came from the surrounding forests. There were 11 water dams in Five Mile Creek between Kanona and its source near Italy Hill. The creeks were used to float logs downstream, and nearly all of the dams furnished power for sawing lumber. Lumbering was big business at the dawn of the 20th century.

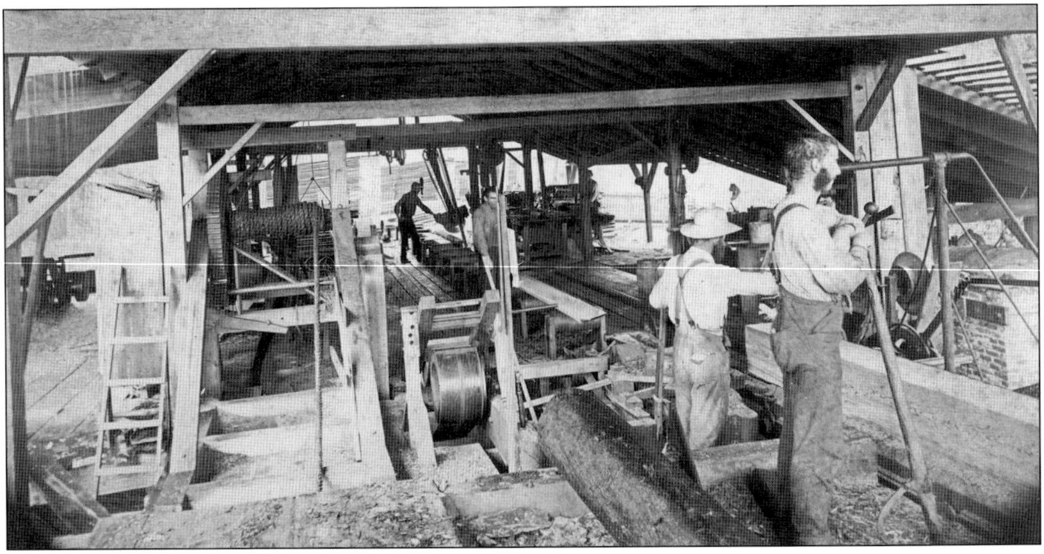

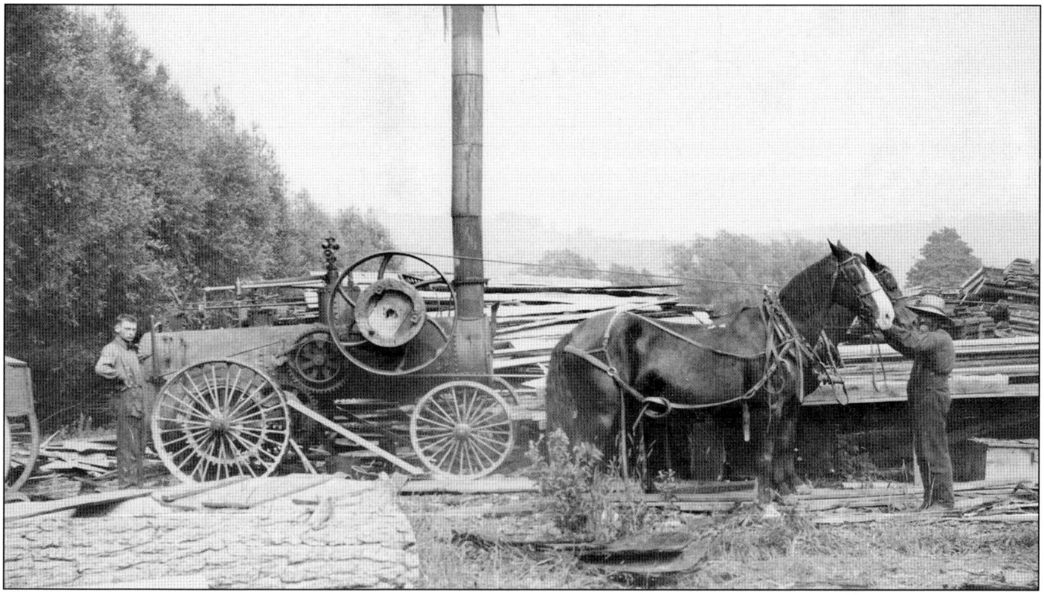

Without modern technology, early residents relied on real "horsepower" to harvest and transport the logs needed for building the town. A good team of horses was invaluable to the operation. The sawmills themselves provided employment for the town and helped create the need for secondary businesses, such as the blacksmith, the furniture maker, and the home builders, which also contributed to the growth of the town.

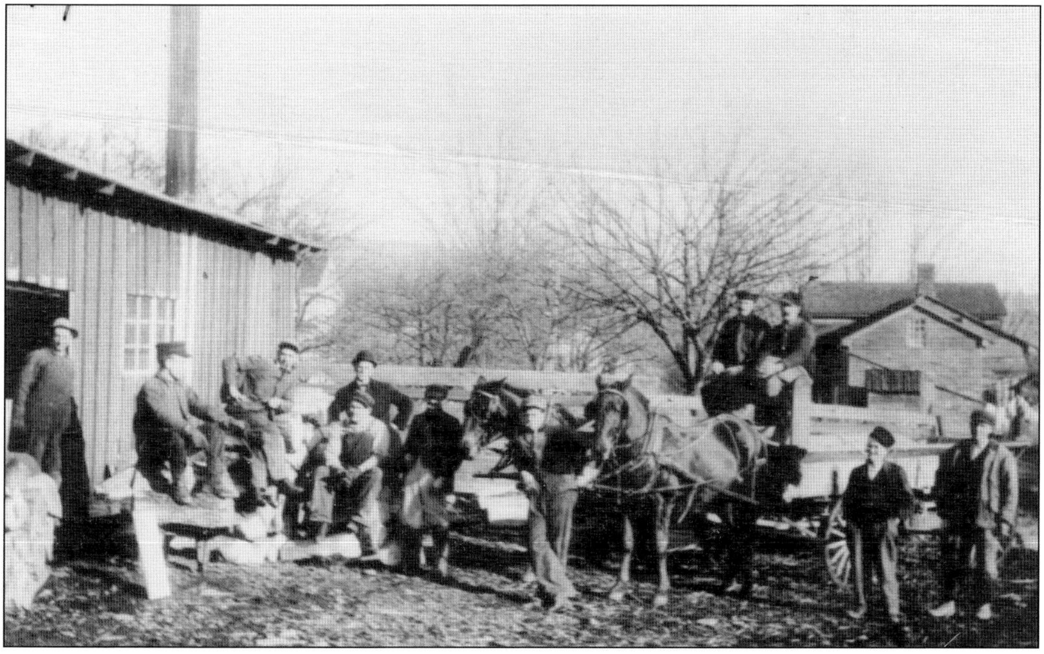

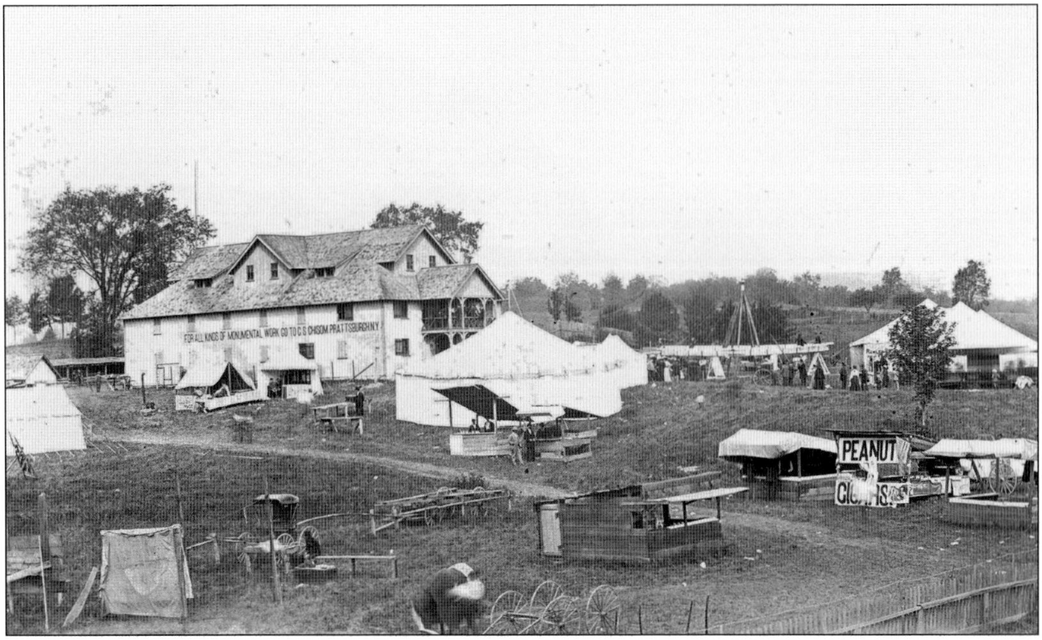

In 1884, the Union Agricultural Society considered having an exhibit of farm and other products from the harvesting season. The first fair was held on October 9, 10, and 11, 1884. A large fair house was built in 1886 to display exhibits, baked goods, and craft items competing for prizes. The bandstand was across the racetrack from the grandstand and was built from proceeds raised through a harvest dance. The fair drew a crowd of 5,400 the first day. Many visitors to the fair came in on the newly constructed railroad.

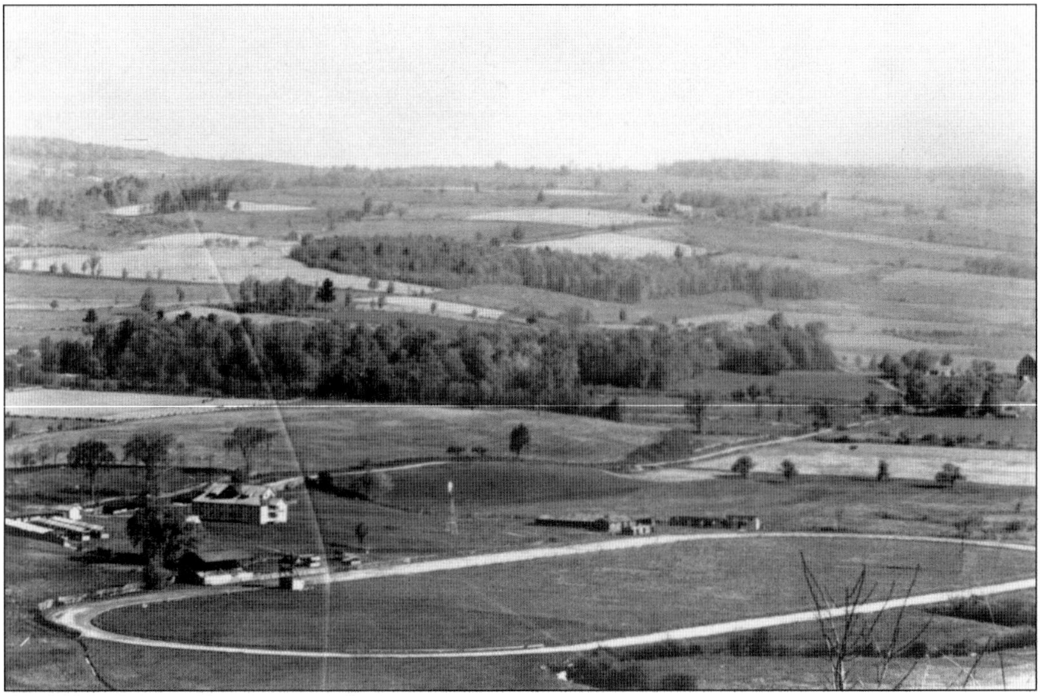

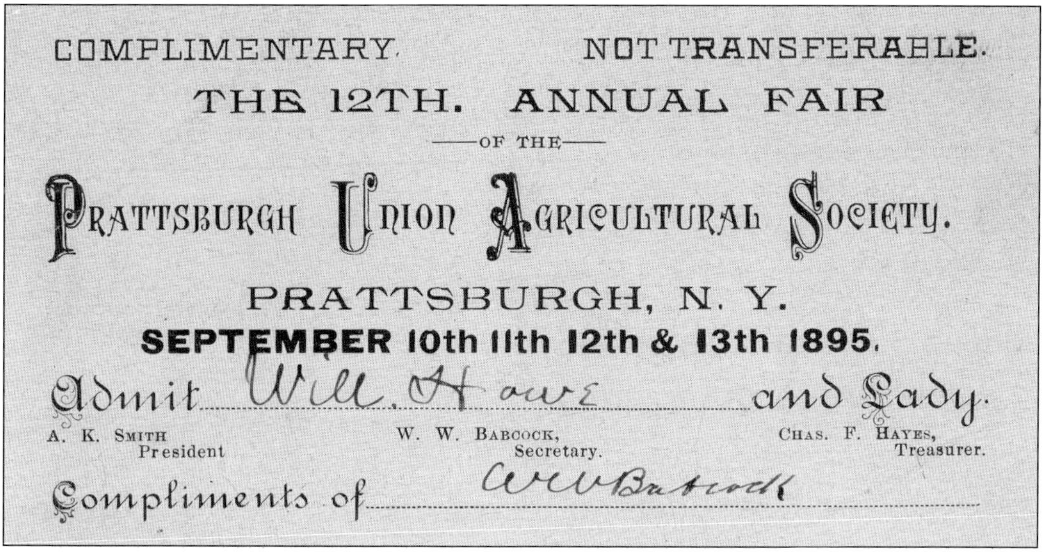

COMPLIMENTARY. NOT TRANSFERABLE.

THE 12TH. ANNUAL FAIR

—OF THE—

PRATTSBURGH UNION AGRICULTURAL SOCIETY.

PRATTSBURGH, N. Y.

SEPTEMBER 10th 11th 12th & 13th 1895.

Admit Will. Howe and Lady.

A. K. SMITH, President W. W. BABCOCK, Secretary. CHAS. F. HAYES, Treasurer.

Compliments of W W Babcock

The fair lasted 25 years and was enjoyed by many who came to view the exhibits and watch the various events, including the bicycle races shown below. By 1907, local interest seemed to be on the decline, largely due to the automobile making it possible for people to travel to larger fairs. There were fewer exhibits, and paid attendance was not as it had been in the past. The fair of 1908 broke even, so it was decided in 1909 to cease operation and hold an auction to sell all buildings—the fair house, grandstand, office, cattle and sheep sheds, hog homes, chicken houses, judge's stand, lumber, and so forth.

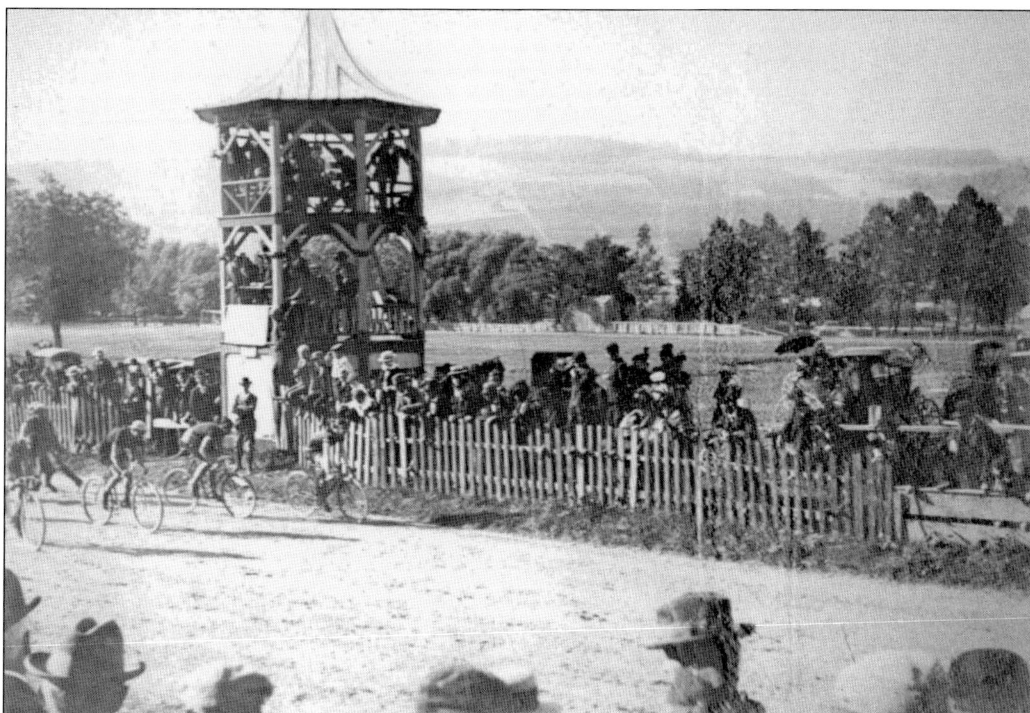

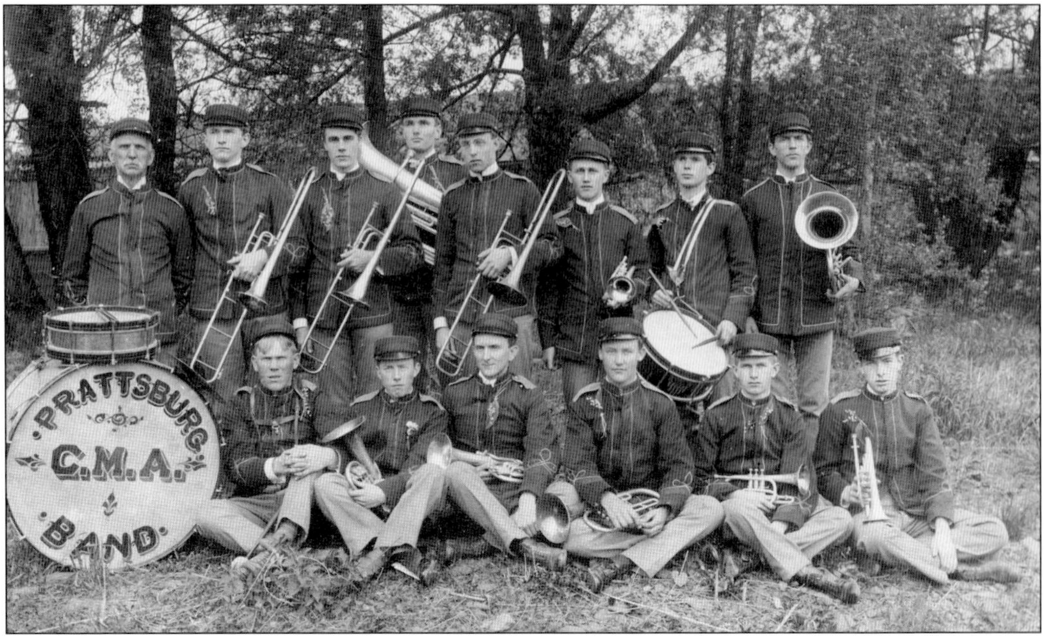

The Prattsburgh Silver Cornet Band was organized in 1890 and consisted of 13 members. It was directed by Frank "Mickey" Montgomery. The band played at dances, the fair, and Memorial Day parades. The band was eventually led by Benjamin P. Austin.

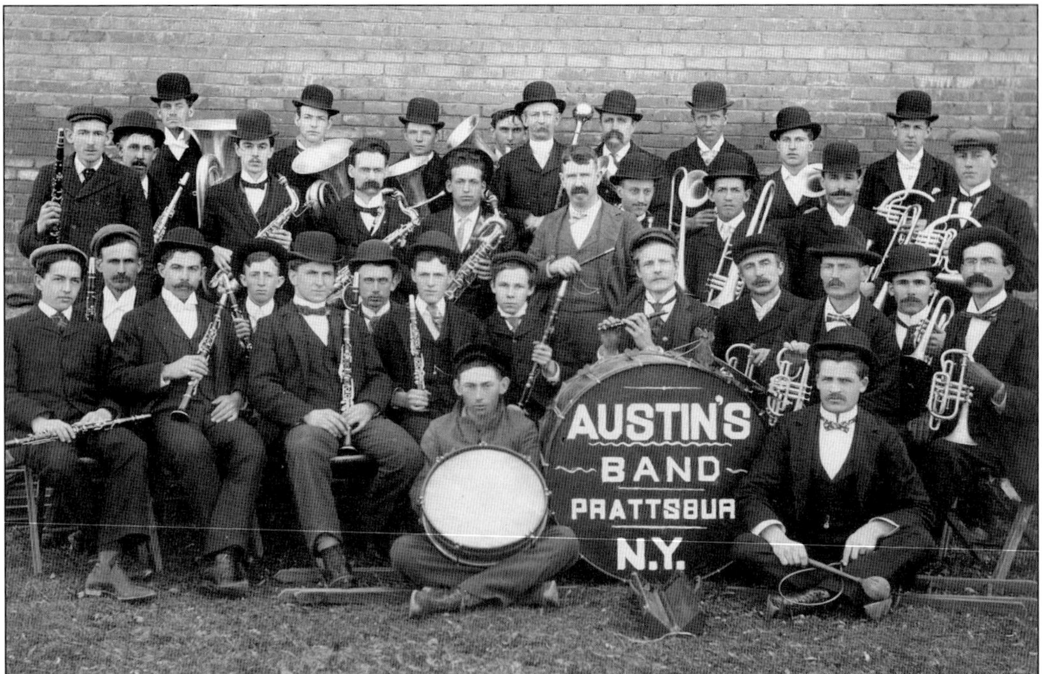

By 1940, the Silver Cornet Band had about 25 musicians from the area, and the name was changed to Austin's Band. The band held many concerts in the park. After Benjamin P. Austin's death, 25 musicians held a memorial concert and played some of Austin's mini compositions. Eventually, the school band took over for the town bands.

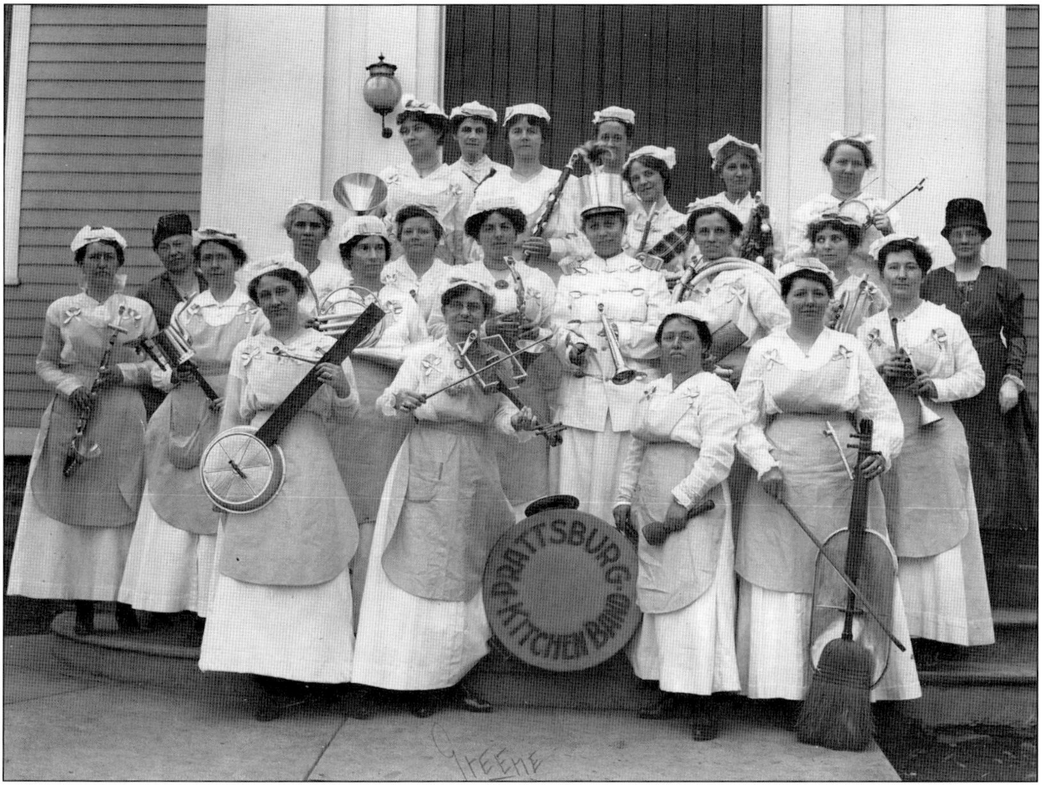

Enjoying and playing music was a popular pastime in Prattsburgh. The all-ladies Kitchen Band delighted residents with the popular songs of the day, putting on performances at such places as the auditorium and Presbyterian church. However, it was not just the adults who performed in town. Boy Scout Troop No. 34 played drum cadence in the local parades and ceremonies.

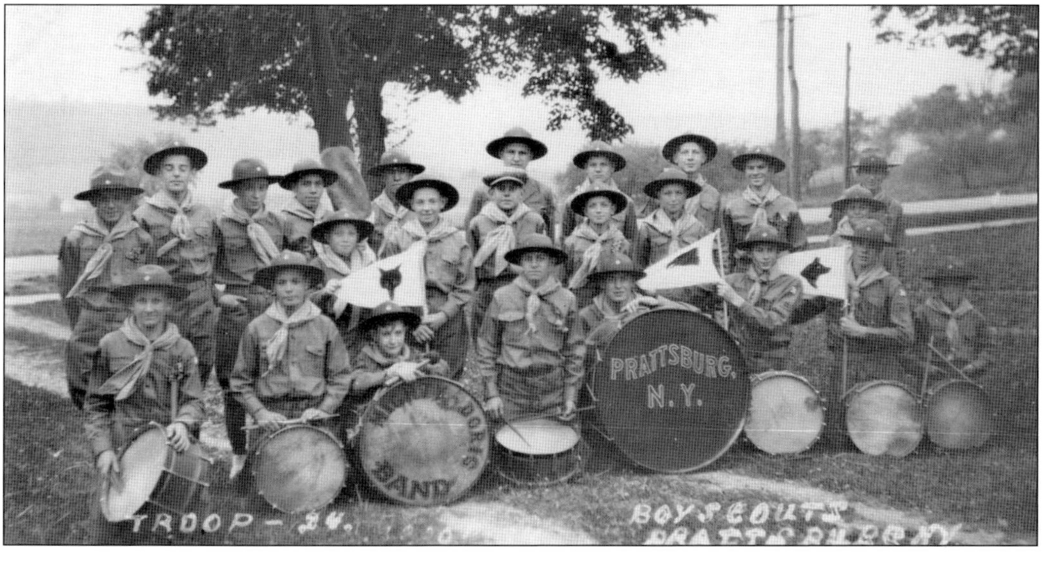

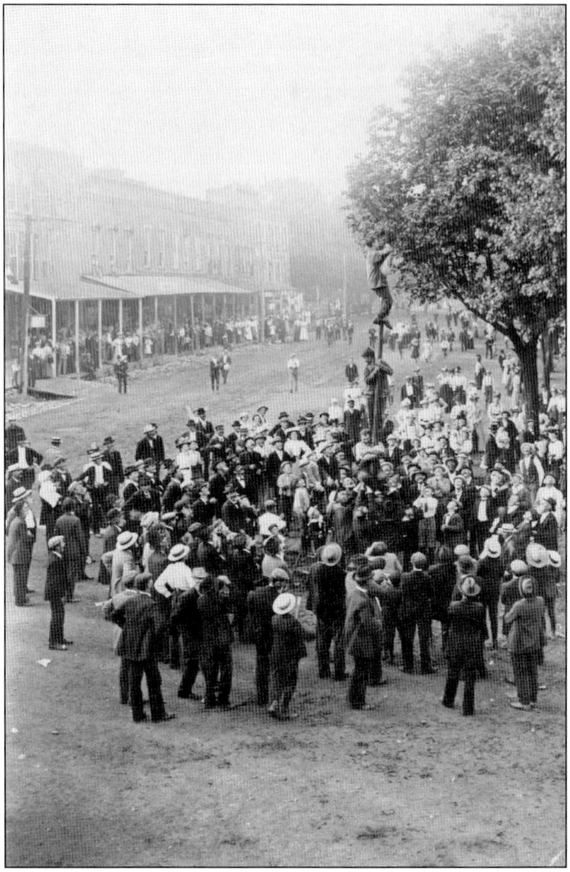

All down through history, starting back as early as 1886, Prattsburgh was known to have wonderful Memorial Day and Fourth of July celebrations. Besides the parade, many competitions were held, such as the greased pig and the greased pole contests, shown here. Without the distraction of modern technology like the television and Internet, these events drew many residents together to enjoy social activities.

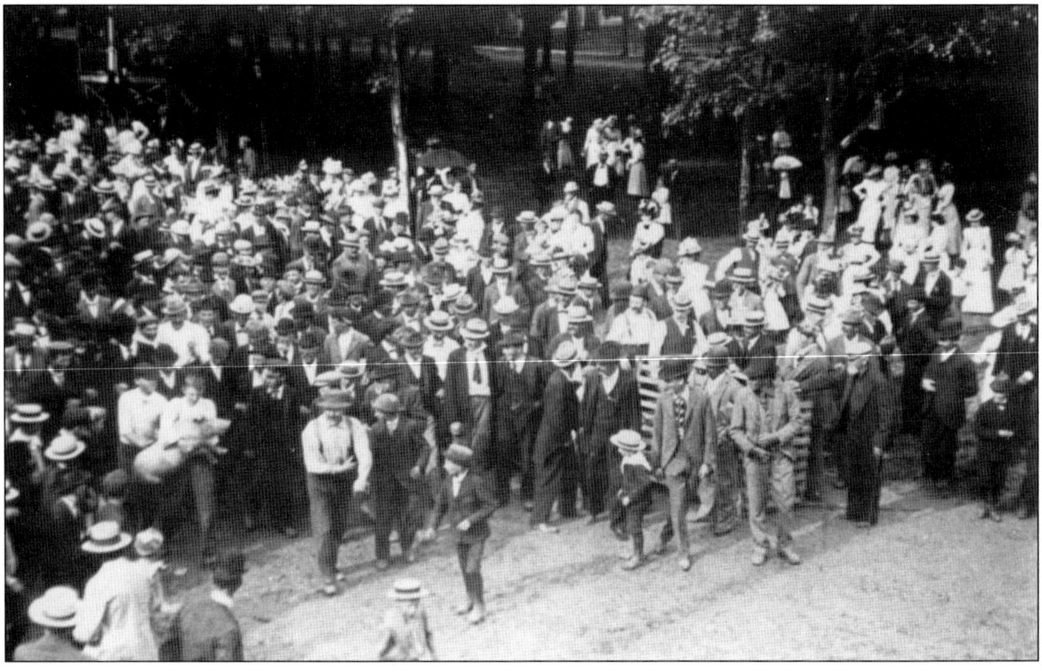

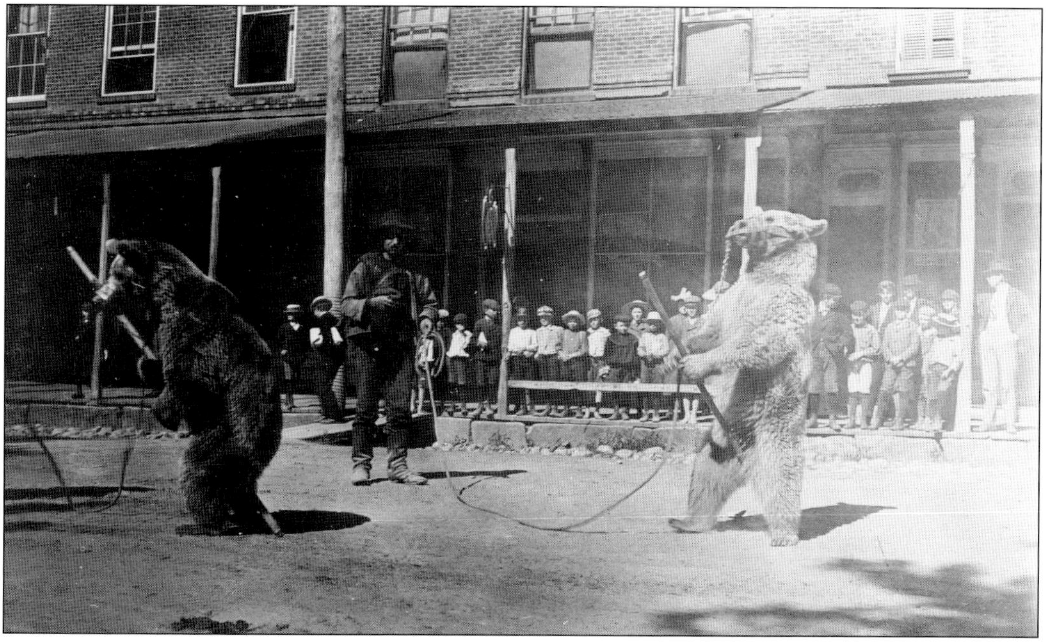

When the circus came to town, residents young and old were treated to a live animal show by the bear trainers in hopes of enticing them to attend the circus. The bears wore muzzles and were held on a leash by the men. The close proximity of the bears to the audience shows the faith they had in the trainers.

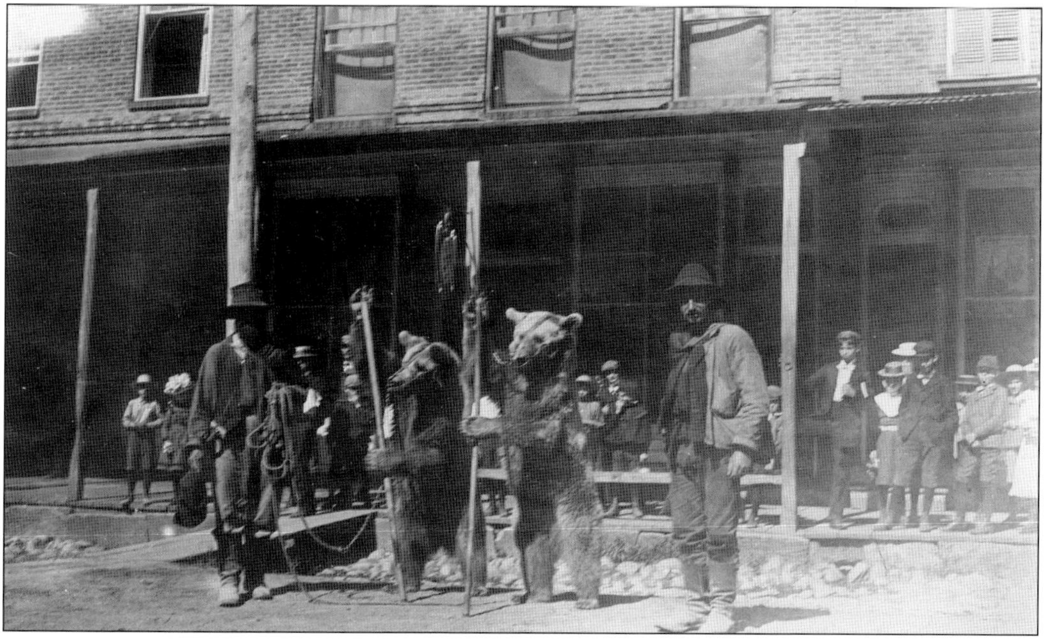

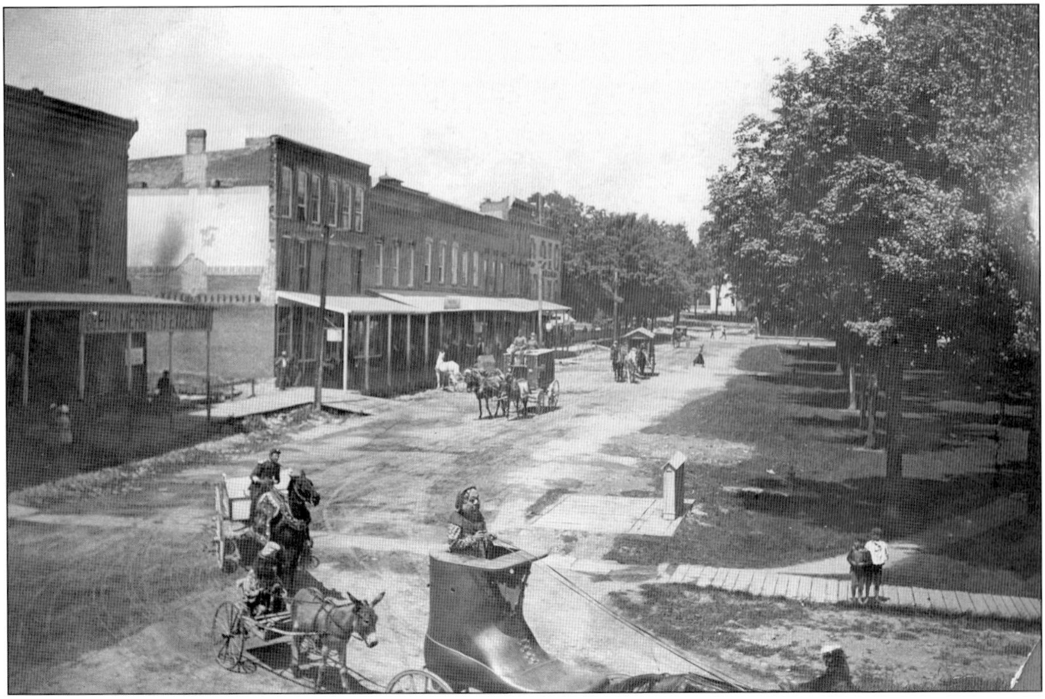

During celebrations like Memorial Day or when the circus came to town, there was sure to be a parade. Residents concocted elaborate floats to the delight of those watching. The parades usually began on Main Street by the school and traveled to Mechanic Street around the park. Even the horses got in the act, sporting decorations fitting to the parade's theme.

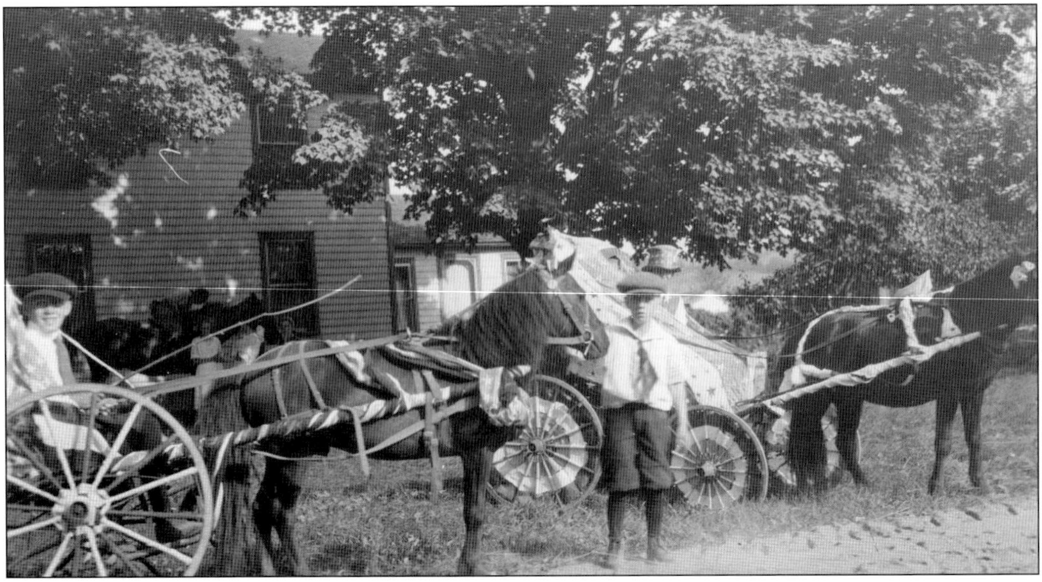

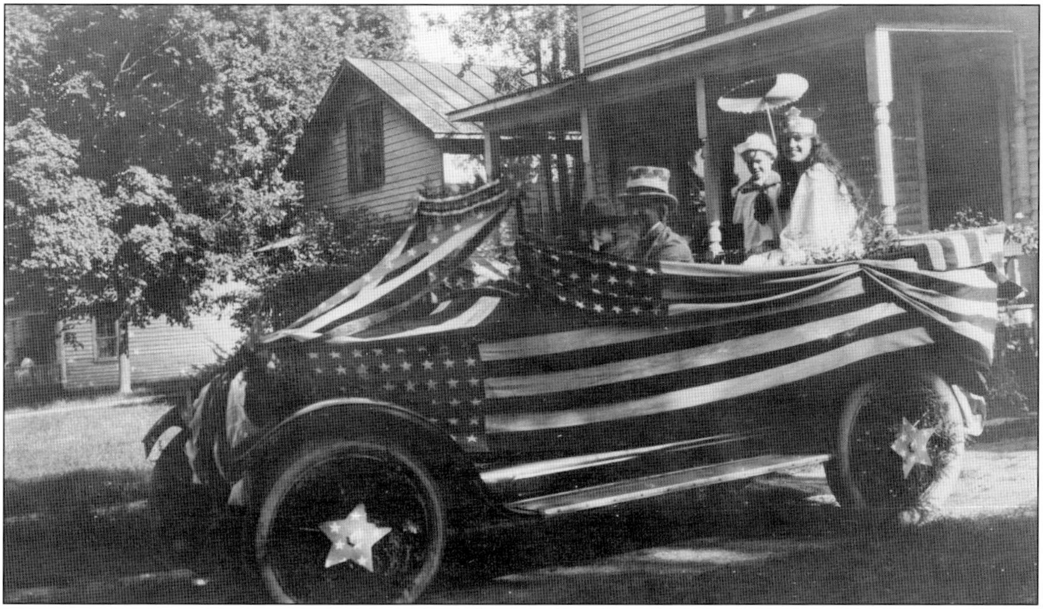

As time went by, the automobile came into being and was the main mode of transportation for the more prominent families. These families were eager to show of this new contraption and enjoyed participating in the annual parades. This flag-draped car took first place in this parade. Eventually, as more and more cars appeared, the parades became more populated with floats.

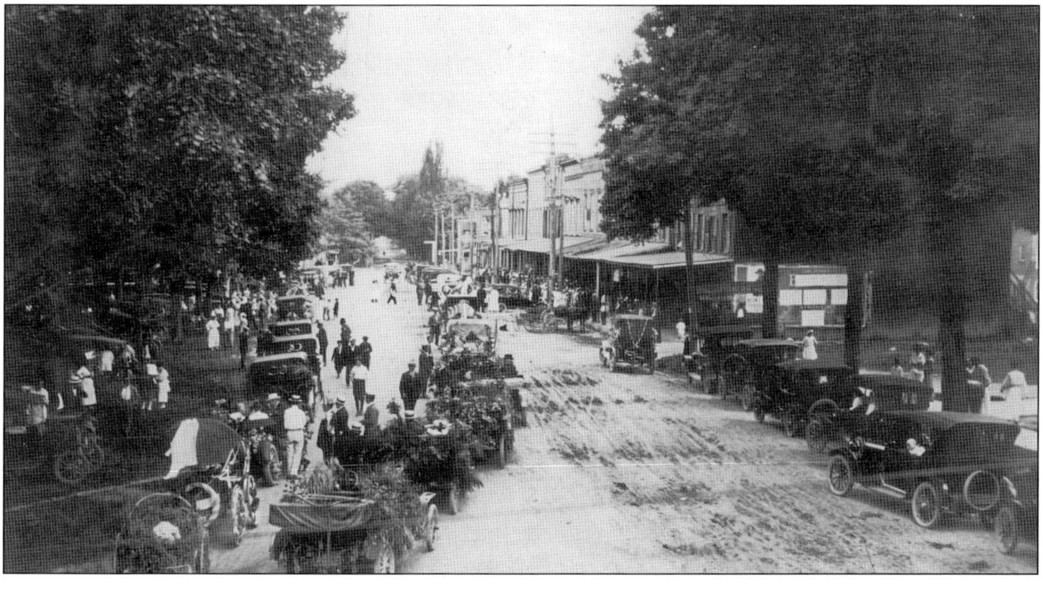

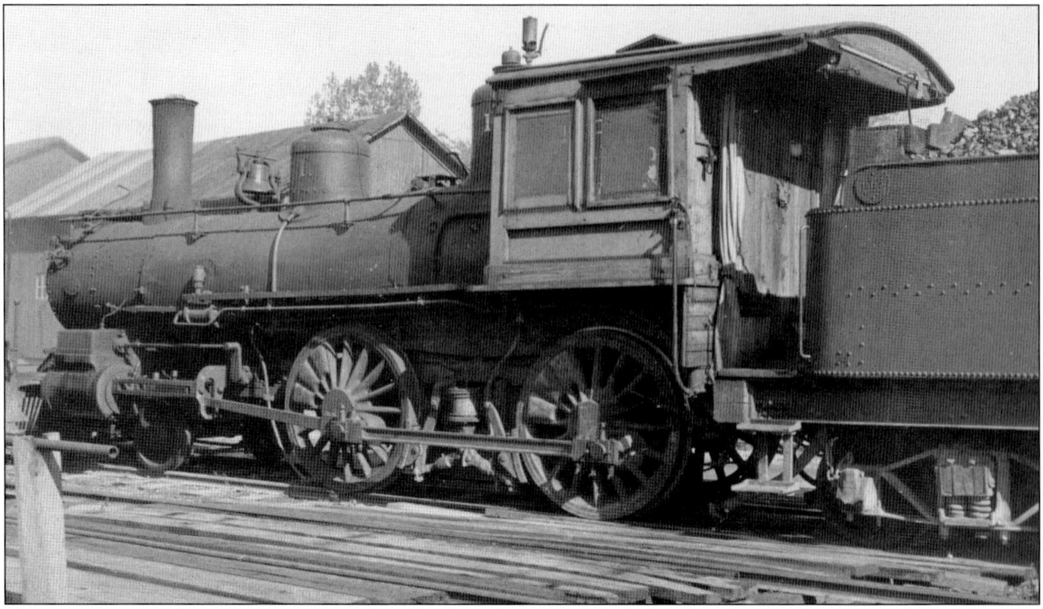

After a few years of difficult negotiations, the Kanona & Prattsburgh (K&P) Railroad was constructed. In October 1889, "Huldy" made her first run, drawing two coaches loaded with passengers from Kanona to Prattsburgh in 28 minutes. The rise of the railroad saw the end of the stagecoach and the transporting of produce by horse and wagon.

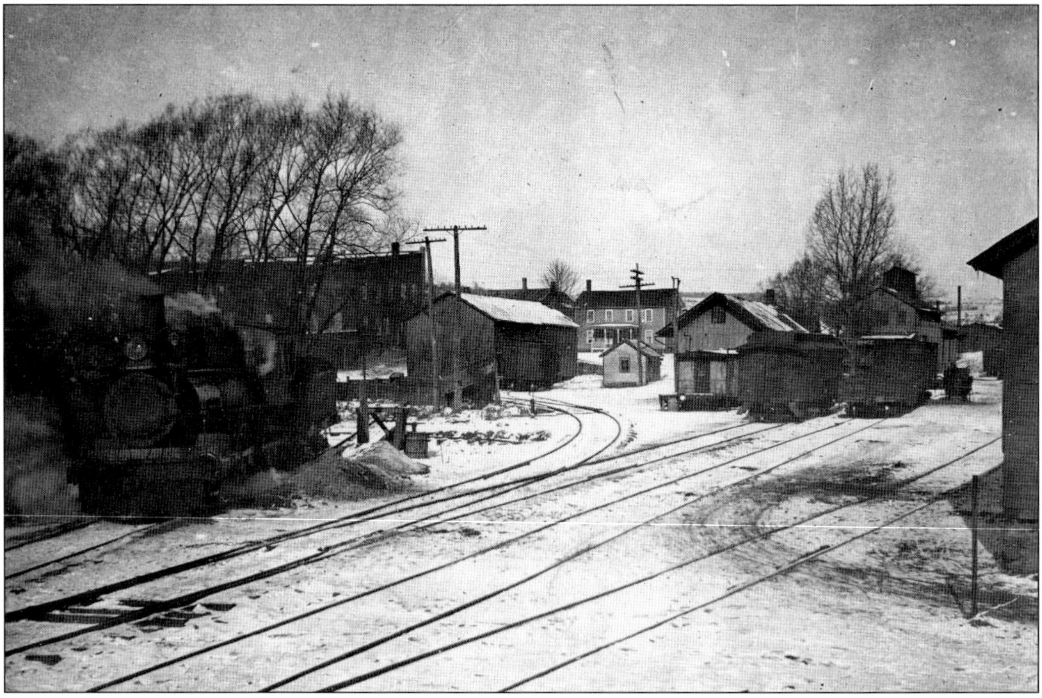

Originally, the train had to make the return trip to Kanona backwards as there was no way to turn around. Eventually, the railroad installed a turntable at the Prattsburgh Depot strong enough to turn the heavy engine around. Huldy now had the pleasure of running forward both ways between Prattsburgh and Kanona.

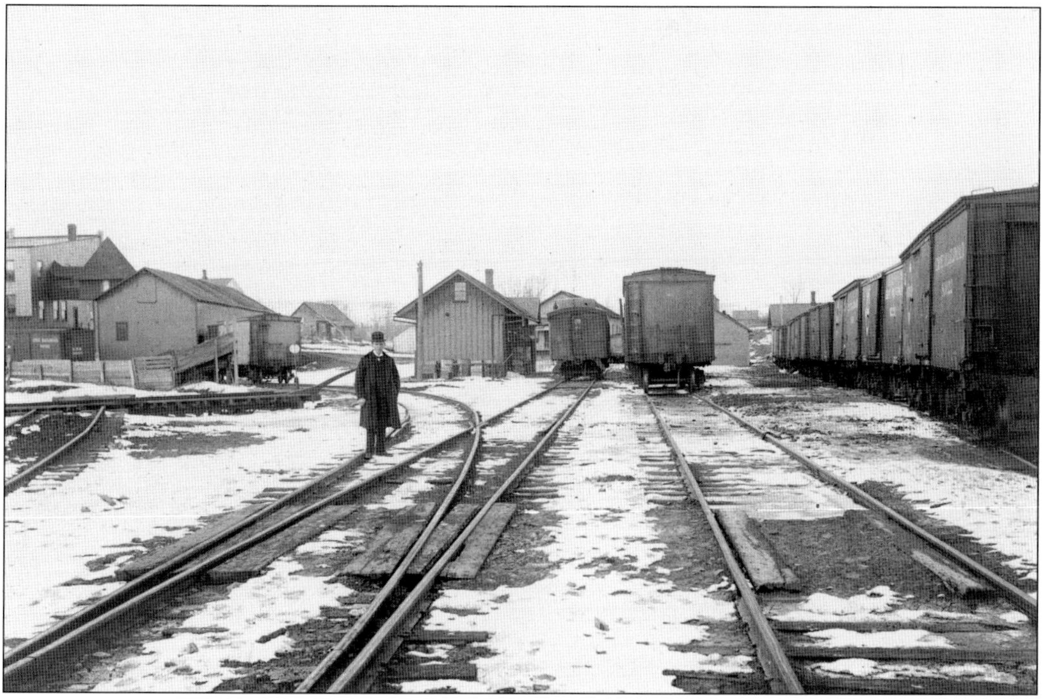

The rail yard on the south side of Mechanic Street behind the depot held the extra cars to be pulled into service when needed. Many of these cars were utilized by the local farmers who would fill them with produce to ship out to be sold.

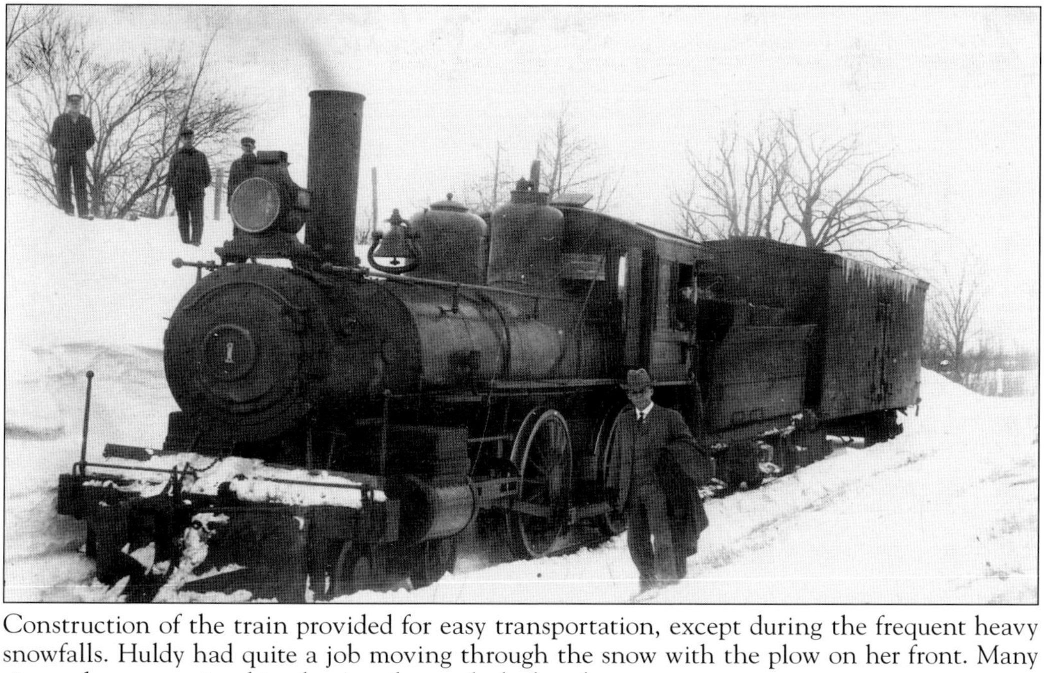

Construction of the train provided for easy transportation, except during the frequent heavy snowfalls. Huldy had quite a job moving through the snow with the plow on her front. Many times, the men assisted in clearing the tracks by hand.

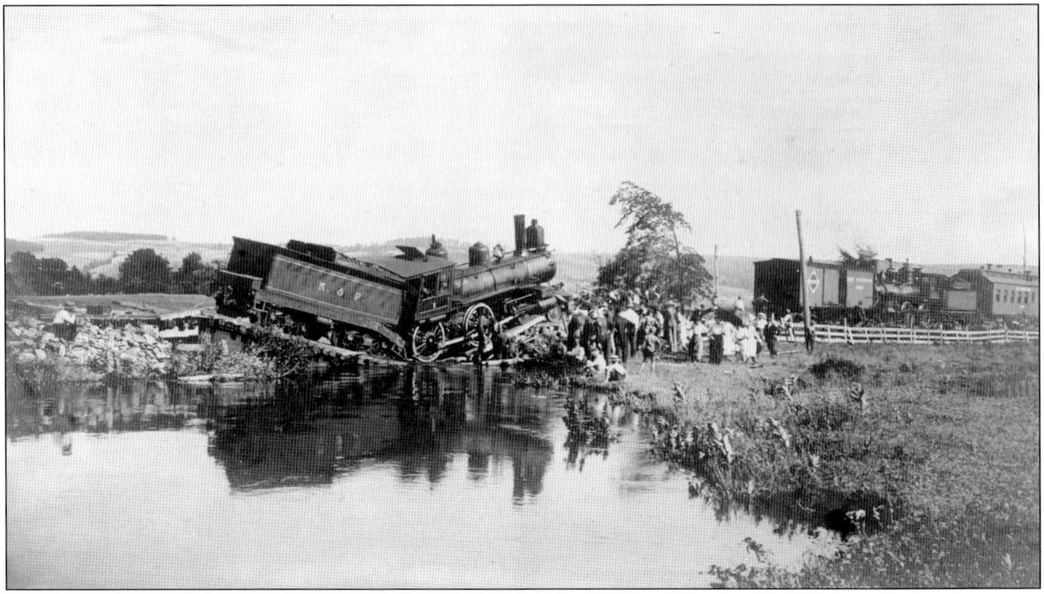

After a heavy rainstorm in July 1902, one of the railroad bridges sank, and the Erie wrecking train had to pull the train back on the tracks.

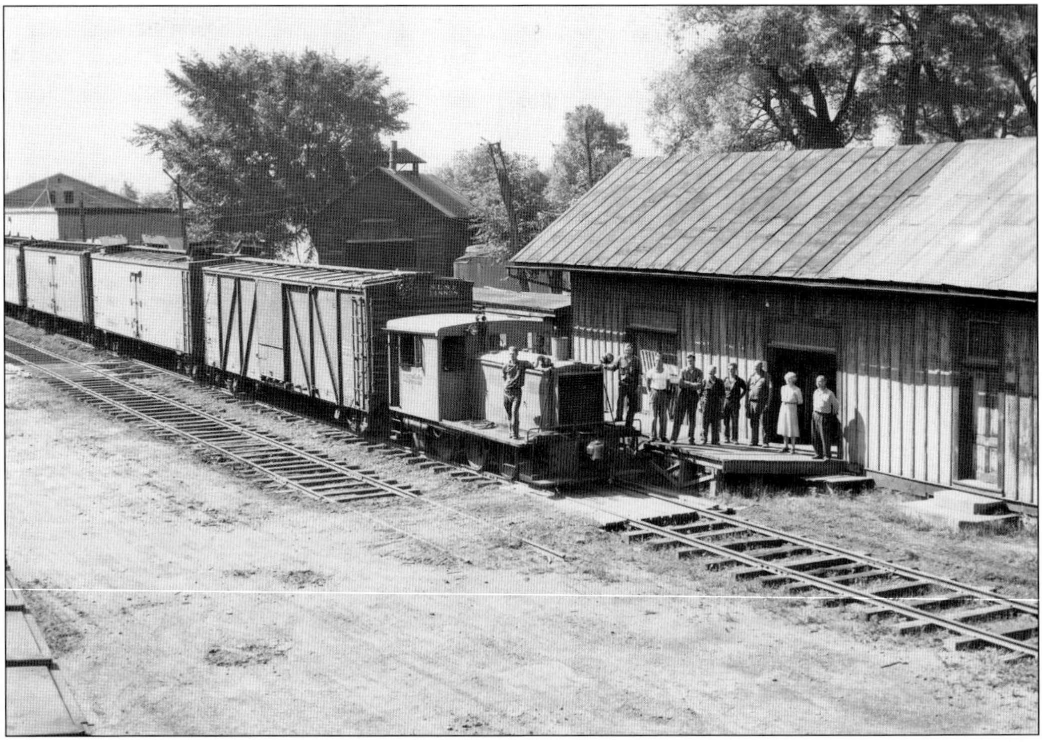

The 11.44-mile trip cost 60¢, lasted 40 minutes, and had seven stops on the route. Eventually, new types of transportation arose. In 1928, the Prattsburgh Bus Lines served passengers, and in 1940, tank trucks made the connections at Kanona to New York City and Buffalo, making rail transport less desirable. The last trip of the railroad was September 29, 1959, and all assets were sold at public auction on June 10, 1961.

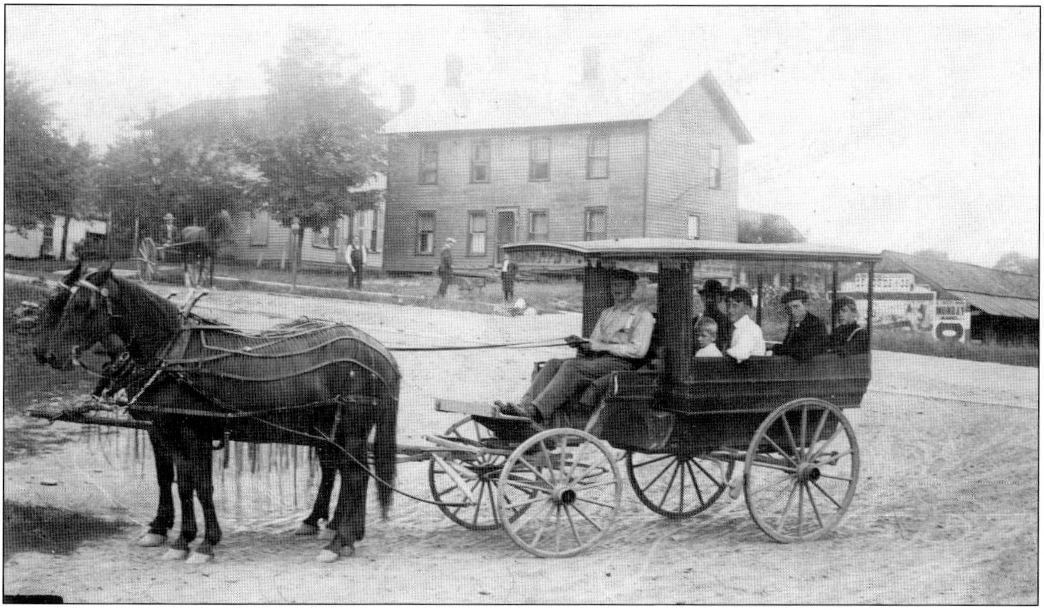

A crew of 30 Italian laborers came to build the K&P Railroad. They settled in a house that once was known as the old Pottery Building, which the railroad company had bought. It was moved 20 rods west and placed on railroad land. After the railroad was built, the house was moved across to 59 Mechanic Street, where it is located today.

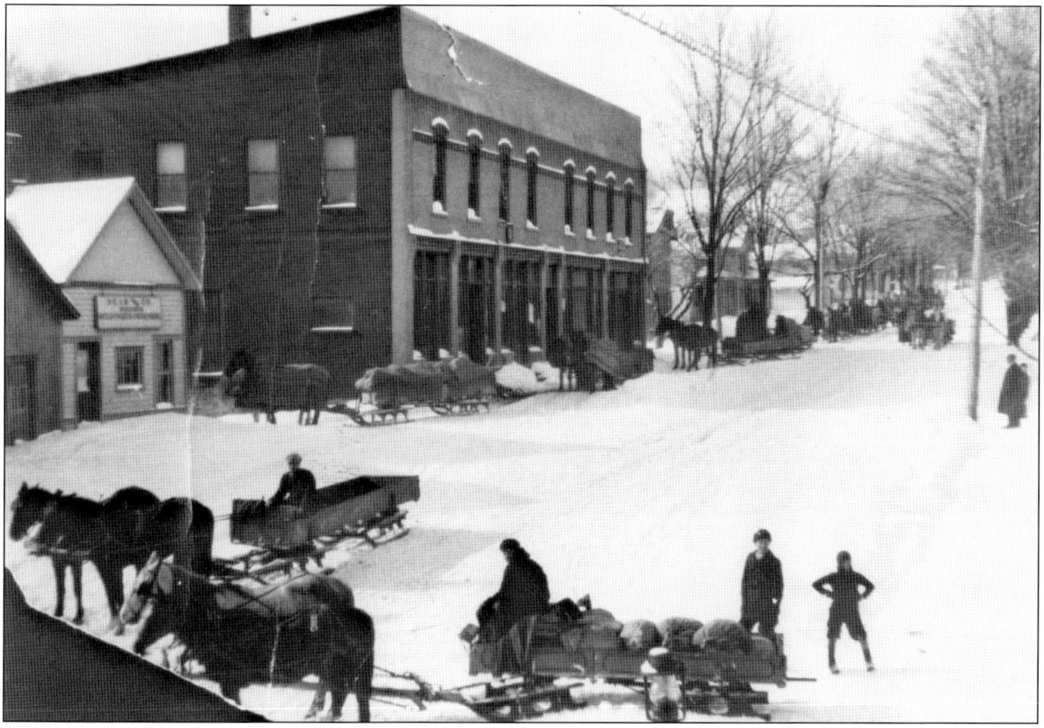

Built near the railroad station, this saloon provided the last chance to get a drink before boarding the train. Next door to the saloon is the scale where farmers brought their crops to be weighed before they were loaded on the train.

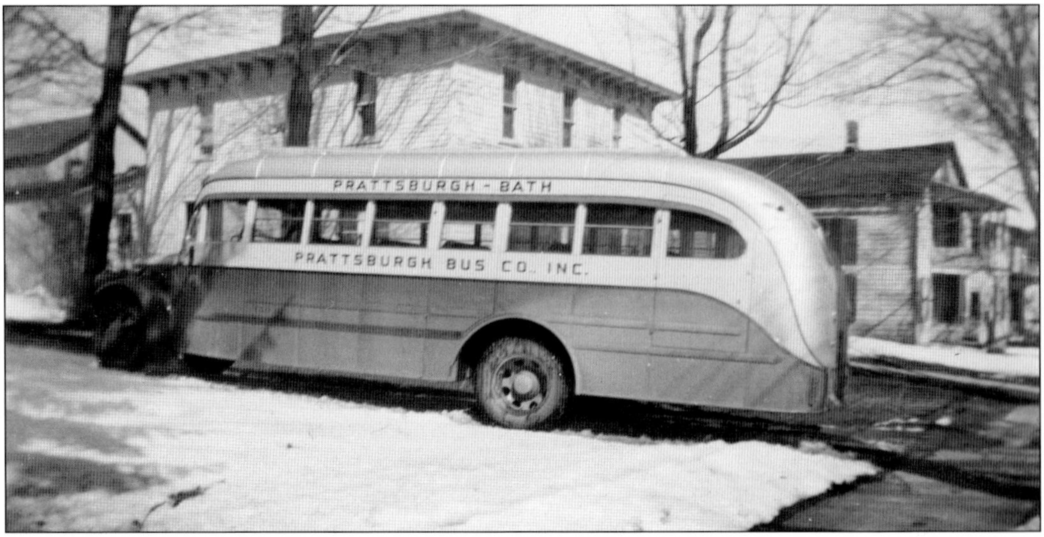

After rail passenger service was discontinued, the Prattsburgh Railway Corporation started the Prattsburgh Bus Company to operate a bus of sufficient size to carry mail and passengers from Prattsburgh to the Erie Railway Station in Kanona. It made its first run on October 28, 1928, and made three daily round-trips. In 1961, the bus company was used solely for school transportation, as it is today. It is now privately owned.

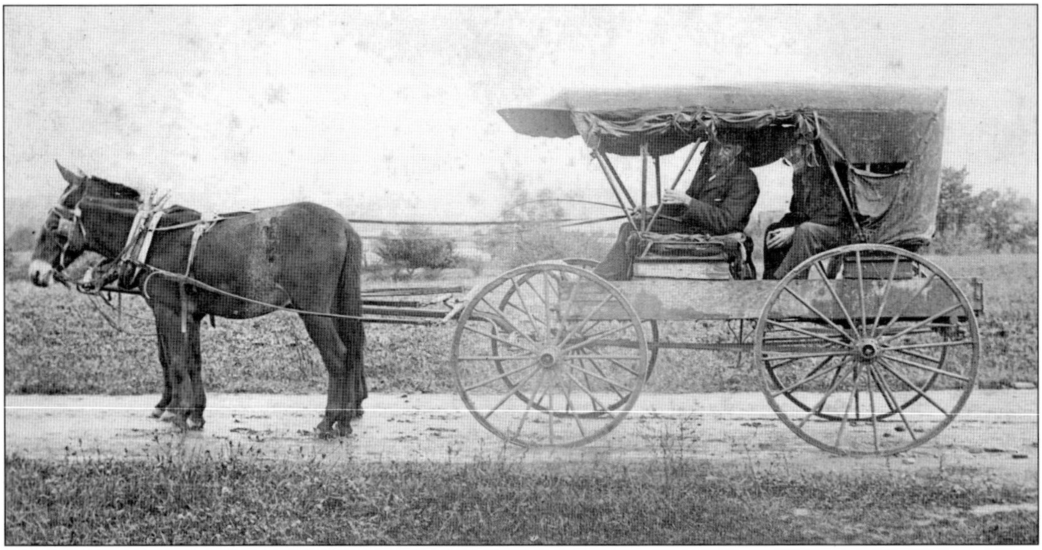

The stagecoach for many years linked Prattsburgh and Bath. This photograph from the 1880s shows James Wheeler and a Mr. Smith aboard the mule-drawn coach. The stagecoach route travelled through Prattsburgh on North Main Street on its way to Geneva, New York. When the railroad came into town, passengers would disembark and take the stagecoach to their final destination.

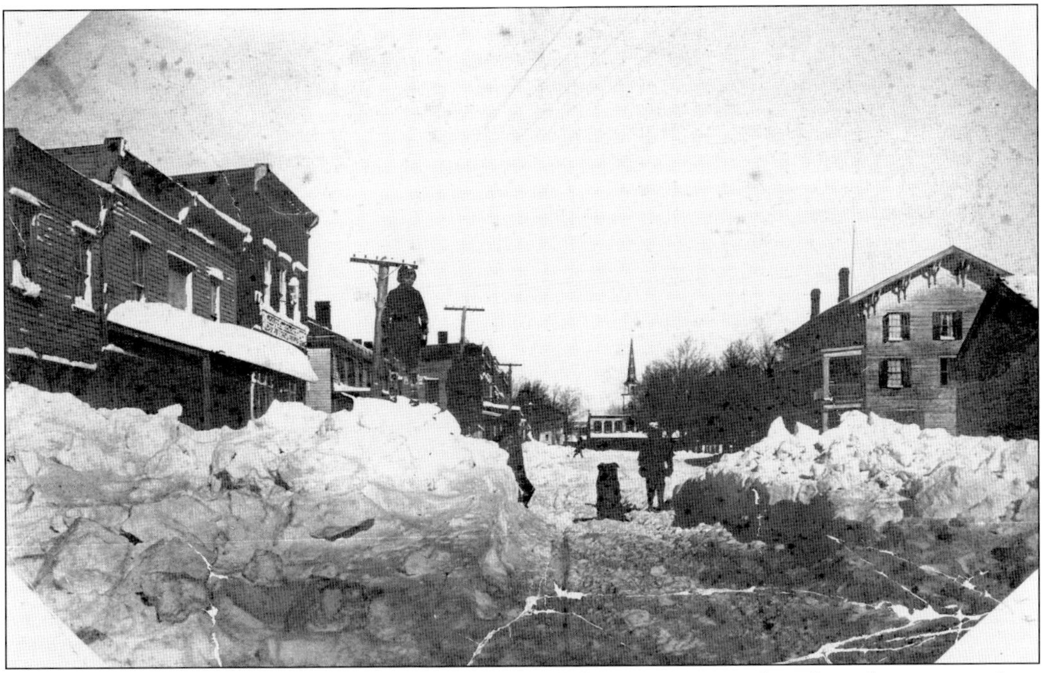

Prattsburgh has always been known for heavy snowfall. Many winters found residents snowed in. People in other towns called Prattsburgh "Little Siberia." One of the reasons might be the fact that Prattsburgh is the highest point of Steuben County. This view of Main Street looking north shows the challenges created by such snowfall for residents.

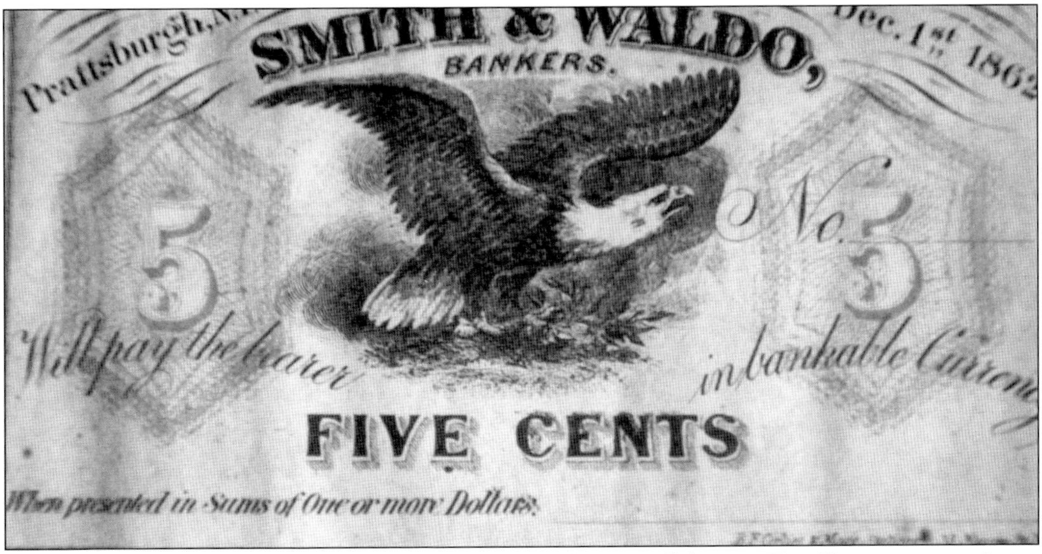

At one time, the town was dry and did not have a bar or sell liquor. To offset concerns that a temperance hotel owner would not meet payroll without liquor sales, temperance people issued this money in 5¢, 10¢, 25¢, and 50¢ denominations in 1862. A large amount was printed constituting a fund subject to taxation if a deficiency in the payroll occurred. The fund was only necessary the first year, as the hotels succeeded despite the lack of alcohol.

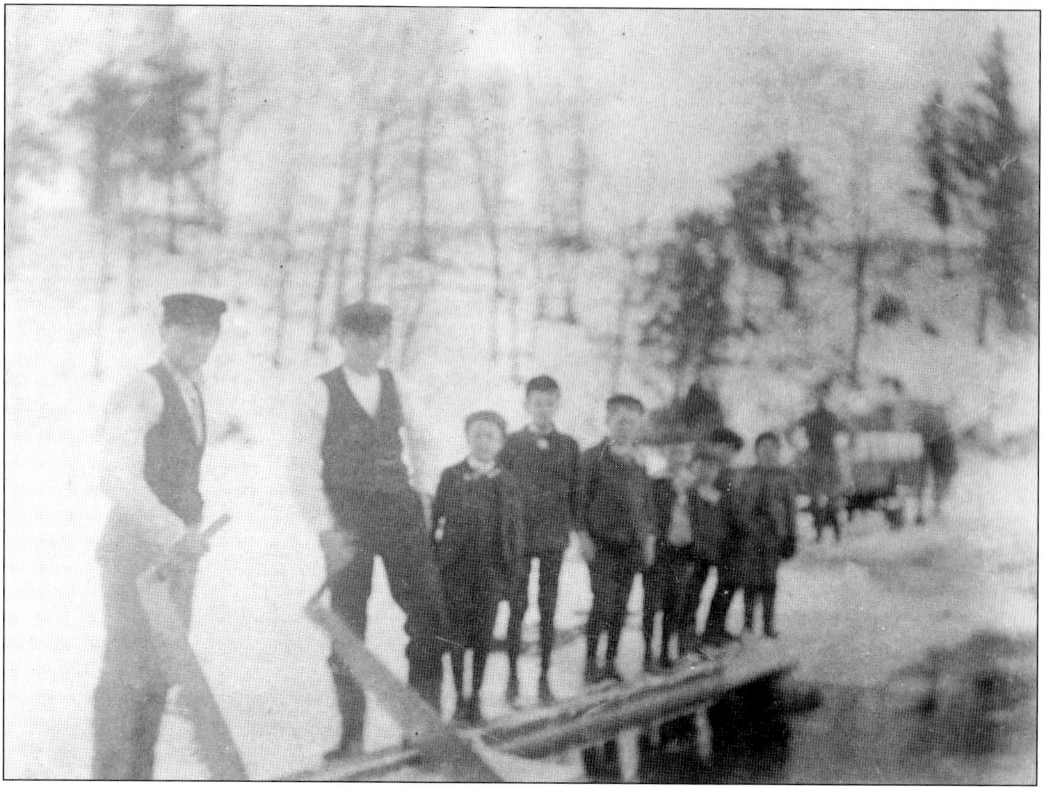

Ice was cut from Mill Pond near where the Cole Mill was located. The ice was stored in sheds and covered with sawdust. This ice was then used in iceboxes in the home and also in milk tanks to cool the milk on the farm. The blocks were cut and pulled from the pond by horses, traveling along makeshift rails made of small trees to a wagon. Eventually, electric-powered refrigerators eliminated the need for these blocks of ice.

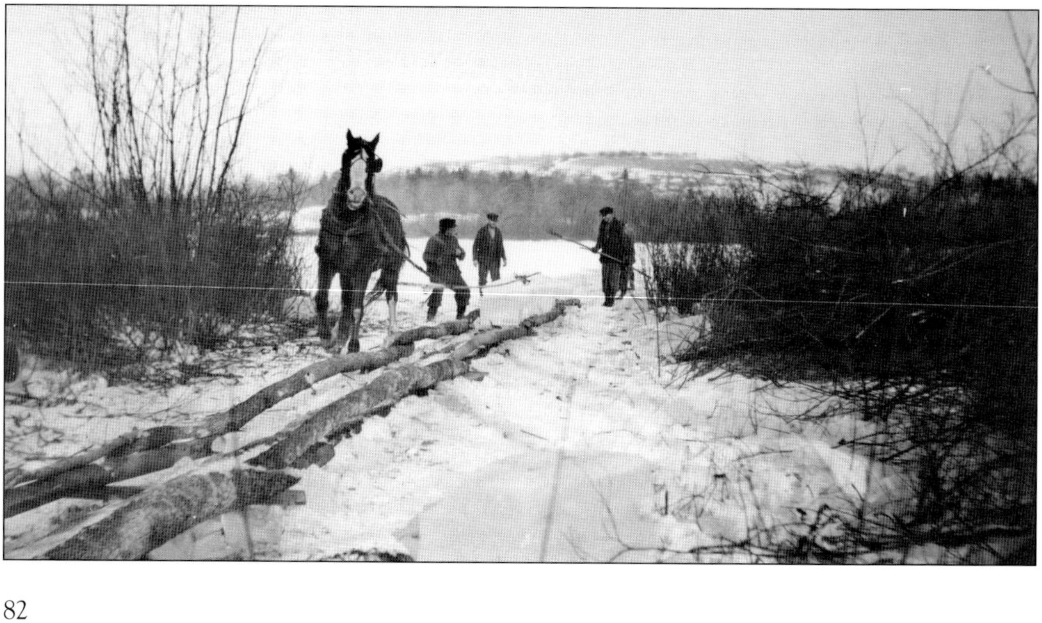

Five

Education

The early settlers of Prattsburgh were well-educated individuals who built successful enterprises. Education was so important to these men that the Franklin Academy was established to provide a place of higher learning for boys and girls from Prattsburgh and surrounding towns. In fact, Robert B. Van Valkenburgh, the first US ambassador to Japan, was a graduate of Franklin Academy. The school produced many successful Prattsburgh businessmen.

In addition, the town boasted 17 district schools spread out over its geographic area. These "little schoolhouses" laid the educational foundation for many a young resident. Present-day Prattsburgh Central School continues to be a leader in educational excellence despite the small size of the town.

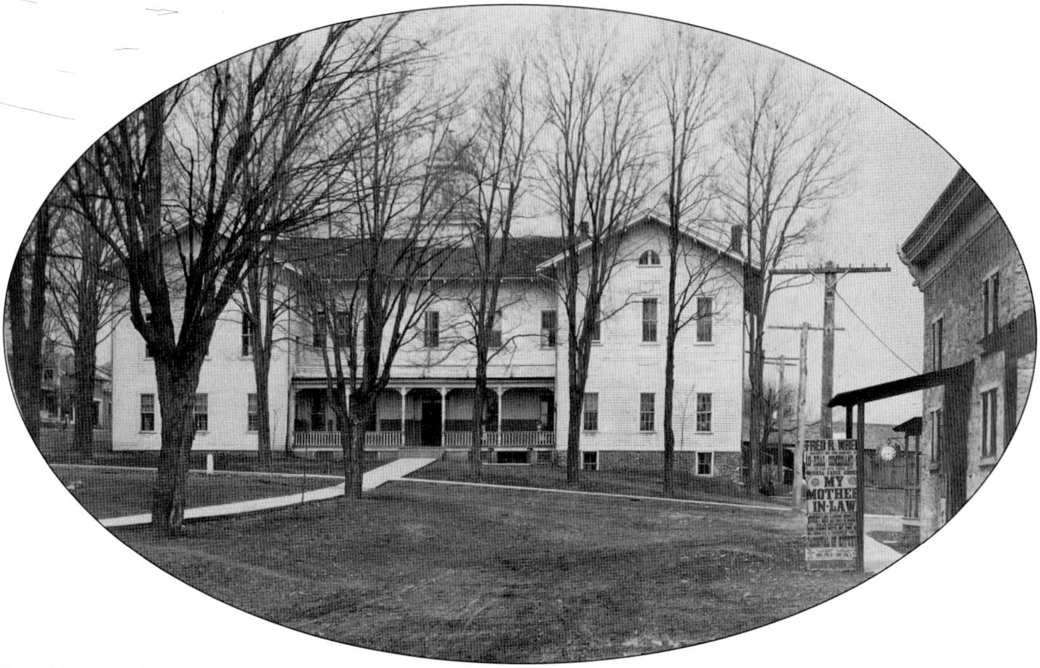

Franklin Academy and Collegiate was built in 1823. At first, it was a boarding school for pupils from in and out of town. A Mr. Beardsley was the first principal, and he made $400 per year. Charles F. West signed up as the first student. Tuition was $3 per quarter. The school took on a religious affiliation from the start. Completion of the course schedule was comparable to a two-year college. In 1828, there were 62 pupils attending, with 37 from Prattsburgh and 25 from other towns. As the picture below of the 1909 student body shows, the school served a diverse age group.

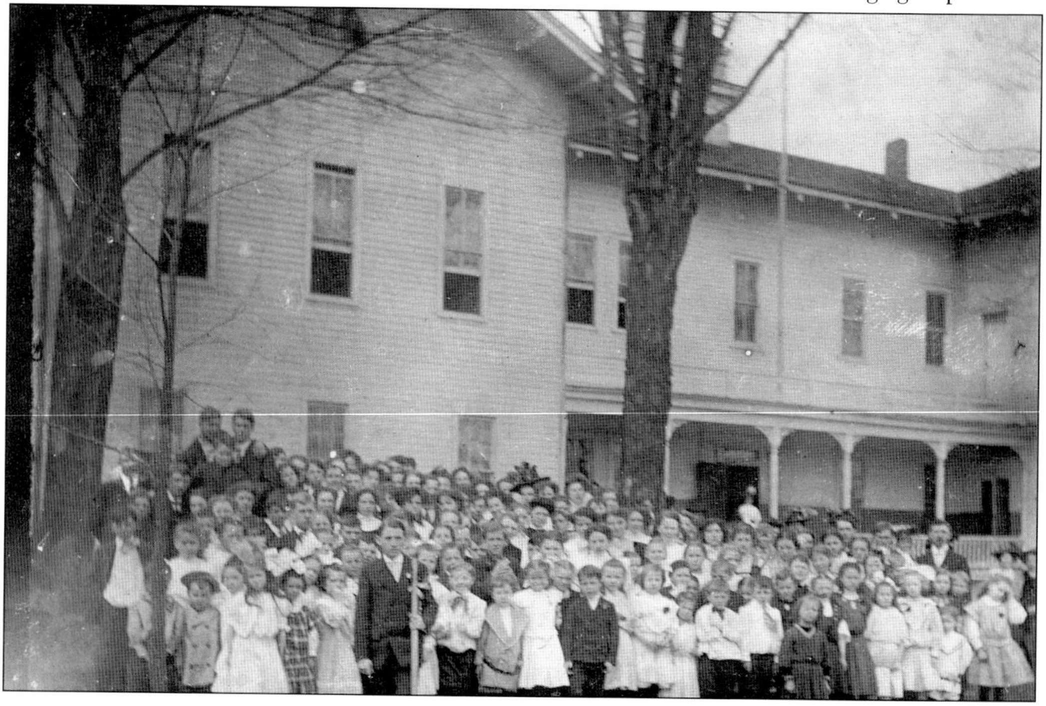

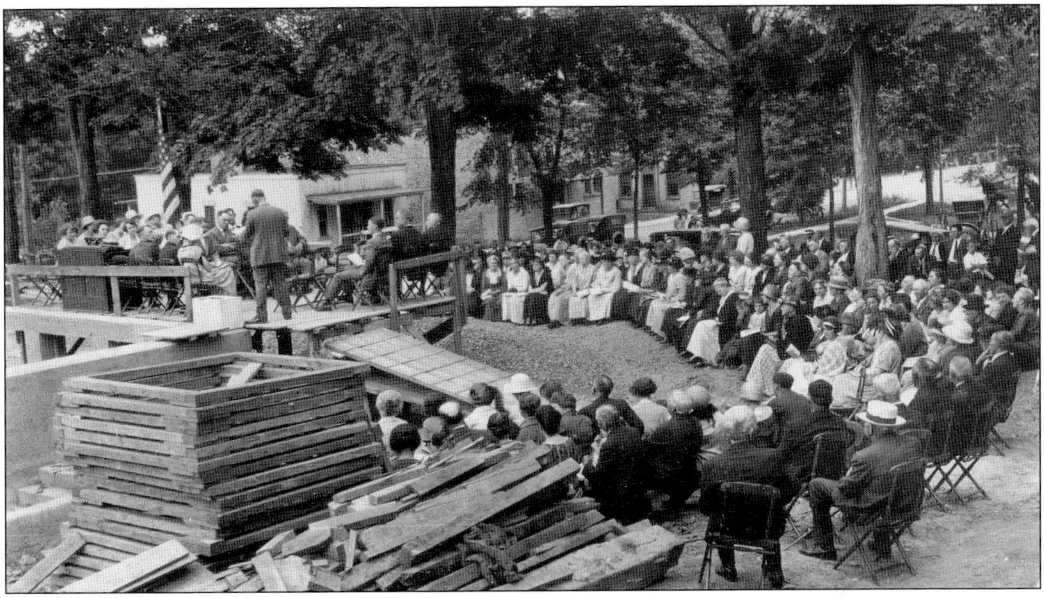

On February 23, 1923, the school and neighboring church burned down. For the time being, classes were held in the Baptist and Methodist churches and the Grange hall. The cornerstone for the new school building was laid in July 1924. Completion of the new school building occurred later in 1924, the construction had to meet the state stipulations on design and size. With the new, larger building, the school could consider centralization and eliminate the small schools.

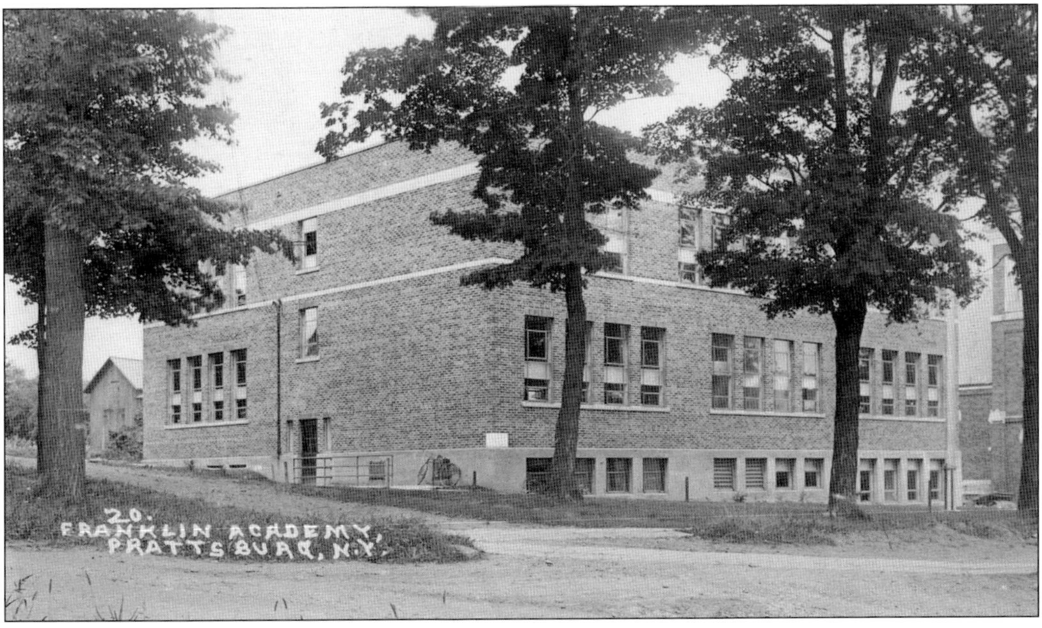

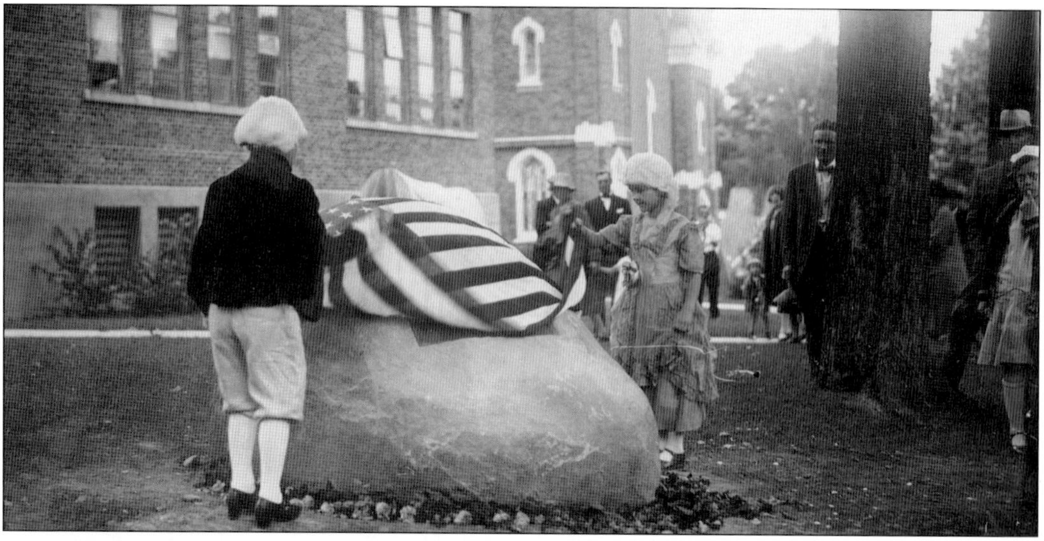

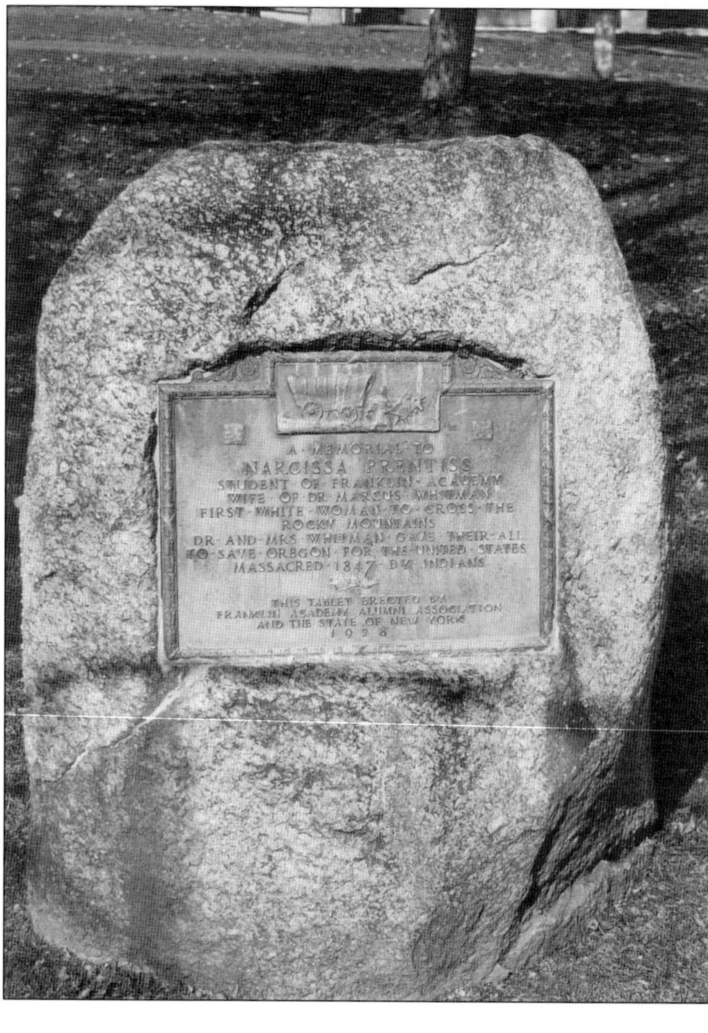

On July 16, 1928, a tablet honoring Narcissa Prentiss was unveiled in front of Franklin Academy. The unveiling was attended by 500 people. The plaque honors Narcissa Prentiss, the first white woman to cross the Rocky Mountains with her husband, Dr. Marcus Whitman. It was unveiled by John and Elsie Skinner who were direct descendants of the Whitman line. The children were dressed in colonial costume and drew back the flag, revealing the tablet. The Franklin Academy Alumni Association and the State of New York erected the tablet.

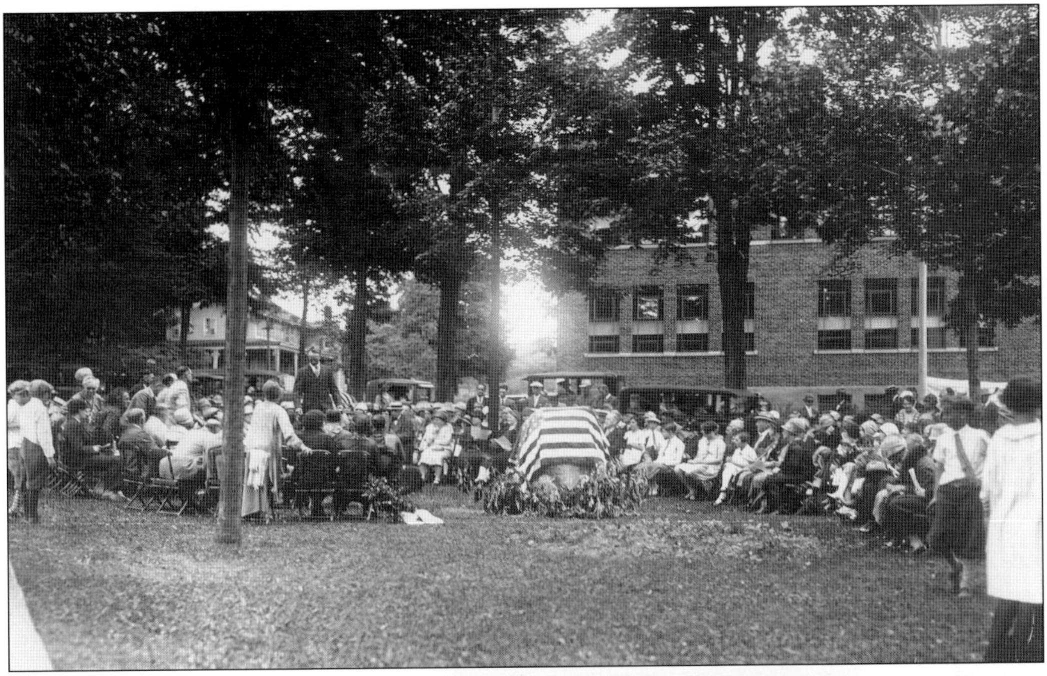

This plaque was installed in 1928 on a large rock on the lawn of the Prattsburgh Central School to honor Rev. Henry Harmon Spalding, who accompanied Narcissa Prentiss and Dr. Marcus Whitman on their journey west across the Rockies. Reverend Spalding was a student of Franklin Academy. The tablet was erected by the Franklin Academy Alumni Association and the State of New York.

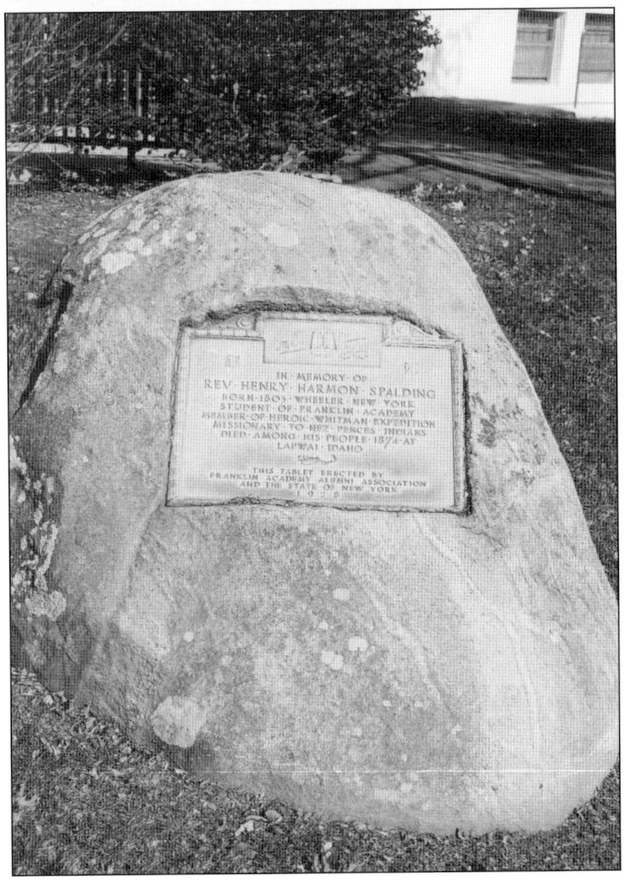

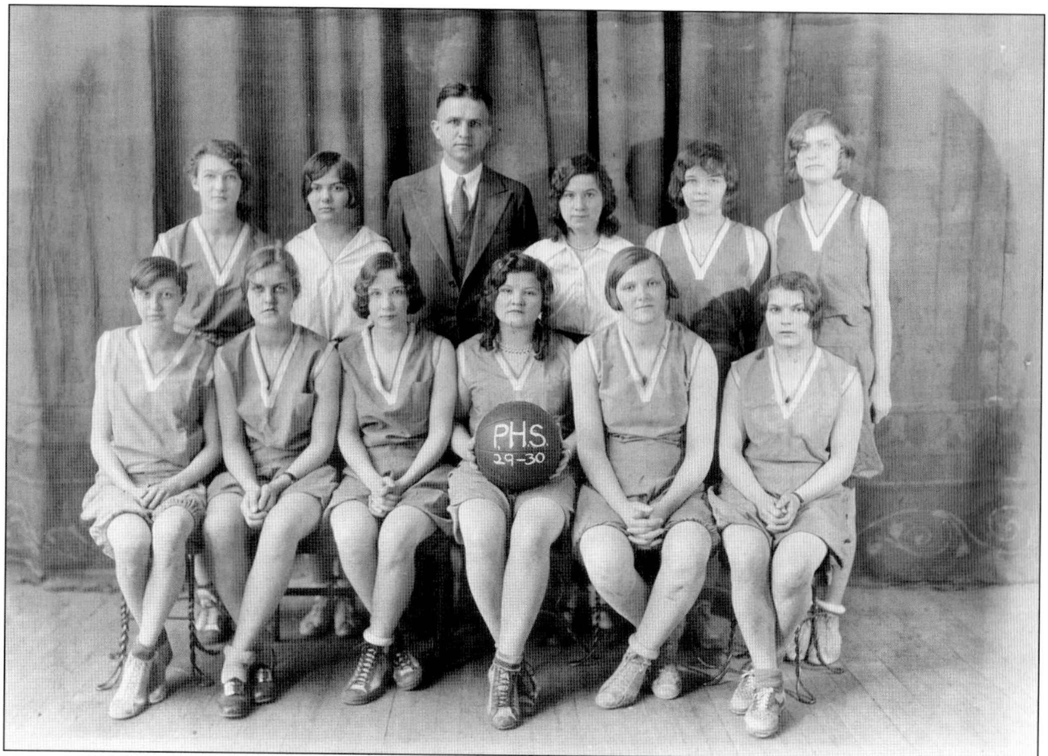

Although Franklin Academy prided itself on academics, the students also excelled in athleticism. Basketball was a favorite sport of the school, and both boys and girls fielded teams. These pictures from the 1929–1930 school season provide a glimpse into the athletic activities pursued by students.

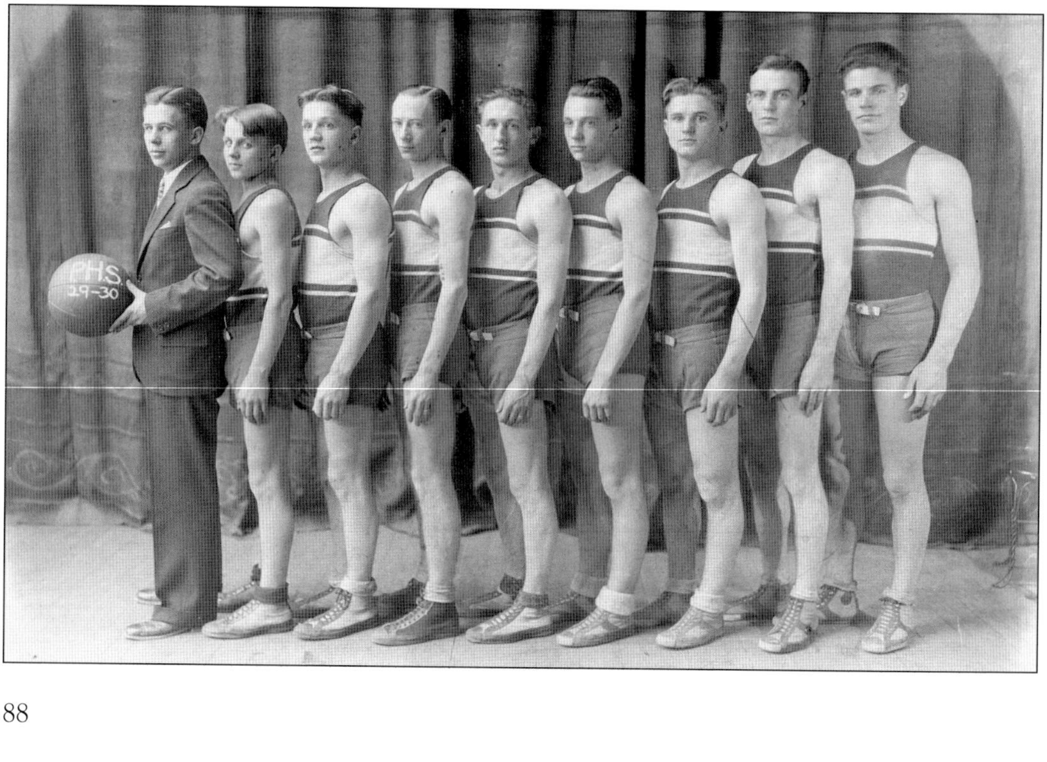

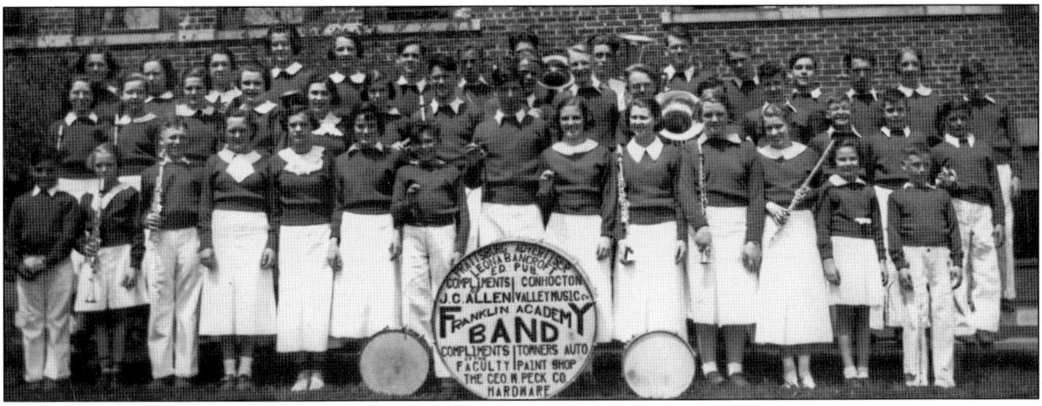

Students at Franklin Academy and Prattsburgh Central School also enjoyed nonathletic pursuits, including participation in bands. In fact, the school band eventually took over the task of performing for the community bands. Through the years, the school band has received many awards for marching and playing competitions with other schools. This picture shows the band during the 1937–1938 school year.

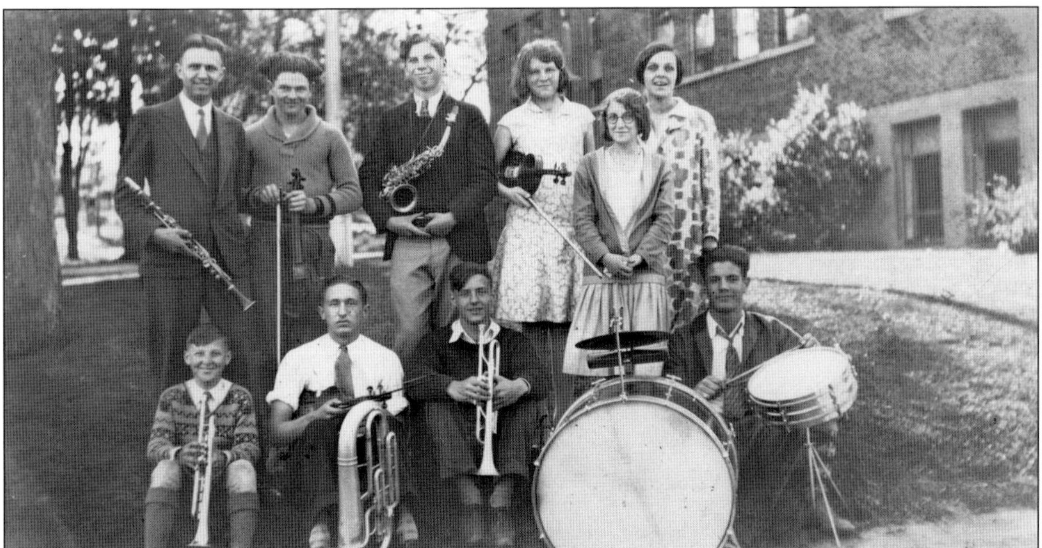

The high school orchestra provided a different sound in the form of classical and jazz music. Each musician played his or her own instrument, as shown here in this 1931 group picture. The orchestra also competed with other schools, winning awards along the way.

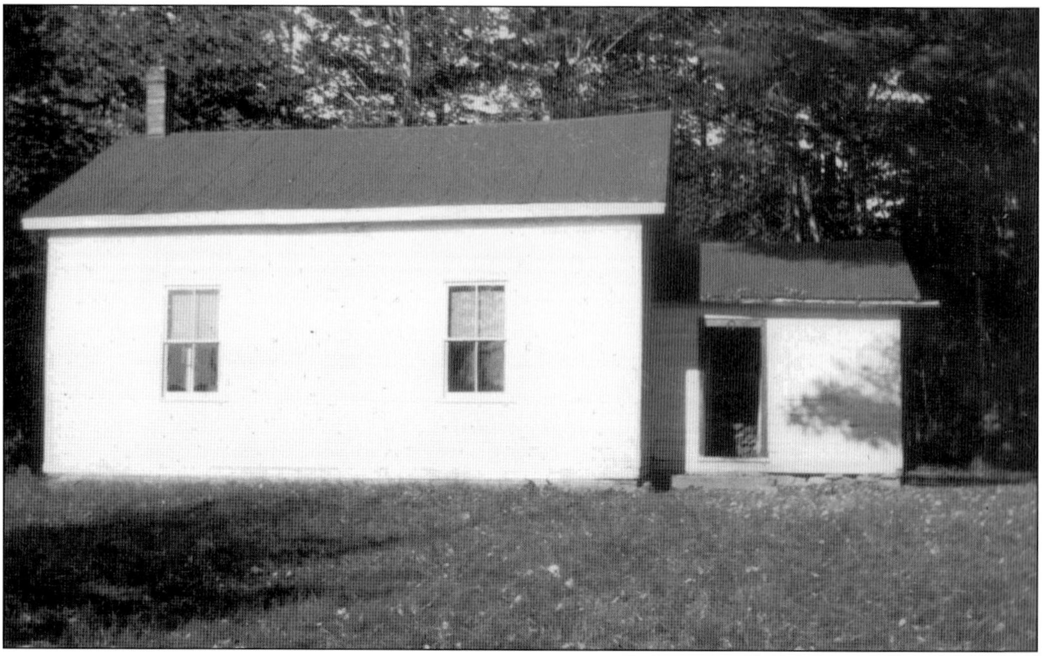

When six to eight families would settle near each other, they formed a school district. One of the families would provide the land upon which a one-room schoolhouse was built. At one time, the town of Prattsburgh had 17 districts, 34 teachers, and an average population of 328 students. The Birdseye School No. 5 (above) was among the first established and located in the southern part of Prattsburgh. Vrooman School No. 7 (below) was located on Twelve Mile Creek on what is now County Route 9.

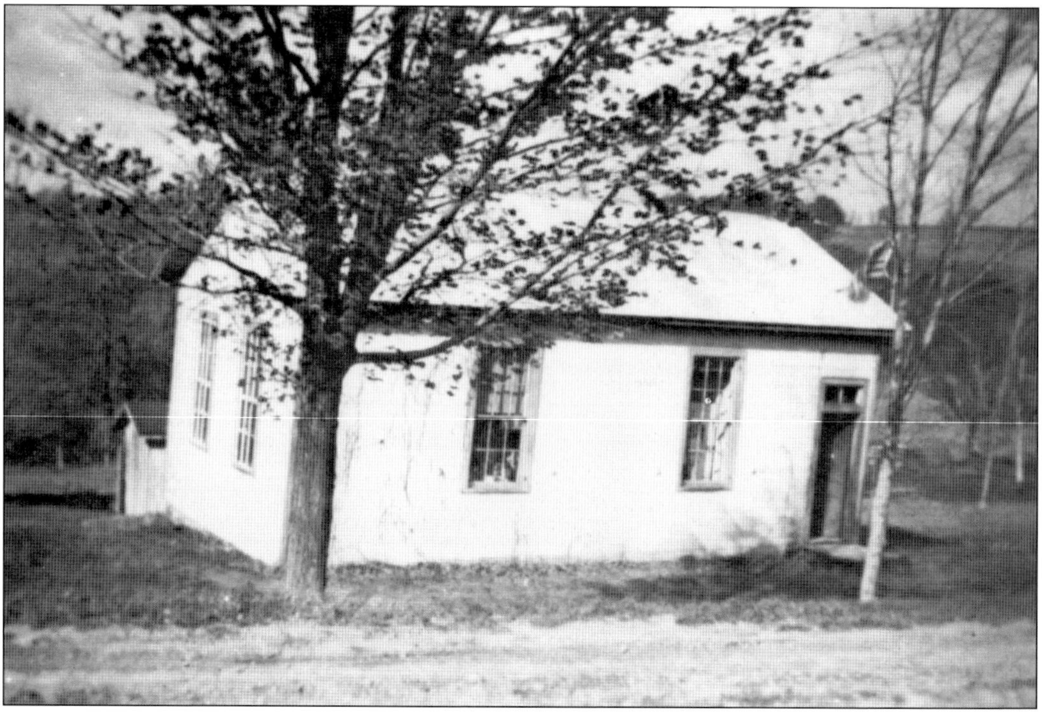

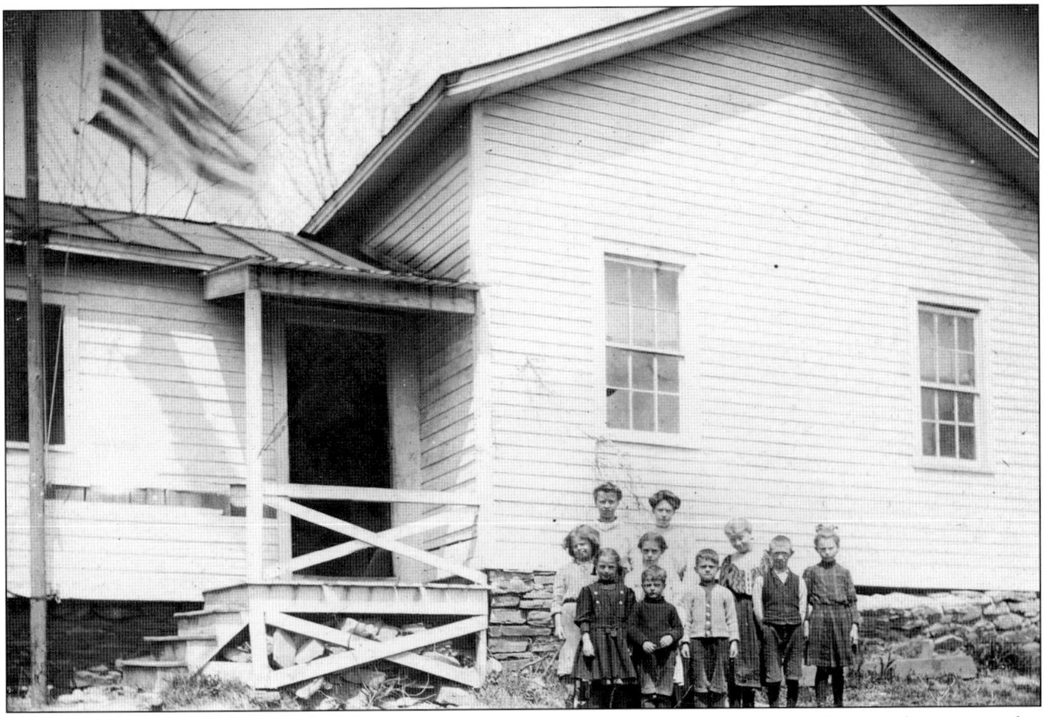

The families in each district would pay a tax that was used to pay the teacher and support the school. The school was visited each year by an inspector of Common School and awarded a certificate of qualification. Each scholar was to furnish one-fourth cord of wood, two feet long, to heat the school. If not, they paid 25¢. Horton's Corner School No. 8 (above) was located at the corner of County Route 75 and Townline Road. Block School No. 13 (below) is on Block School Road at the corner of Burke Road. This building has been restored and is a seasonal residence.

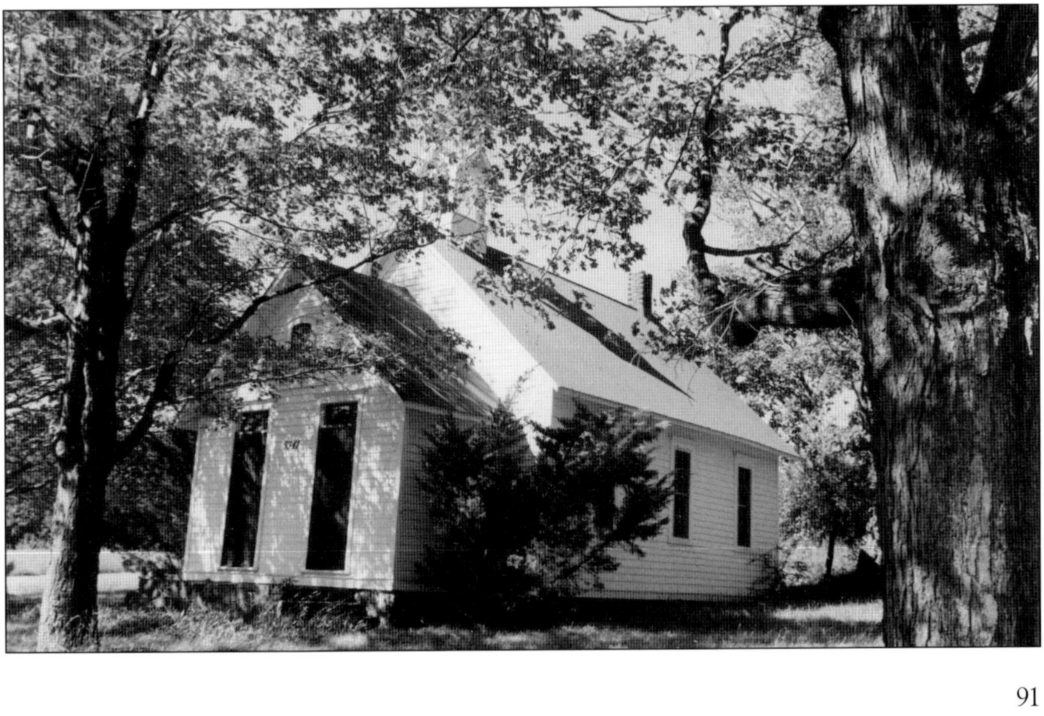

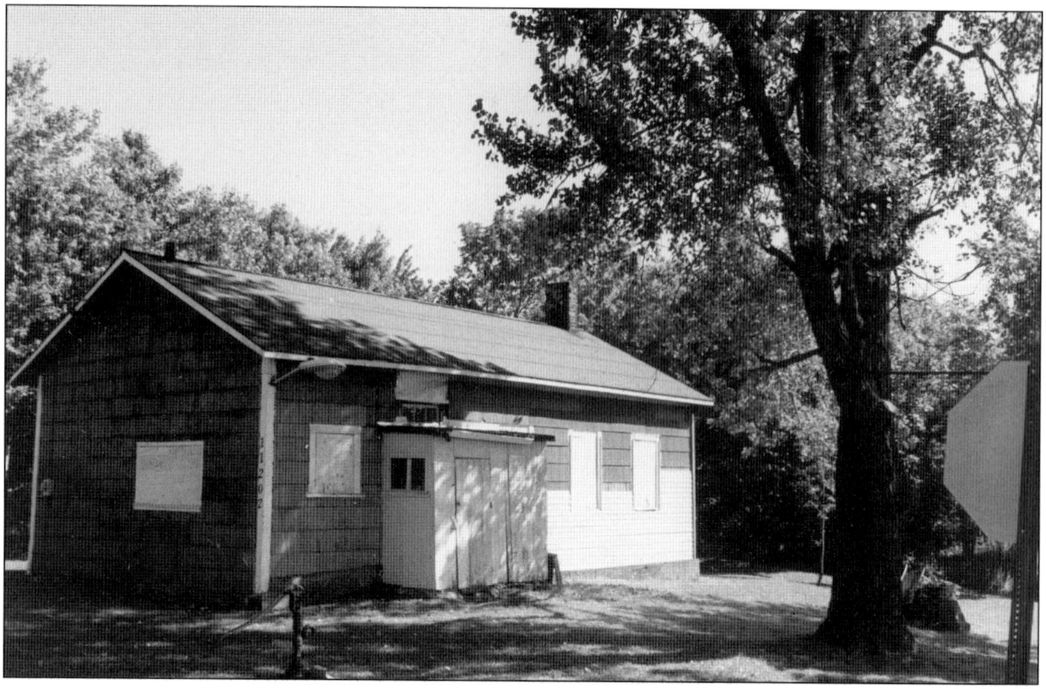

When the school needed to purchase supplies, they would raise the tax by $5 to purchase such things as a shovel, broom, pail, blank books, and plastering cloth used for book covers. The average attendance at each schoolhouse was around 39 students. The Red Schoolhouse No. 14 (above) is located on the corner of Mattoon and Cook School Roads. School No. 17 (below) was located on State Route 53 about a mile south of town.

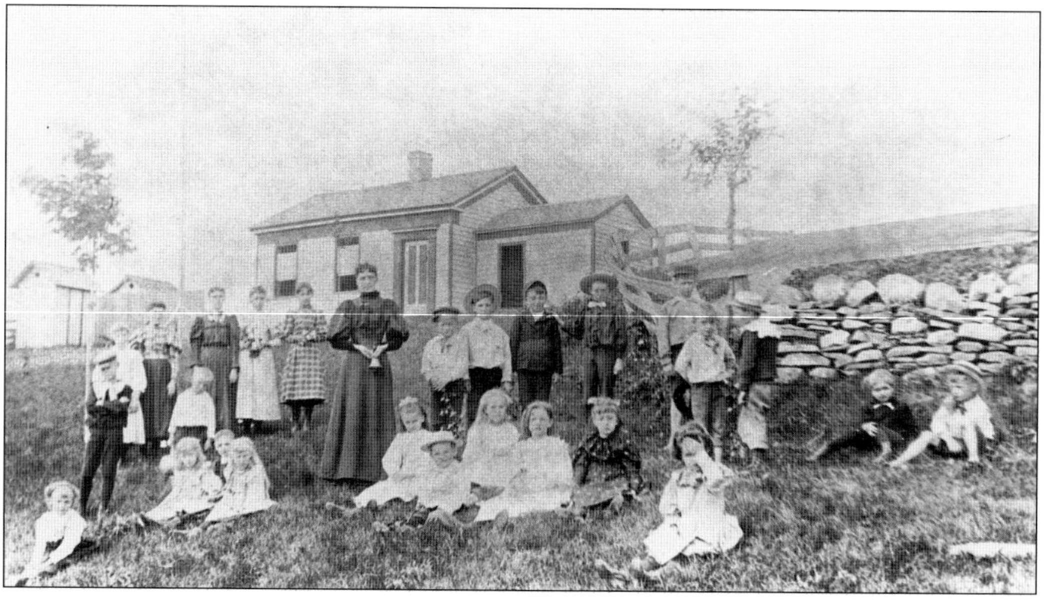

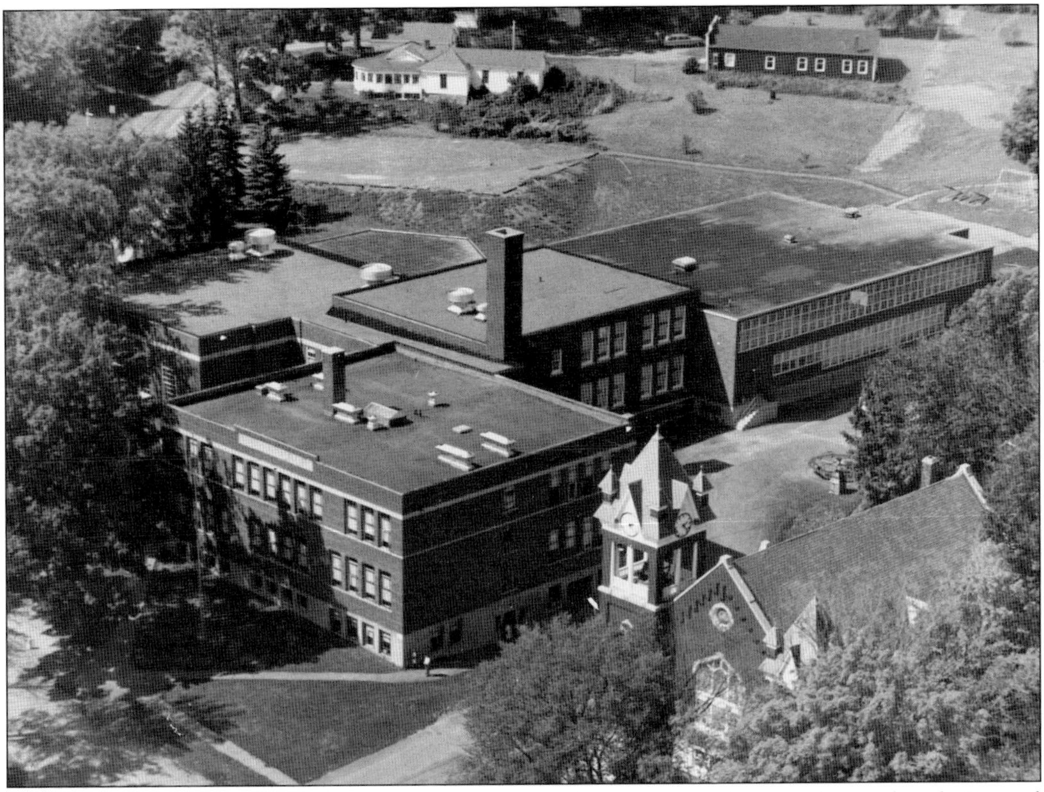

In 1936, the school centralized and became known as Franklin Academy and Prattsburgh Central School. At this time, the one-room schoolhouse era came to an end and all students attended the one large school. This centralized school began serving the towns of Urbana, Wheeler, Pulteney, Italy, and Jerusalem. A wing was added to the 1924 building to house the gymnasium, library, and additional classrooms, as shown in the above photograph. Over the years, as the population grew, the school expanded even more, adding a larger gymnasium, a wing for pre-kindergarten through the third grade, a cafeteria, an auxiliary gymnasium, and choral suite. The photograph below shows just how far the school has come since 1924. (Both, courtesy of Franklin Academy and Prattsburgh Central School.)

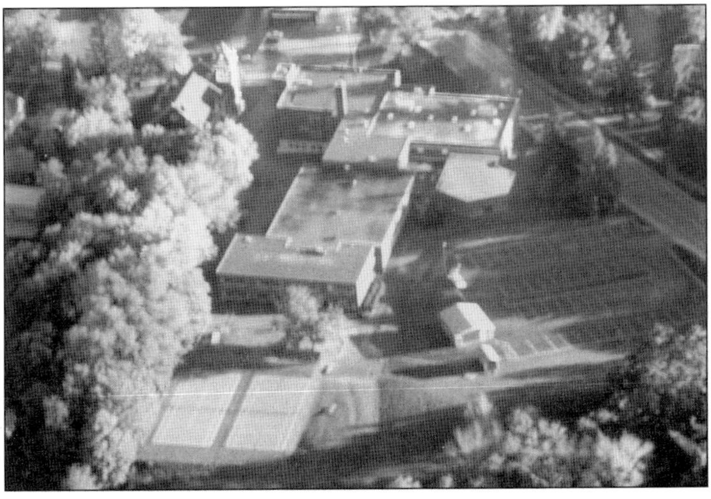

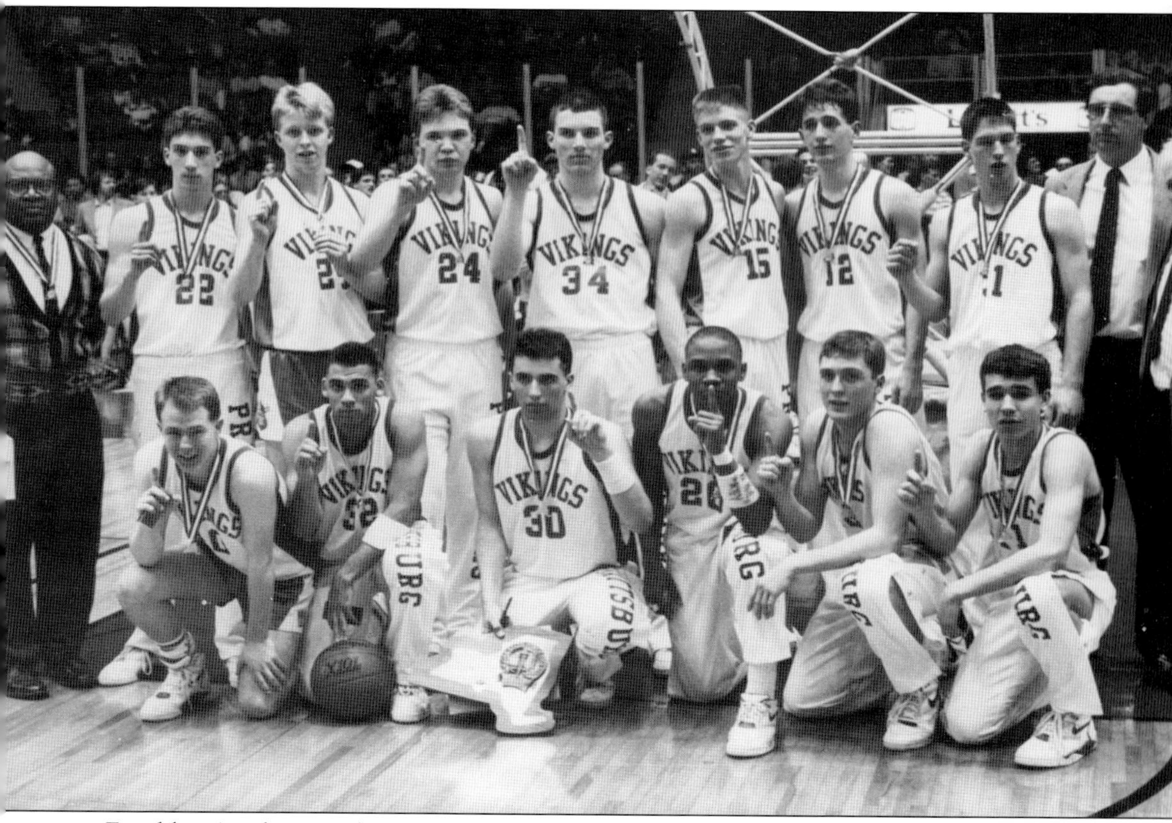

Franklin Academy and Prattsburgh Central School has realized much success in its history. One of the crowning achievements was the winning of the basketball state championship in March 1991. The winning team, pictured here, is the only team to win a state championship, the culmination of a 29-0 winning season. Members are, from left to right, (first row) Chris Robbins, Charlie Hicks, Brain Putnam, Alton Shaw, Marc Clements, and T.J. Carpenter; (second row) coach Wayne Hicks, Brady Zimmer, Bob Adams, Gary Day, Zach DeVoe, Andy Grodis, Jon Jackson, J.B. Sokolowski, coach Jeff Gifford, and head coach Jim Burke. (Courtesy of Franklin Academy and Prattsburgh Central School.)

Six

INGLESIDE

The first settler to this area was Michael Keith in 1807 who traveled to Naples along a rustic towpath for supplies. Then, in 1810, Thomas Riker and William Drake came from Delaware County and gave the area the name Riker's Hollow. In 1882, the name was changed to Ingleside by a vote of the inhabitants. The word Ingleside means "fireside."

As Ingleside grew, so too did its commercial area. By the late 1800s, there were several general stores, two blacksmith shops, a brass band, and three churches. The hamlet has three cemeteries—one by the Christian Church, one south of the church on County Route 9, and one on Twelve Mile Creek.

Over time, the commercial center of Ingleside disappeared, leaving only residences and farmland. Those living in Ingleside now conduct business mainly in Prattsburgh or Naples. The post office that once served the community is now on display at the Rochester Museum and Science Center.

Ingleside is represented by the Prattsburgh Town Board, pays Prattsburgh Town taxes and Steuben County taxes, but pays Naples Central School taxes.

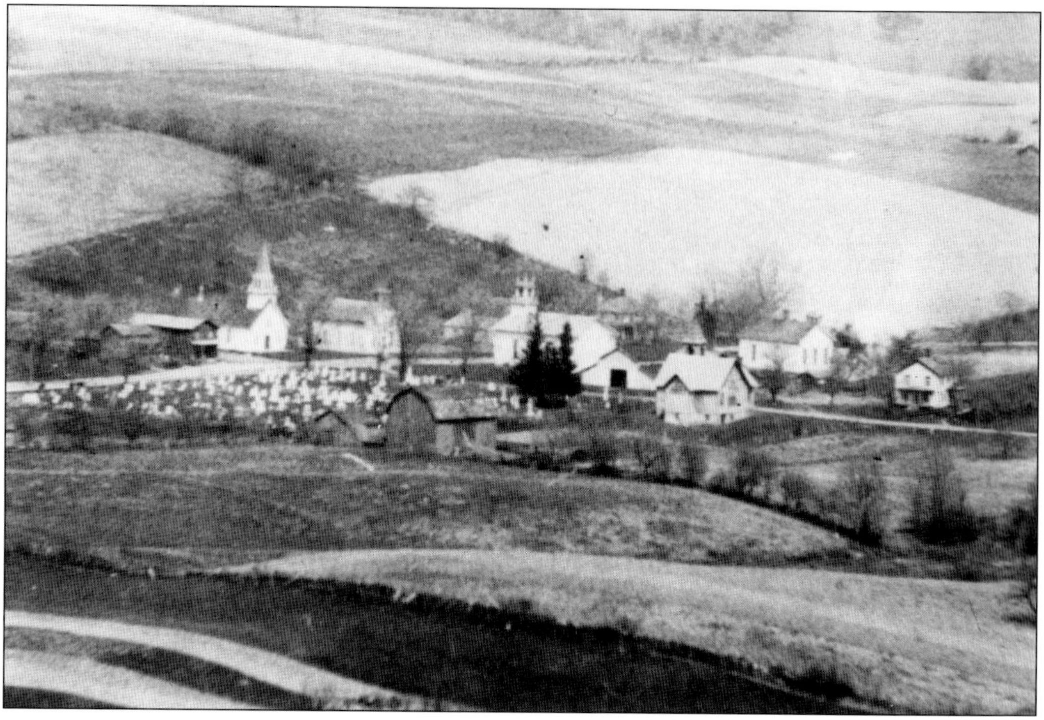

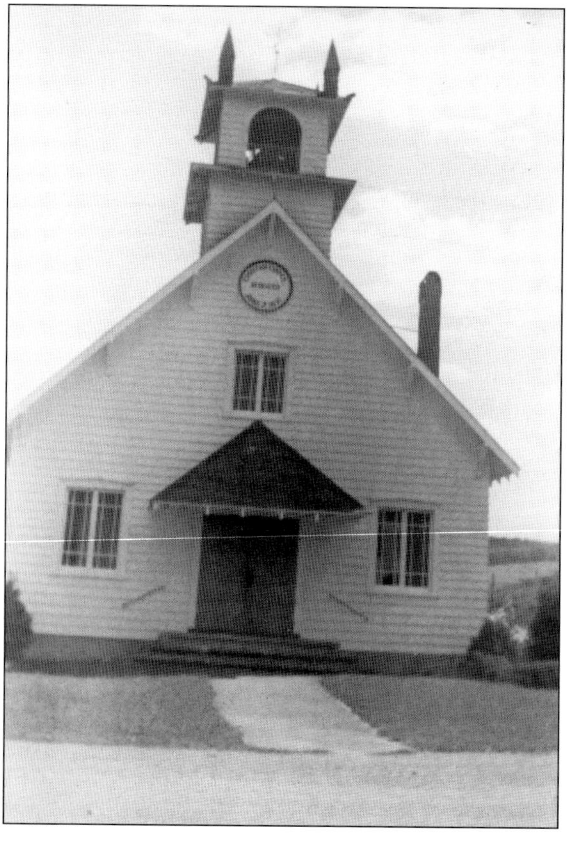

The hamlet of Ingleside was a thriving community in its own right. Agriculture was a key industry, as shown by the vast open fields in the photograph. As in any community, the church played a central role in the lives of the families living there.

The original Ingleside Christian Church, or meetinghouse as it was called, was built in 1869 on a property owned by George and Louisa Hare. On May 16, 1930, the Ingleside Christian Church and its sheds burned to the ground. The members of the church and others of the community constructed a new church building on the site of the old one. In just a little over a year, on June 7, 1931, the new building was dedicated. The Ingleside Christian Church continues to have a dedicated membership.

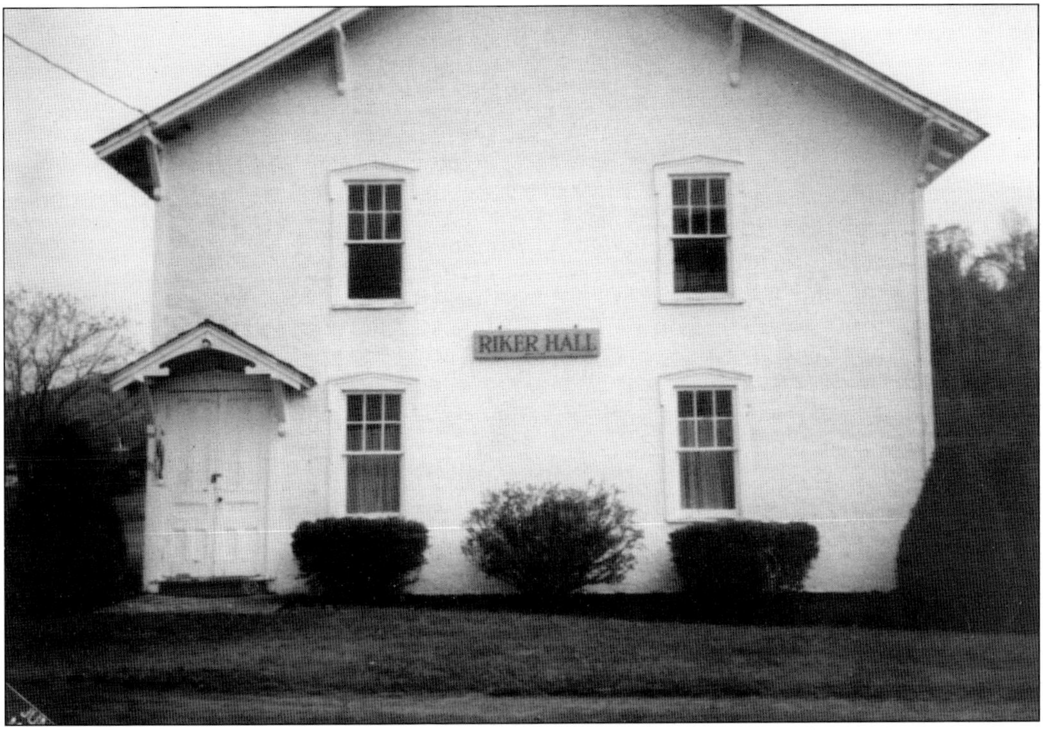

The Ingleside Grange was organized in December 1879 with Harrison Briglin as the first master. At first, meetings were held in Briglin's home, but the Grange later purchased a building that was rejected by the school in 1881. In December 1931, the hall was destroyed by fire and was rebuilt in October 1932. There was a Junior Grange organized in 1932, and the Grange continued to be a part of the community for many years. After the Grange disbanded, the building became owned by the Christian Church and was named Riker's Hall. It has since been torn down.

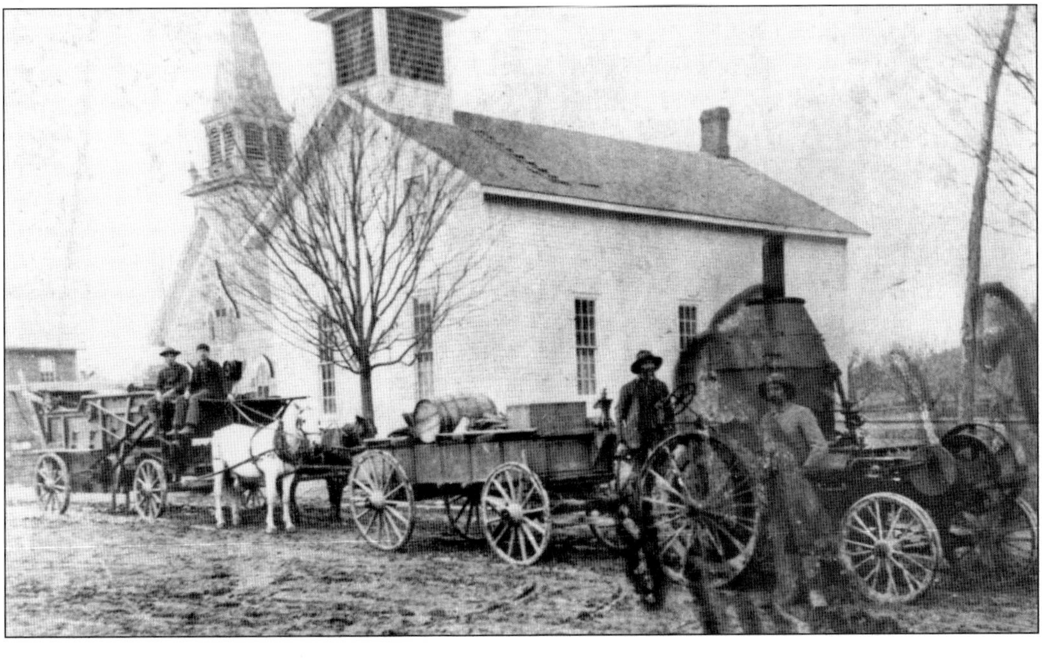

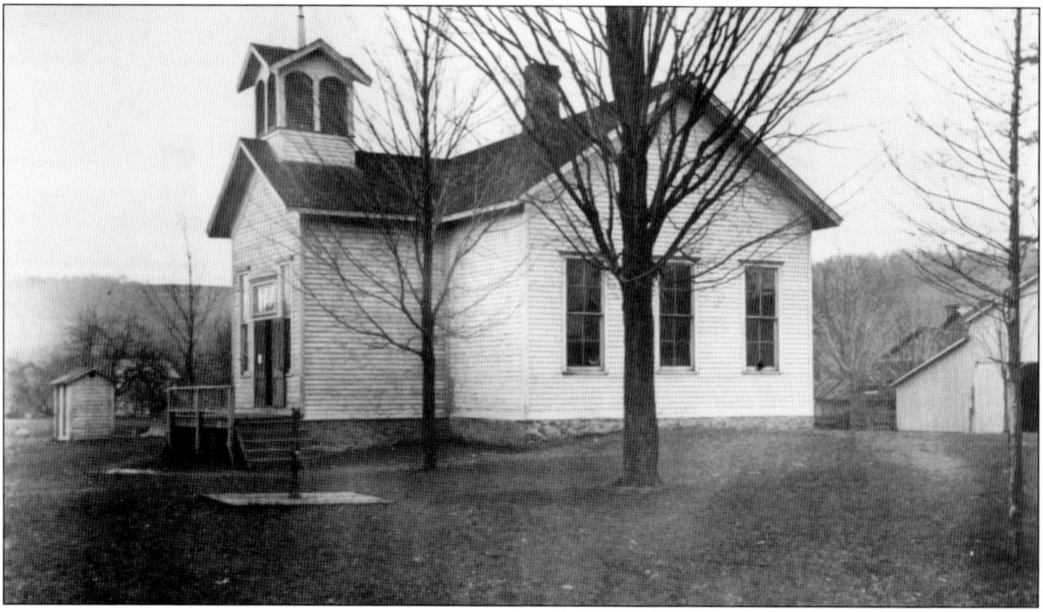

The school building was erected in 1878 beside the church on the east side after the original structure constructed for this purpose was rejected. It was later remodeled into a two-room schoolhouse. Once the school centralized with Naples, the building was donated to the Primitive Baptist Church. It was torn down in 1990.

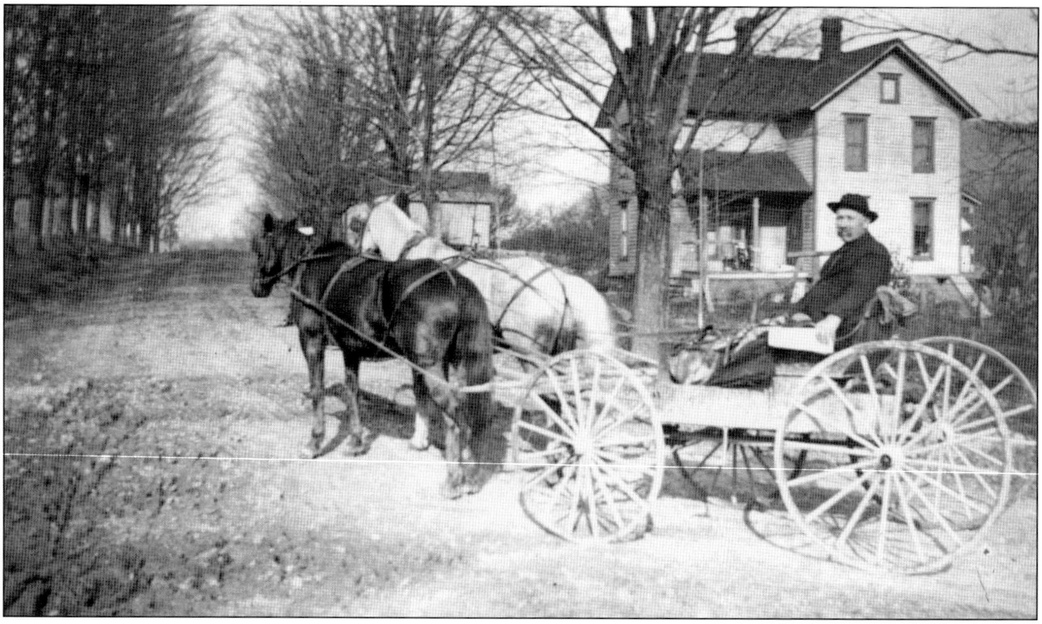

A. Mr. Lounsberry was the mail carrier for Ingleside. The mail came in by rail from Atlanta, New York, and was picked up by a carrier. At one time, Ingleside had its own post office but is now served by the Naples Post Office. The Ingleside Post Office is now a permanent exhibit at the Rochester Museum and Science Center.

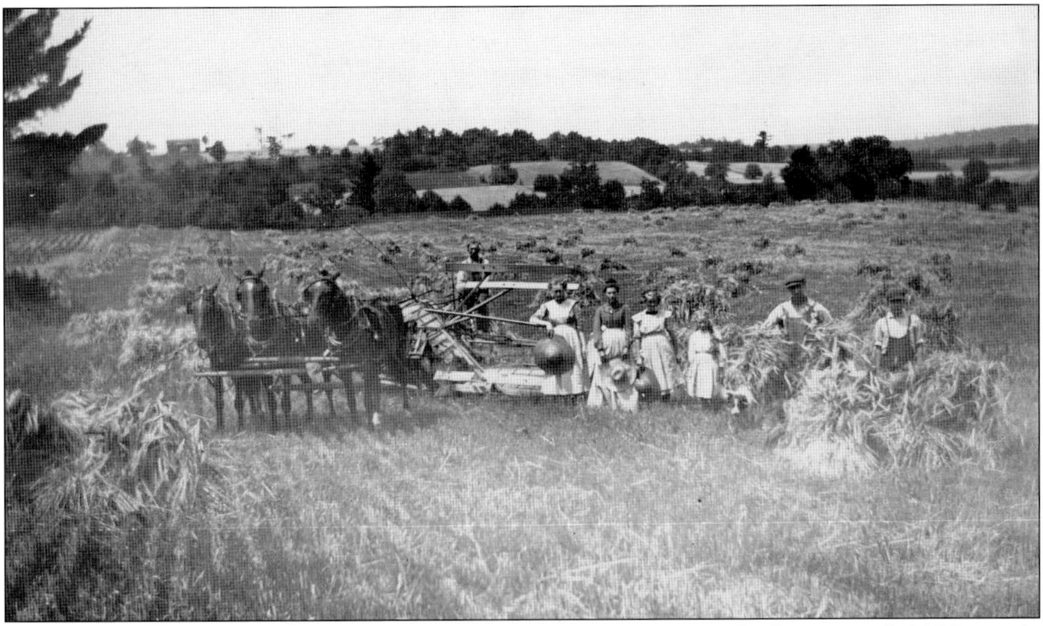

The biggest event ever held in Ingleside was the farmers' picnic, which attracted 6,000 people on August 12, 1933. The day's activities for children consisted of 50- and 100-yard dashes and three-legged, sack, and paper races. Adults competed in cradling, plowing, and potato-planting races and a pie-eating contest, which was actually for both adults and children.

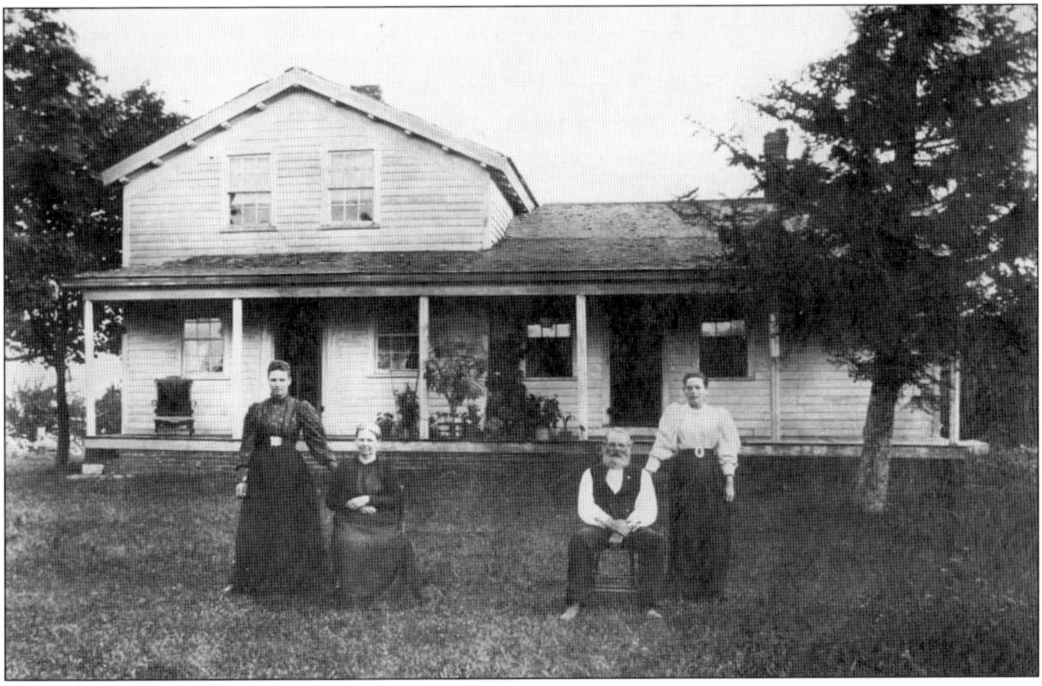

The Graves family was among the earliest to settle in Ingleside, and they were very active across several generations. Both the men and women in the family held offices in the Grange, including master, treasurer, secretary, and pianist. This picture shows the farm of Charles Graves located on Burke Road. Charles was the Grange Master in 1893, 1894, 1898, 1899, and 1900.

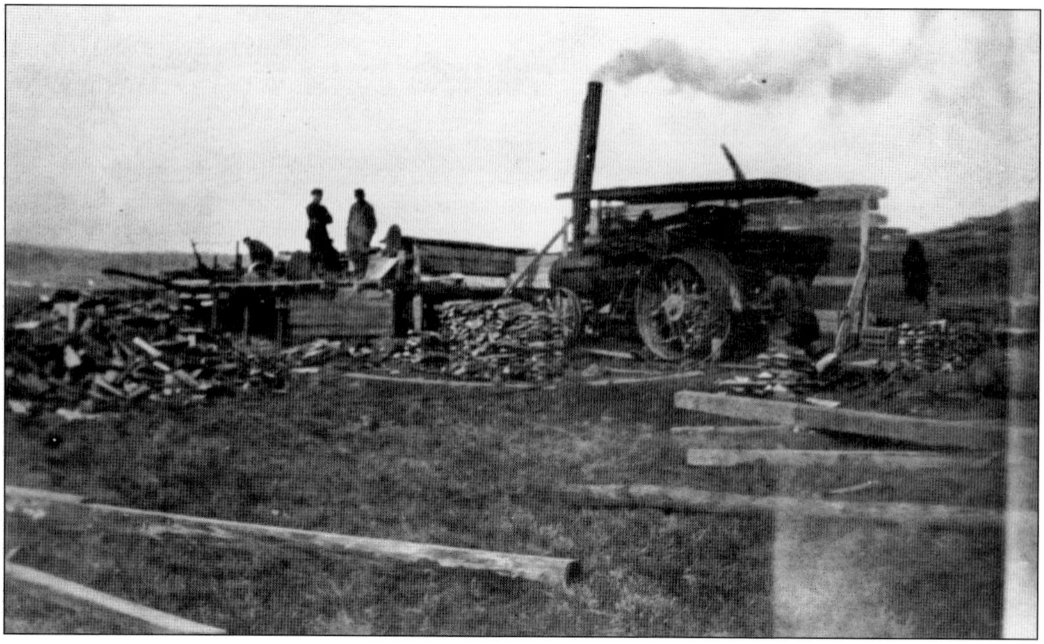

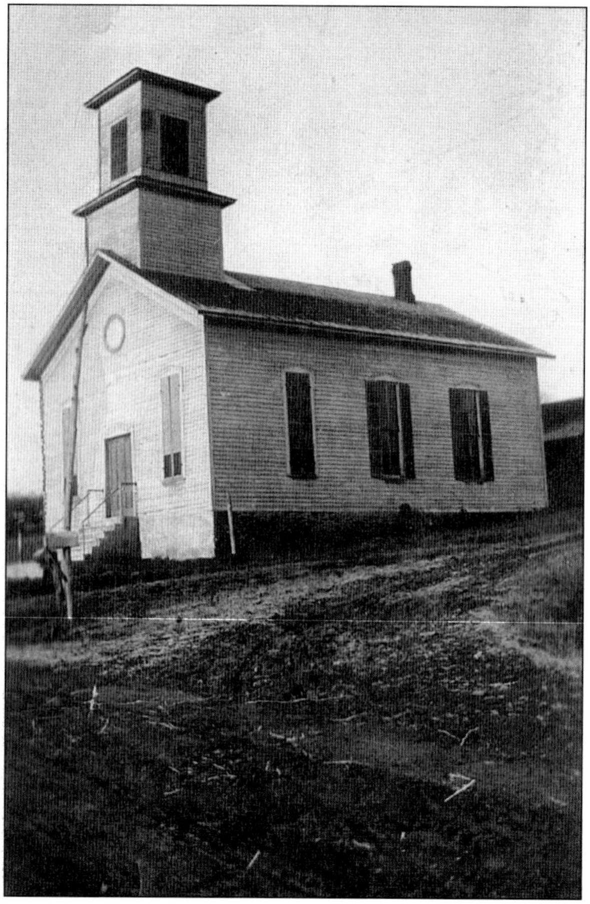

As soon as settlers began arriving, there arose a need for lumber to build the hamlet. Twelve Mile Creek provided a prime spot near which to operate a sawmill. Fred Presler, who was among Ingleside's earliest settlers, operated this sawmill.

The hamlet of Lynn was along County Route 7 to the south of Ingleside. In 1876, the Methodist congregation dismantled the church there and moved it to Ingleside. This became the first church in Ingleside. It burned down in the late 1800s.

Seven

Wheeler

Wheeler was first settled by and named after a Revolutionary soldier, Capt. Silas Wheeler, in 1799. Captain Wheeler's son Gratton H. Wheeler was named after Lord Henry Gratton, who helped Silas escape from British forces in Quebec. Over time, Gratton was elected to the state assembly, state senate, and the US Congress. In 1840, he served as a presidential elector supporting General Harrison.

Wheeler is just south of Prattsburgh, having been formed from Prattsburgh and a small portion of Bath. It contains two centers, Wheeler Center, found at the four corners, and Mitchellsville, located on the southeast border along County Route 13. There is a strong Amish community in Wheeler.

The first religious society was formed in 1810. Later, the Methodist and Presbyterian Churches were formed, sharing the same building for a period of time. Today, only the Methodist Church exists in Wheeler. Wheeler, at one time, boasted two general stores, two sawmills, a school, a feed mill, blacksmith shop, and one hotel. There was also diverse agricultural activity in Wheeler. This included sheep raising, lumbering, wheat growing, and tobacco farming.

Today, there is very little evidence left of the commercial center; however, agriculture still continues to thrive in this community.

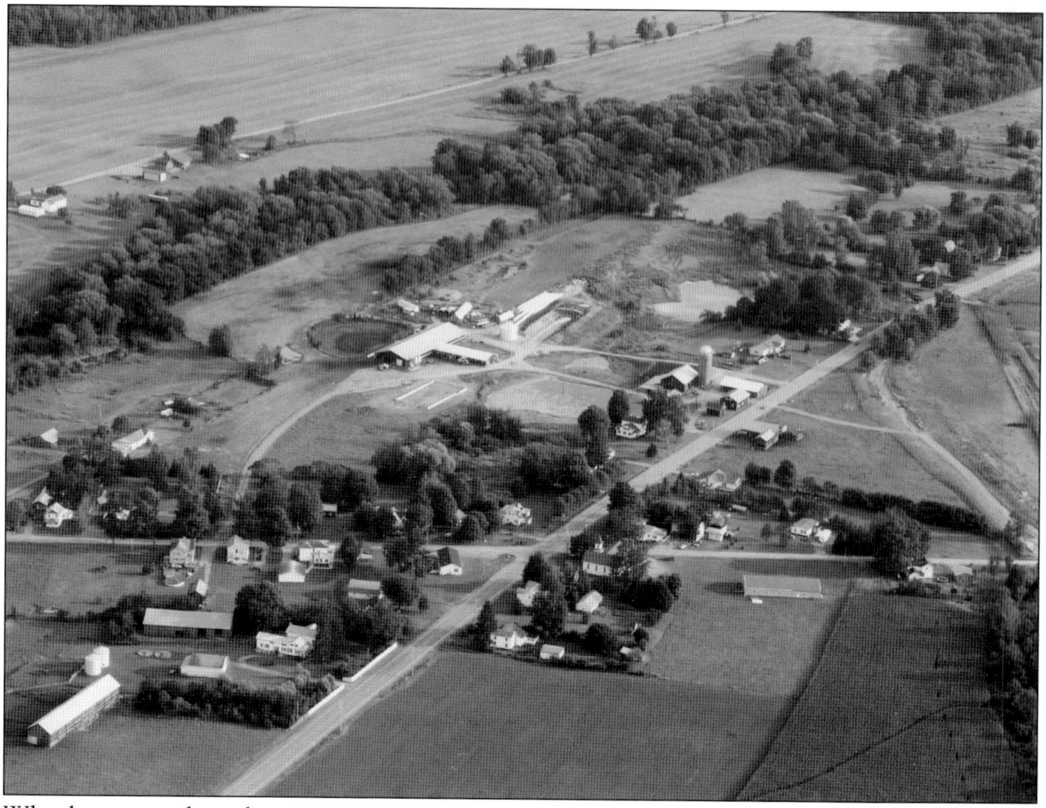

Wheeler received its charter in 1820. The population peaked in 1850 to almost 1,500 but now has just a little over 1,000 residents. Many of the original buildings have been lost to fires and age, leaving just memories of their existence. Wheeler Center now consists of the town hall and the Methodist church.

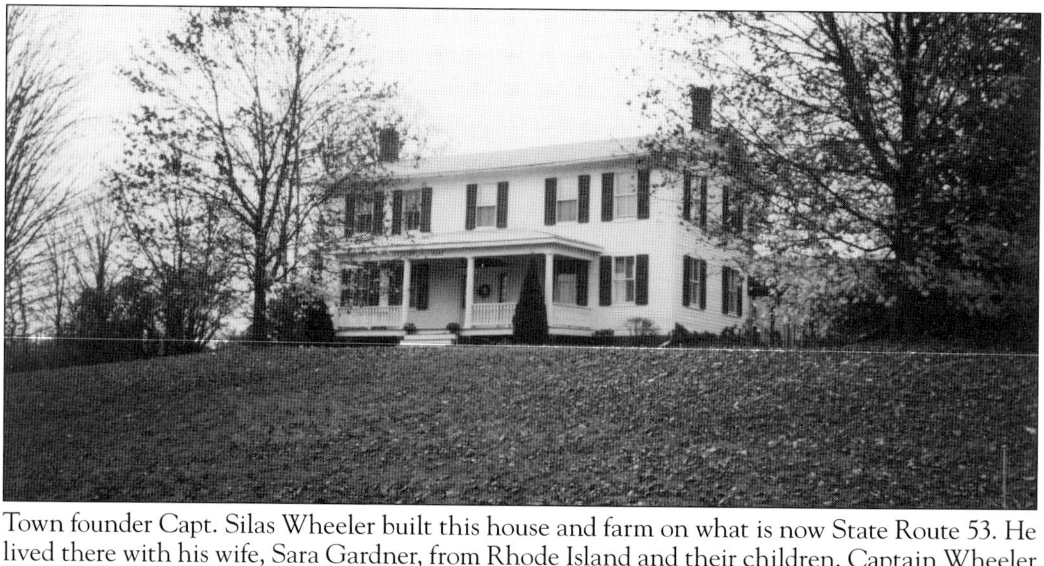

Town founder Capt. Silas Wheeler built this house and farm on what is now State Route 53. He lived there with his wife, Sara Gardner, from Rhode Island and their children. Captain Wheeler opened the Gulf Road to Bath through Mitchellsville. He also began the first sawmill in Wheeler and ran it with his son Gratton in 1809. (Courtesy of Barbara Monroe.)

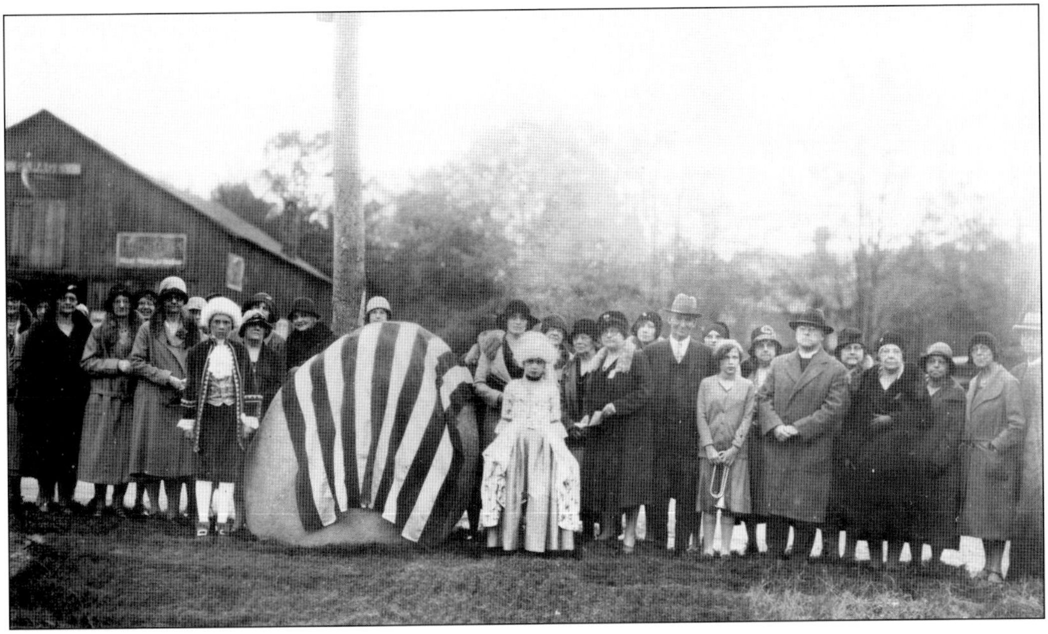

Dr. Marcus Whitman served as a medical doctor in Wheeler from 1828 to 1835. He married Prattsburgh resident Narcissa Prentiss and together they travelled west, being the first to cross the Rocky Mountains and administer to the Indians. He and his party met an untimely death during an Indian massacre in 1847. On October 3, 1930, children in Wheeler dressed in colonial costume to unveil a bronze tablet that tells this remarkable and tragic story to future generations. The stone is located in the center of town at the four corners in front of the town hall.

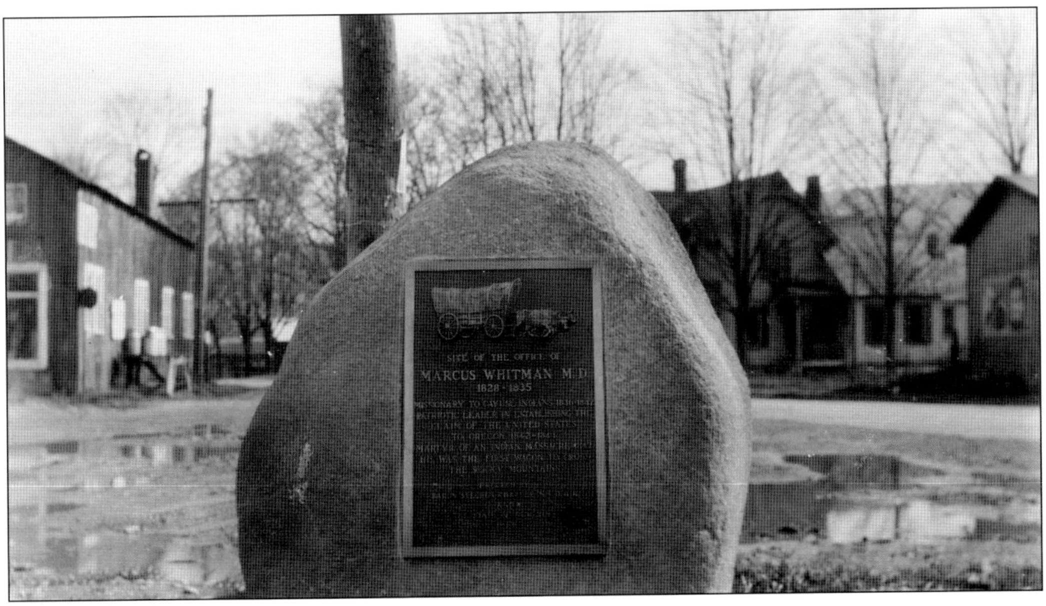

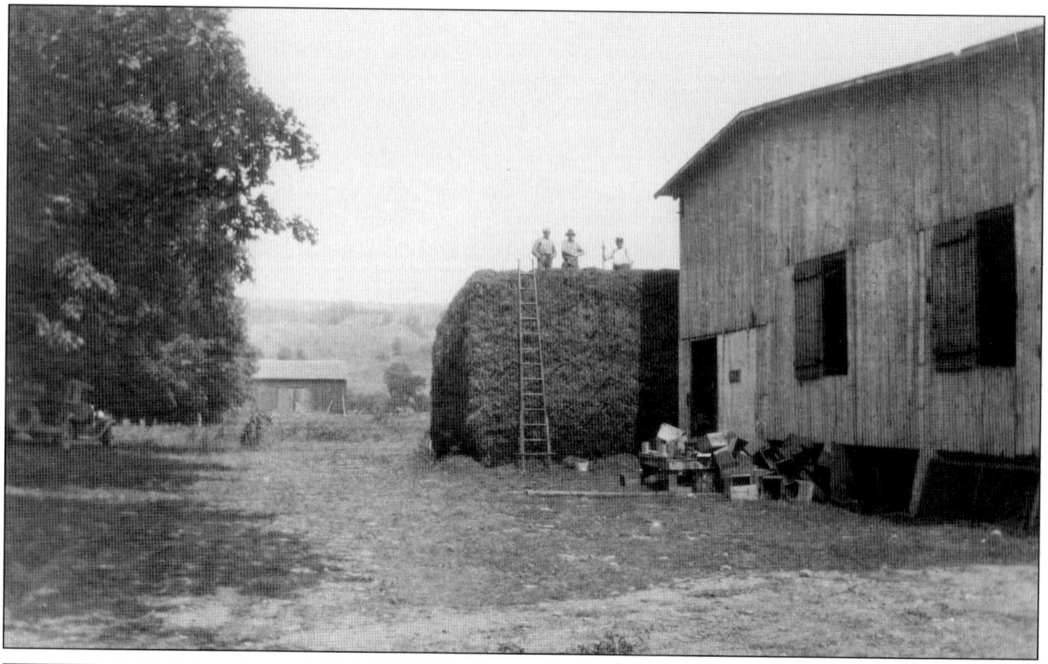

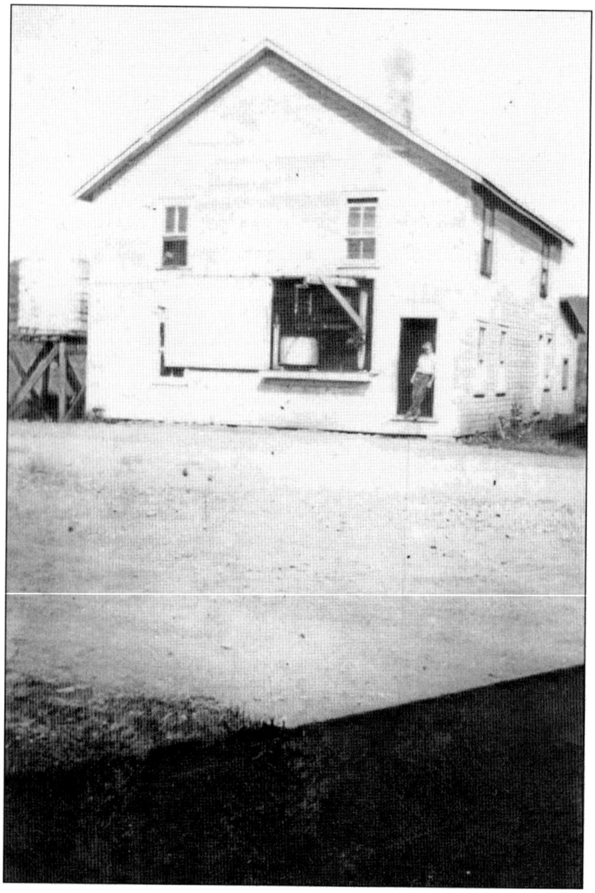

The pea vinery, located on State Route 53, was used to thresh peas. Farmers would haul the peas on the vines to the vinery. The peas were unloaded and put into a pea sheller. The peas would be put into boxes and shipped to the cannery. The vines would be stacked so they could ferment. In the winter, farmers would use the fermented vines for cow feed.

The Wheeler cheese factory was one of many businesses serving Wheeler. Local dairy farmers would take their milk to the factory for processing. It was sold to the Wetmiller Dairy and Farm Products Corporation on April 22, 1924. (Courtesy of Sandra McDougal.)

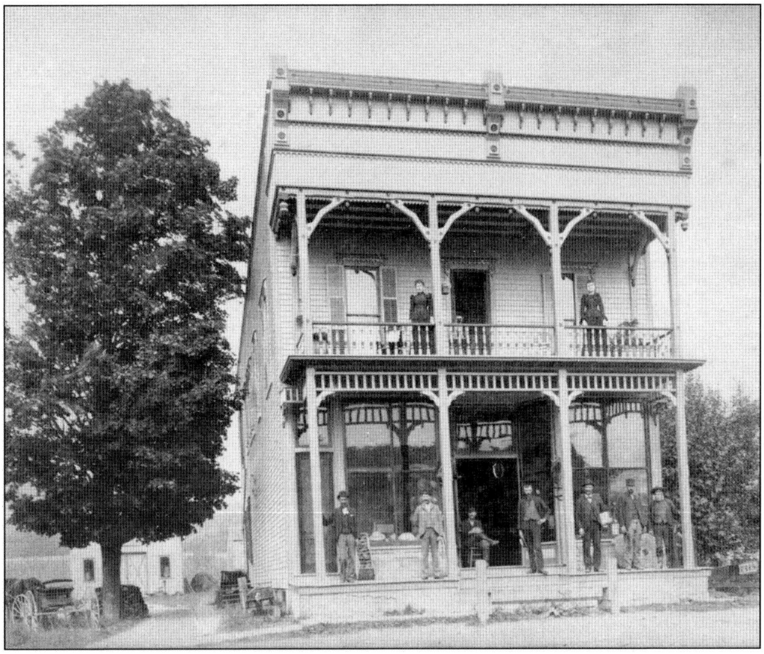

The Kendall Derick Store was built in 1887 on State Route 53 next to the church. It, along with the church, burned in 1901 and was not rebuilt. The store provided residents with food and dry goods necessary for daily life. (Courtesy of Sandra McDougal)

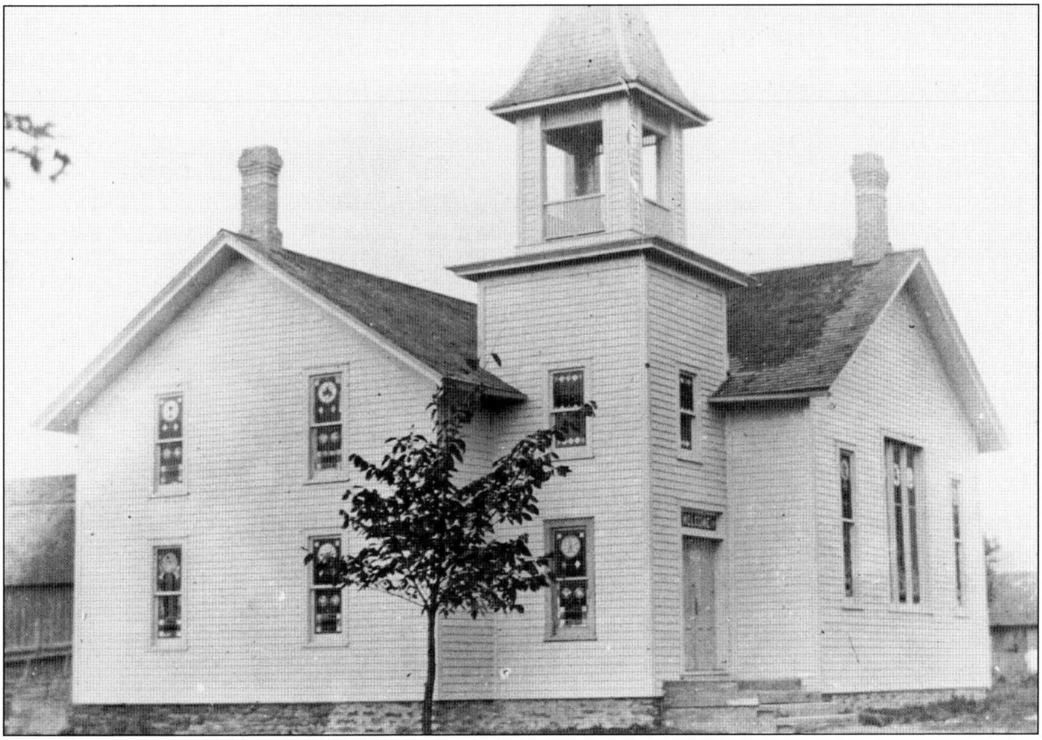

The first Methodist Episcopal Church burned down in 1900. After that event, this newly built Methodist Episcopal Church was constructed of wood from a torn down tobacco barn. Later, a two-story addition was added to include a kitchen, dining room, and a second-floor meeting hall used by the Grange. In 1954, the ladies of the Wheeler church started a Wheeler Community Club. The club serves meals during the week of the Steuben County Fair each year.

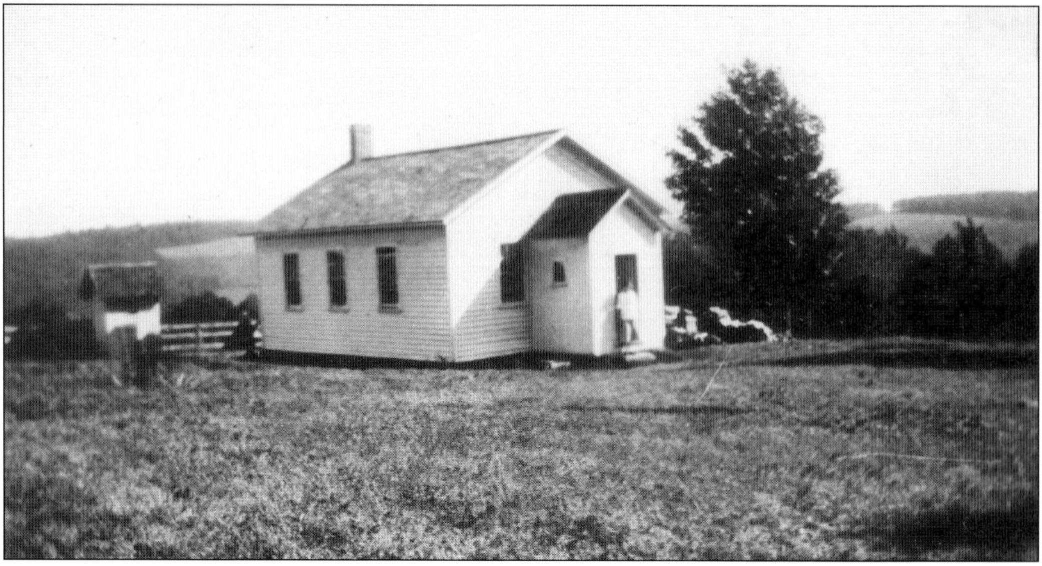

At one time, Wheeler had three little schoolhouses to serve the population. All eight grades were taught by the same teacher. Two, like the one shown here, were located on Kanona-Wheeler Road (now State Route 53) and one was on Bean Station Road. Uriel Chapin, Capt. Joel Pratt's brother-in-law, taught at the first school in Wheeler.

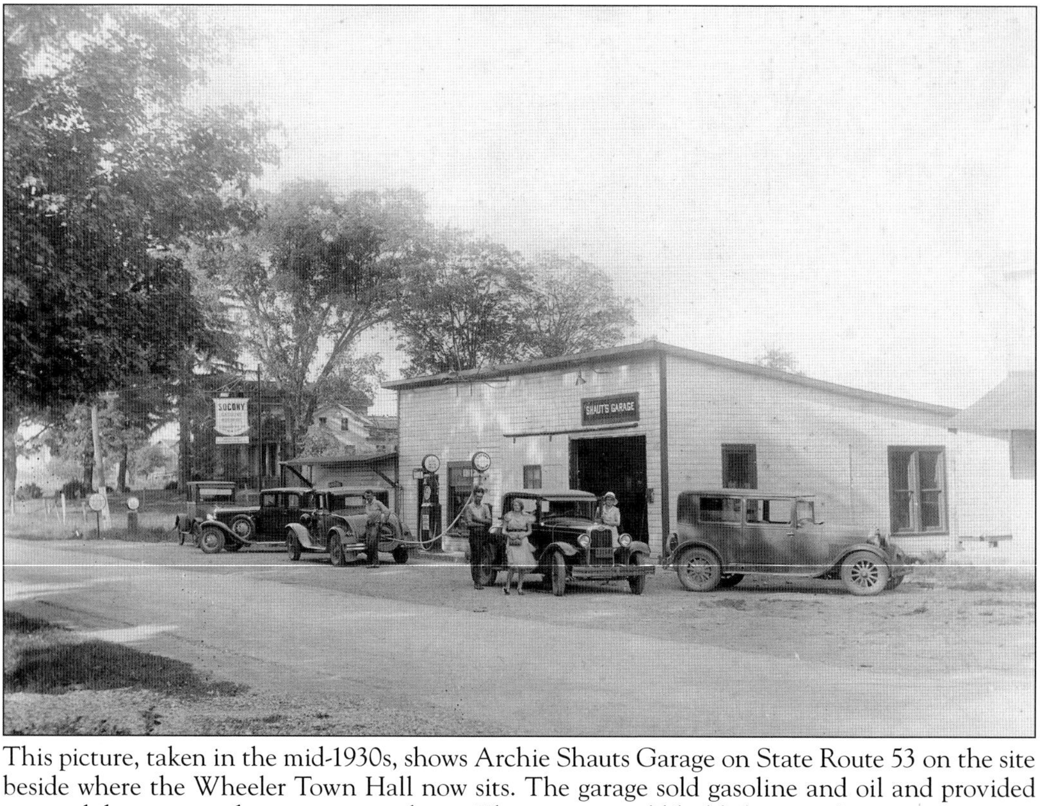

This picture, taken in the mid-1930s, shows Archie Shauts Garage on State Route 53 on the site beside where the Wheeler Town Hall now sits. The garage sold gasoline and oil and provided automobile repair and service to residents. The garage could hold three to four cars for repair work, making it a busy place. (Courtesy of Sandra McDougal.)

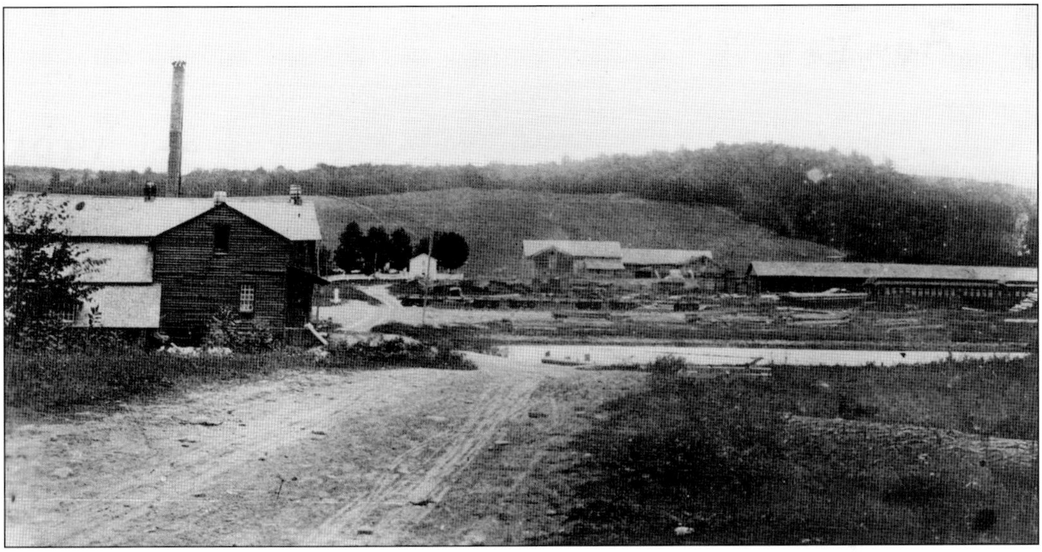

The largest business in Wheeler was Renchan's sawmill, located where County Route 13 crossed Five Mile Creek. The mill was owned and operated by George Renchan. Renchan was a poor boy and had a very little opportunity for education. But, in 1852, he built this large mill, which is said to be one of the largest in the state. He successfully ran his business for about 25 years. Eventually, his son Charles took over the business but was later forced to sell the mill. The mill was both a feed and sawmill in 1879. The train made a stop here on its daily trip. On December 6, 1905, the mill caught fire from a tractor engine passing by. Several saws, belts, and very little lumber were saved. The loss was figured up to nearly $1,500. (Below, courtesy of Barbara Monroe.)

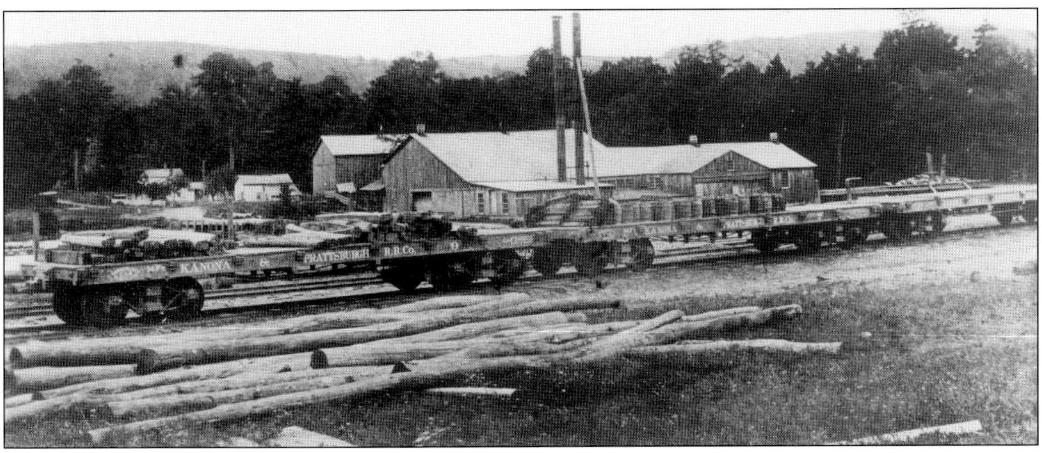

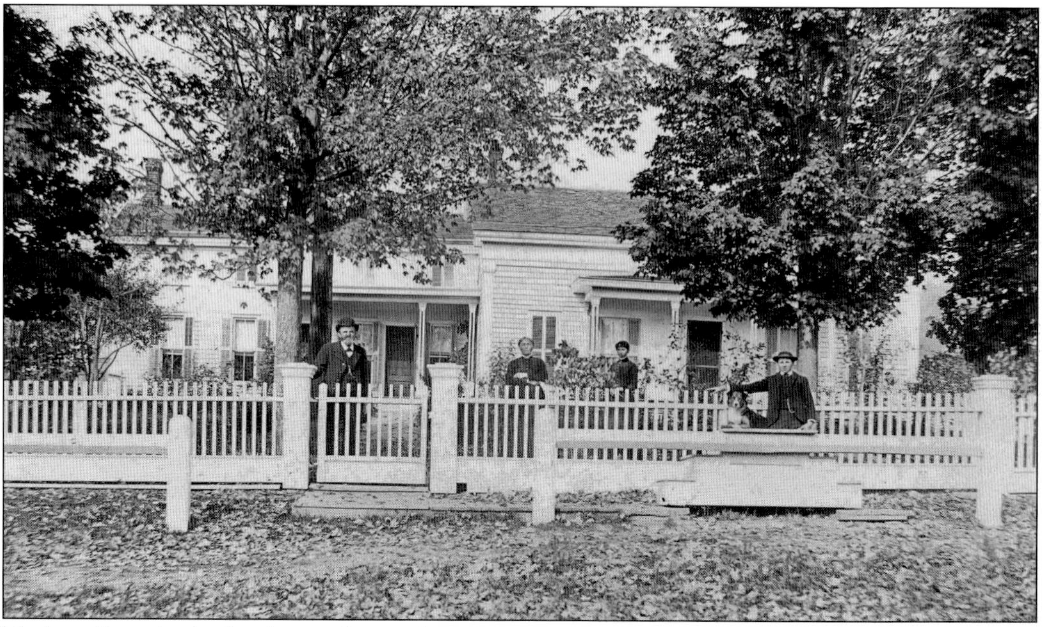

Nathan Rose built this home, located on State Route 53, in 1848–1849. His daughter Sarah married sawmill owner George Renchan. In 1930, the home's residents, Francis and Margelia Phillips Foster, established Foster Fields Farm and raised registered Ayrshires for 60 years. The farm passed to the children, Carl F. Foster and Barbara F. Monroe, who continue to raise dairy cattle there. (Courtesy of Barbara Monroe)

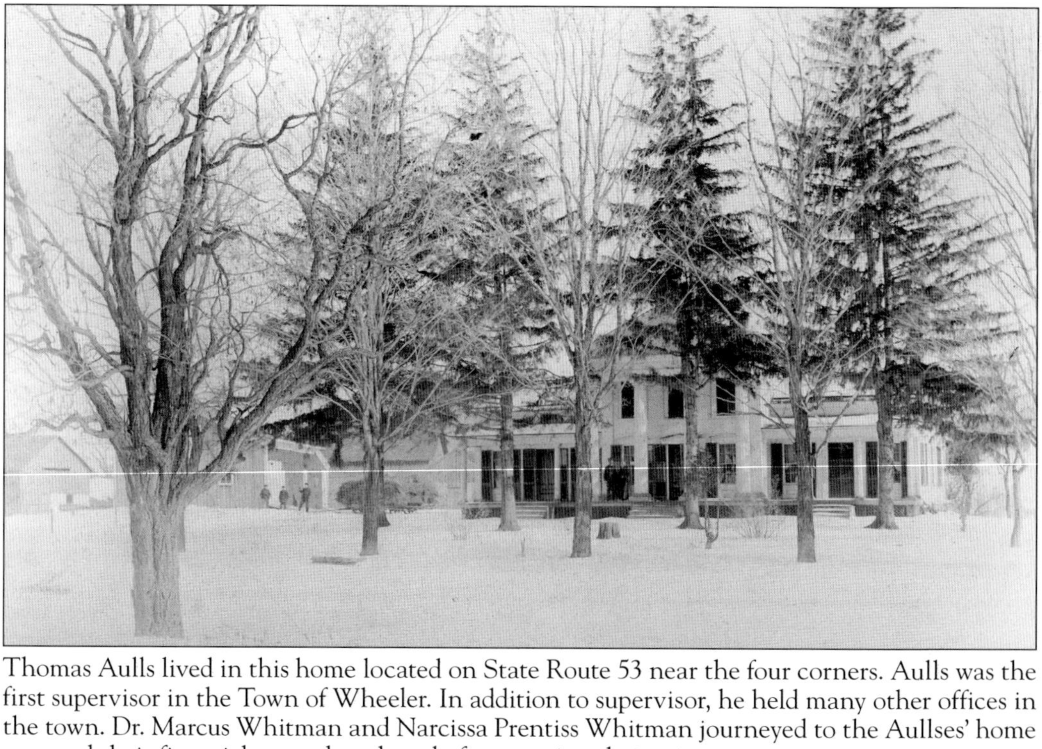

Thomas Aulls lived in this home located on State Route 53 near the four corners. Aulls was the first supervisor in the Town of Wheeler. In addition to supervisor, he held many other offices in the town. Dr. Marcus Whitman and Narcissa Prentiss Whitman journeyed to the Aullses' home to spend their first night together there before starting their trip west.

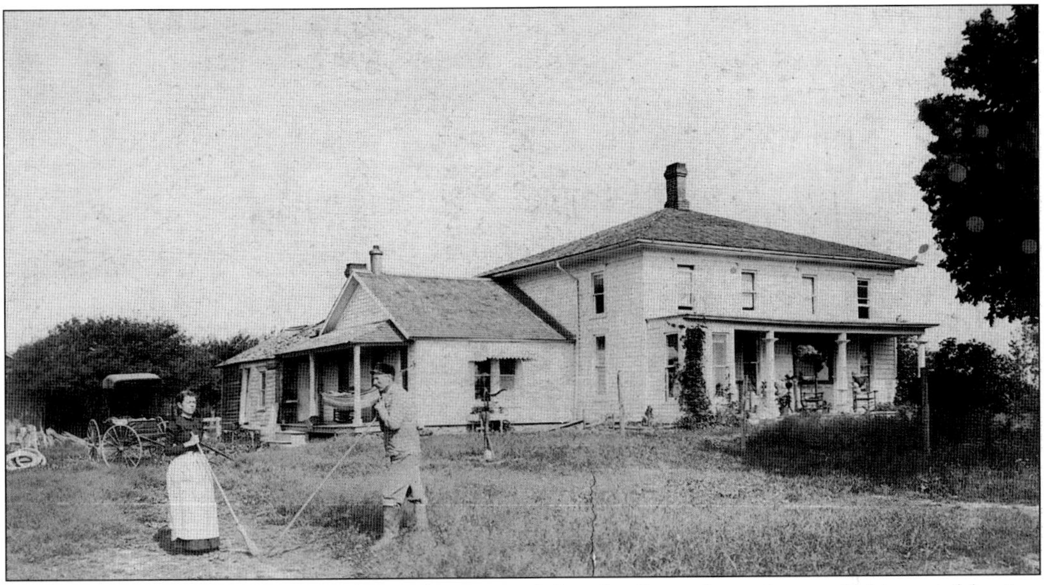

Jacob R. Partridge was the grandson of Jonas and Amelia Partridge, who settled in neighboring Prattsburgh. Jacob built this house sometime before 1850 on Zimmer Road in Wheeler. Jacob and his wife, Laura, lived there and worked the farm until 1918.

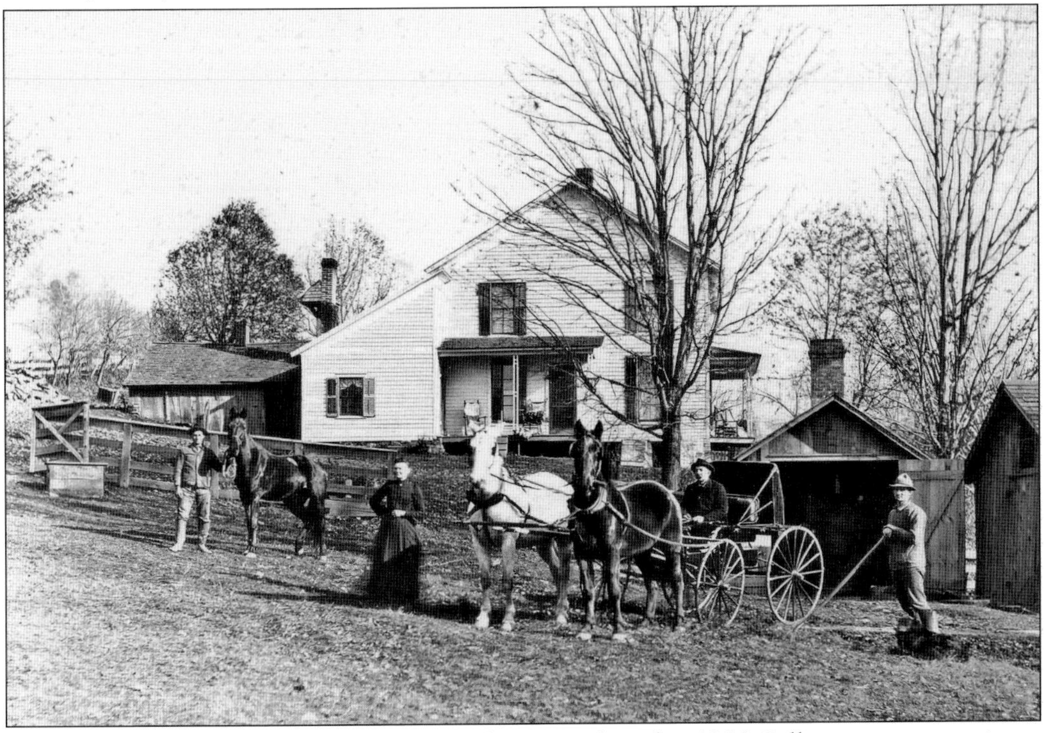

The George N. Bellinger farm on West Creek was purchased in 1866. Bellinger was a prominent farmer in the community for many years. The farm was passed on to his son George H. Bellinger, pictured in the buggy. George H. served as the Wheeler Highway superintendent and later was elected to the office of supervisor, serving a term as the representative to the county board of supervisors. He was a member of the Grange and Presbyterian Church, among other things.

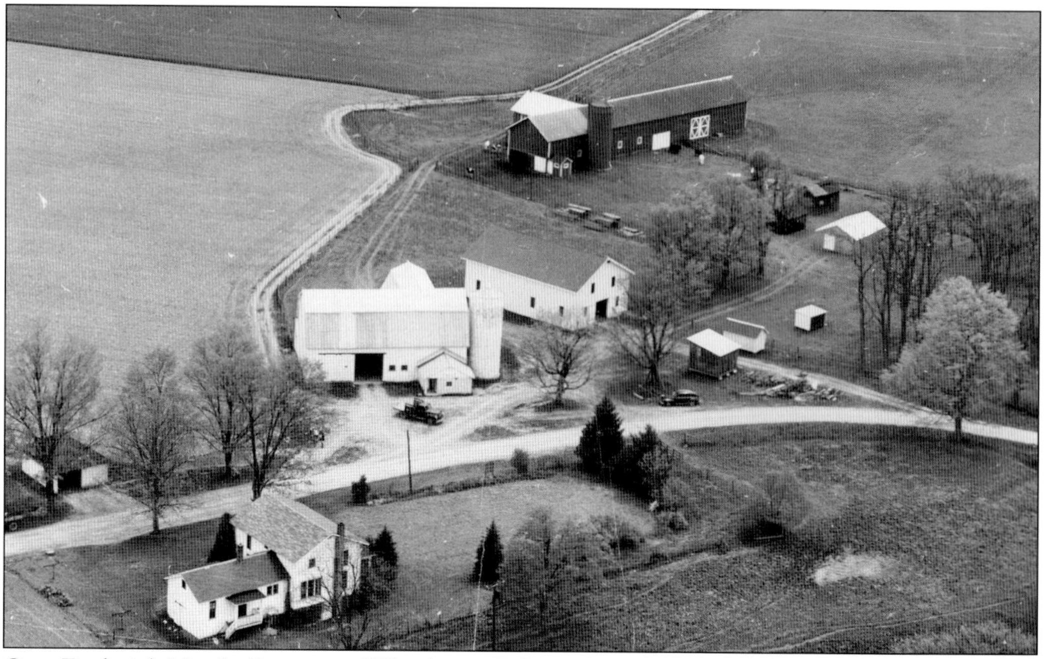

Otto Frederick Marshall came to Wheeler on February 22, 1810. He cleared 200 acres of land on Larue Road to operate a farm. The property has changed hands several times but continues to operate as a farm. (Courtesy of Charles Butts.)

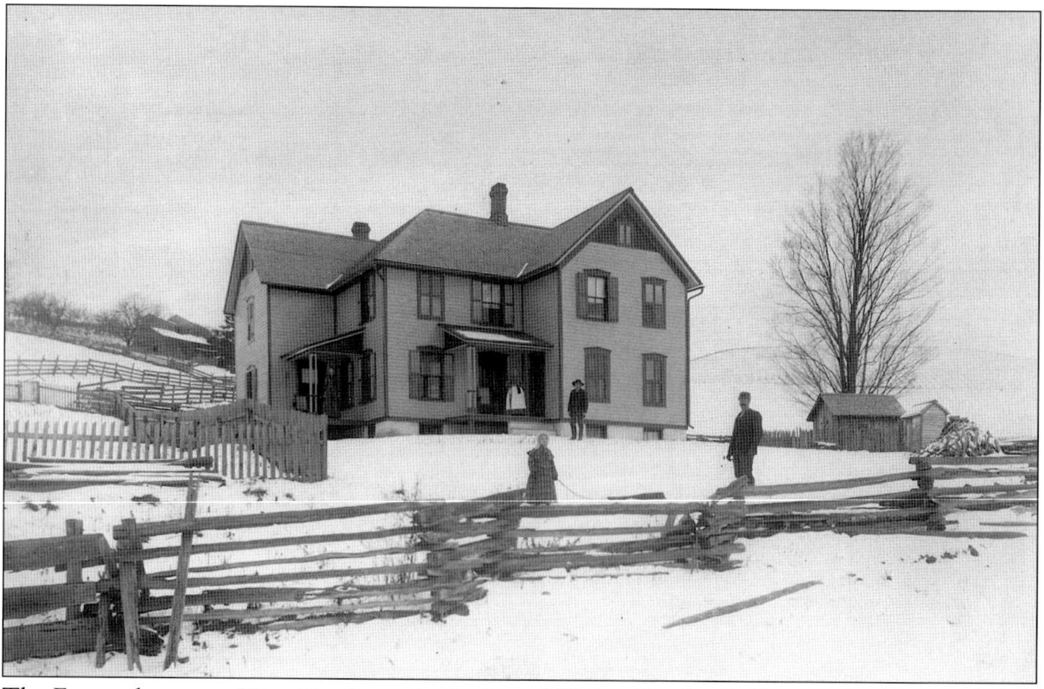

The Everett house on West Creek was built about 1885 by Charles H. Everett on a 160-acre farm cleared by Charles's grandfather Jesse Everett about 1817. Charles became owner of the farm after the death of his father, Levi Everett, in 1891. Charles was a successful farmer and bred Jersey cattle and chickens for a living. The house was torn down in the early 1980s.

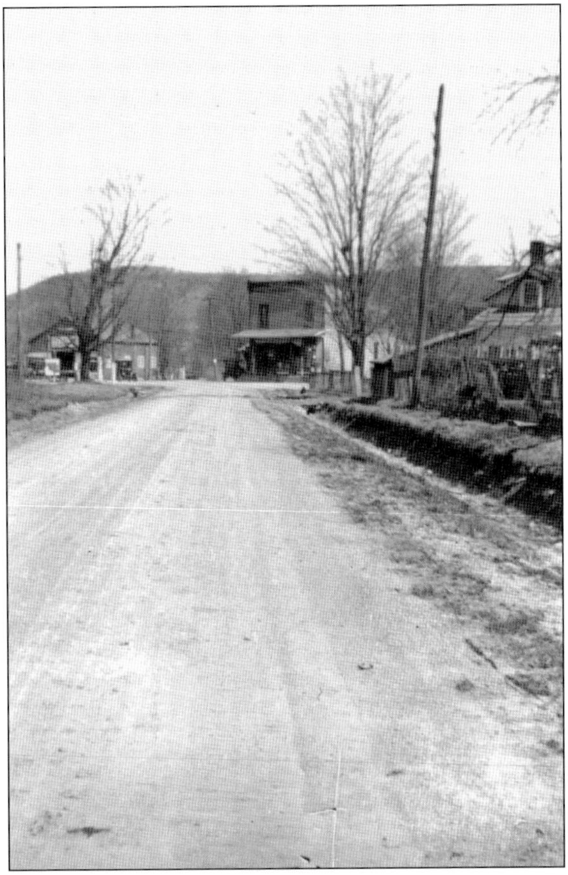

The Wheeler Supply and Grocery store, the first in Wheeler, was located on State Route 53 on the east side of the four corners. It was a large two-story building. On the second floor was the Grange where many parties and other functions were held. The store itself was loaded from floor to ceiling with canned goods, produce, and other necessities. In later years, the store served as a bus stop for passengers making the trip to Bath. The bus would also take on mail and packages for transport to and from Bath. Like most stores, this one served as a gathering place for locals.

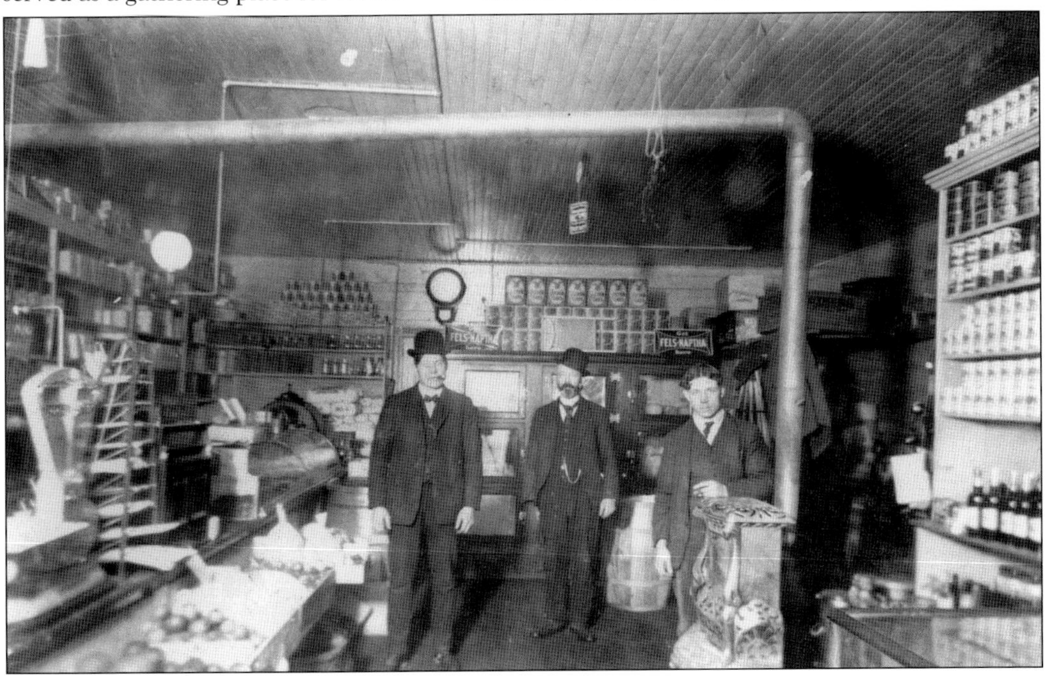

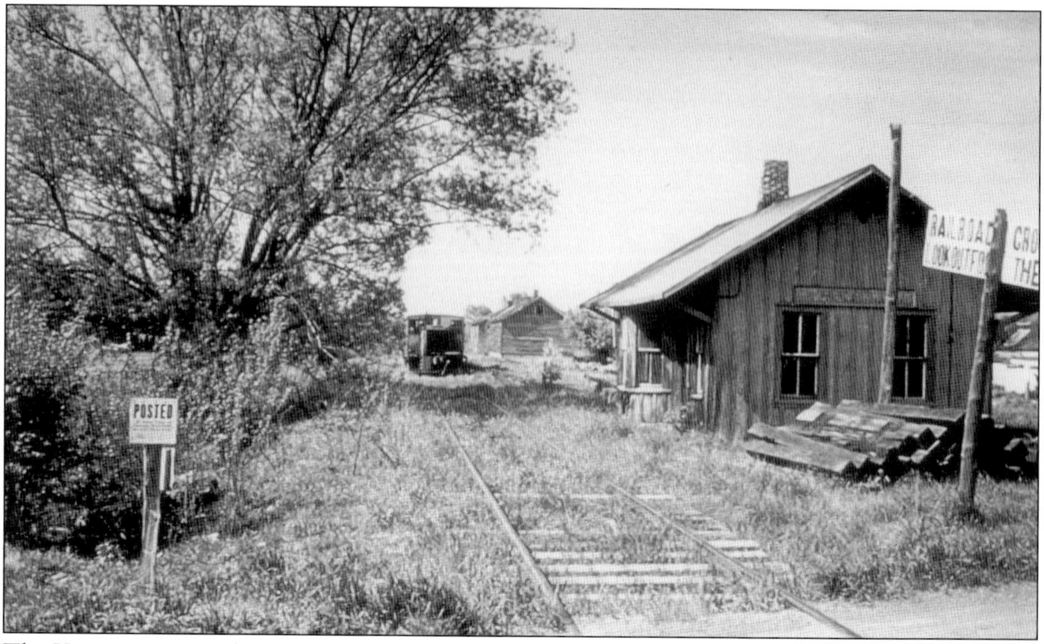

The Kanona & Prattsburgh Railroad passed through Wheeler on its way to Bath. The train made two trips per day and four during harvest season. The depot, shown here, was built in 1889 and contained the Wheeler Post Office. The structure on Gardener Road still stands today and is now a single-family dwelling.

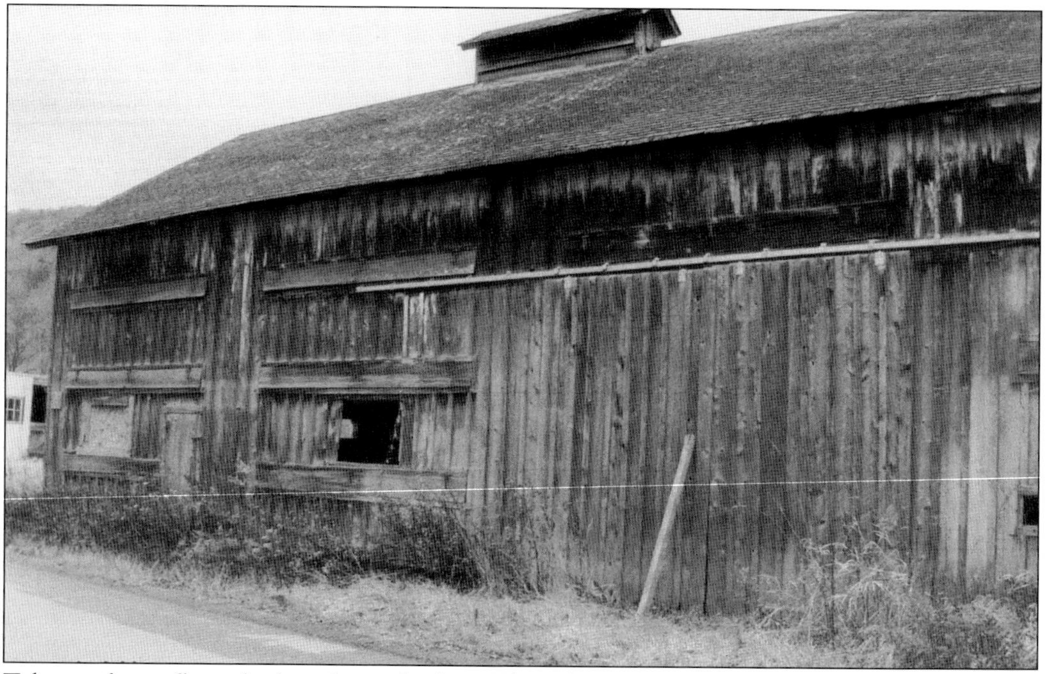

Tobacco farms flourished in the early days. The tobacco barns were about 160 feet long and designed to open on the sides to allow for air flow. After the tobacco was picked, it was hung upside down in the barn. Located on Gardener Road, this is one example of a tobacco barn, which still stands today.

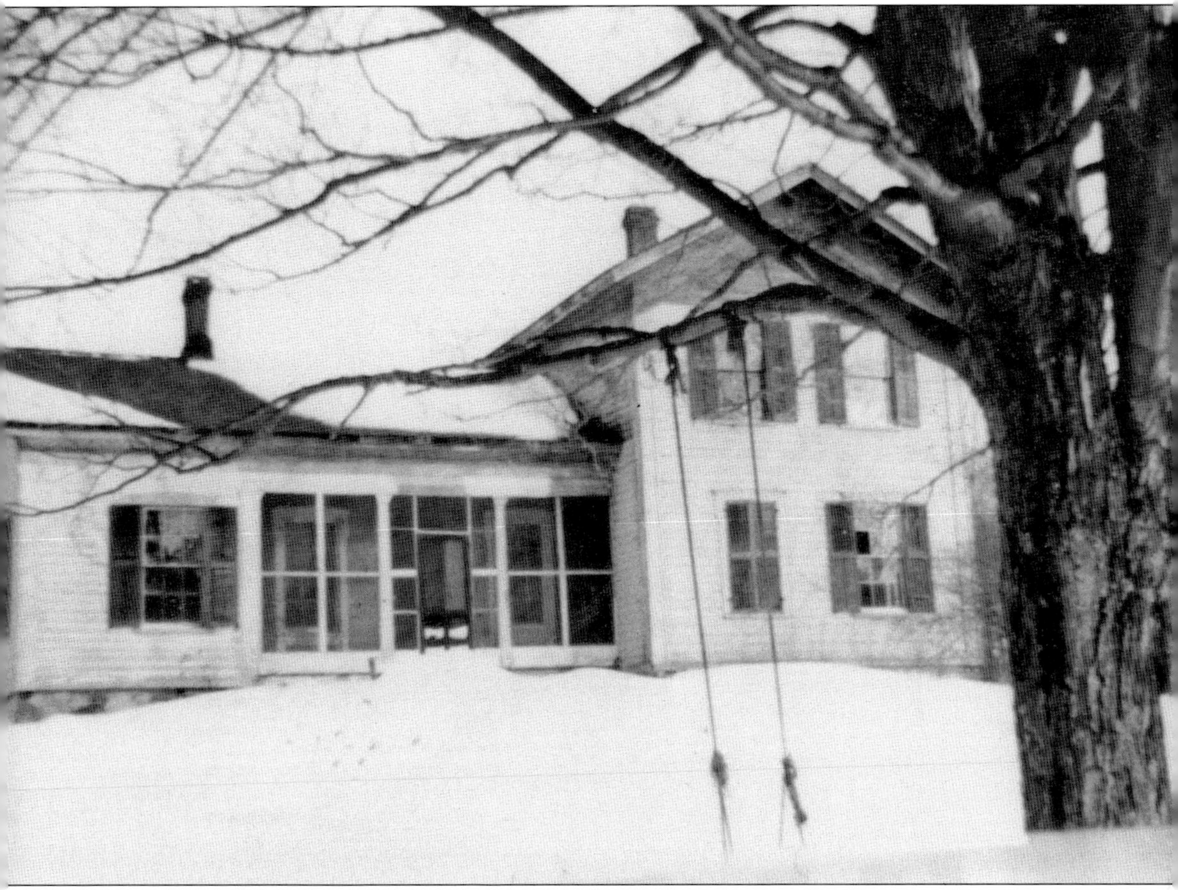

Early settler John Storms built this large home on West Creek Road in the early 1800s. It was later owned by his granddaughter Ella and her husband, Elmer Olmsted.

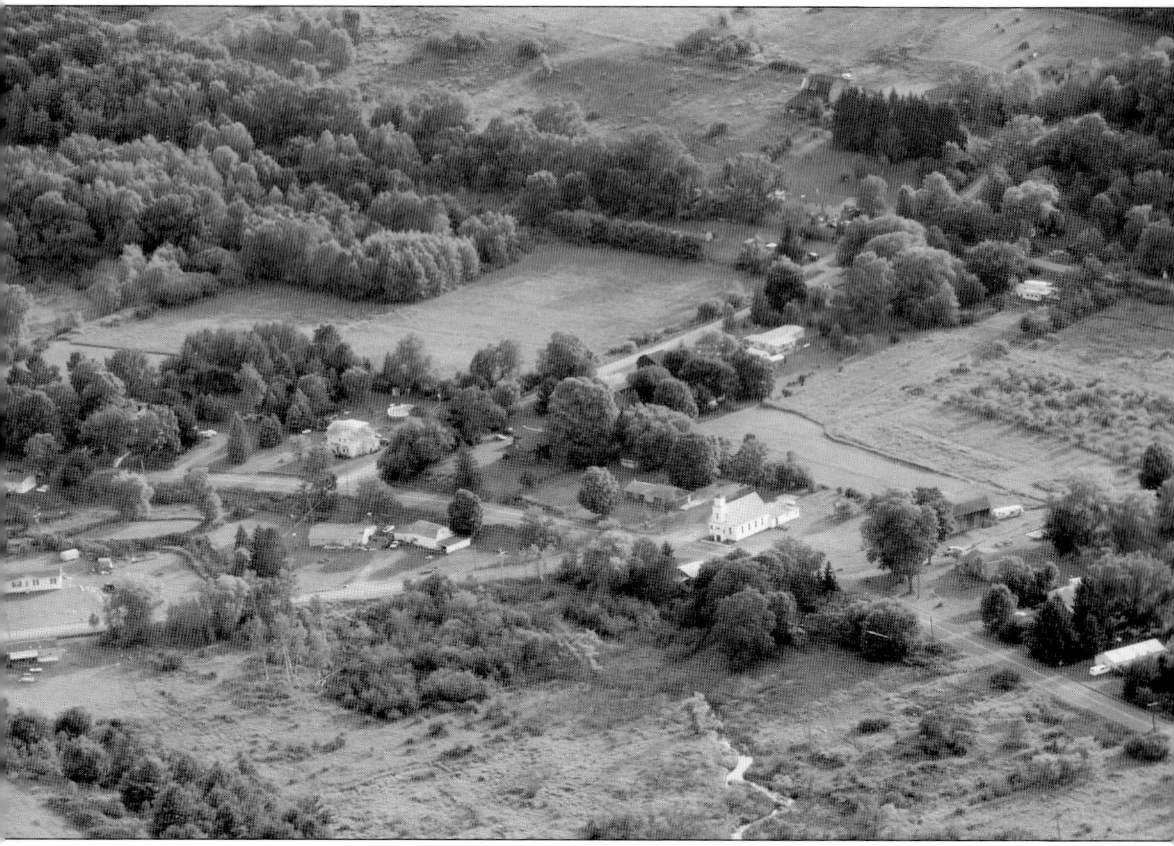

The hamlet of Mitchellsville is located at the southeastern border near the town of Urbana. The only public building left in Mitchellsville now is the Methodist church. An old schoolhouse that was located on the corner of Newton Road is now a private home. Across the road was a general store, and down the road was a hotel and cider mill. The corner grocery store later became a ceramic shop but has since been razed, leaving only a cement pad.

Eight

PULTENEY

Pulteney is located in the northeast corner of Steuben County on beautiful Keuka Lake. The town was named after Sir William Johnstone Pulteney, who, along with a group of English investors, purchased the town from Robert Morris in 1790. The land was acquired from the remaining unsold land of the Phelps and Gorham tract originally owned by Massachusetts and the local Indian tribe. Ironically, Pulteney never came to America to see the town that bears his name.

The first settlers to Pulteney encountered dense pine forests. As their numbers grew, little settlements began to appear. These included Harmonyville (the center of town), Bluff Point (South Pulteney), Scuttsville (Elmbois), Catawba (Gibson's Landing), and Pine Grove. Over time, the people discovered that grape growing adapted well to the area and vast expanses of vineyards were planted.

Pulteney was much larger than it is now. Parts of it eventually went to Prattsburgh, Urbana, Yates County, and Hammondsport, leaving only a little more than 33 square miles. Though small in size, Pulteney has a rich history.

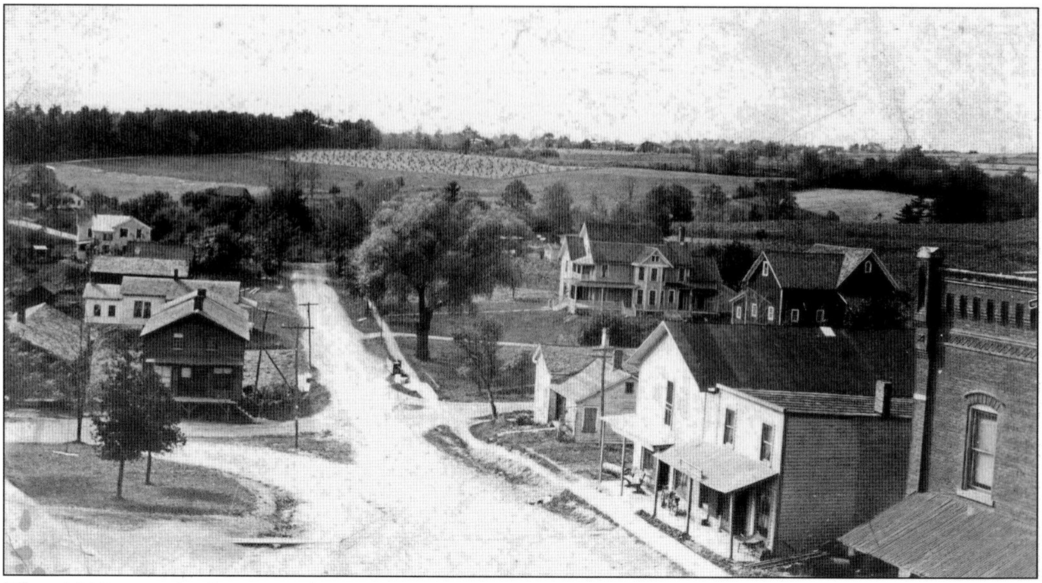

This 1890 view looking south on Main Street bears little resemblance to modern-day Pulteney. Here is where one could shop for groceries and dry goods, fill prescriptions, and take in a meal at the Oasis restaurant. Pulteney was such a thriving place that anything needed could be purchased here without leaving town. All that remains now are the homes, two churches, and the vineyards, which thrive to this day.

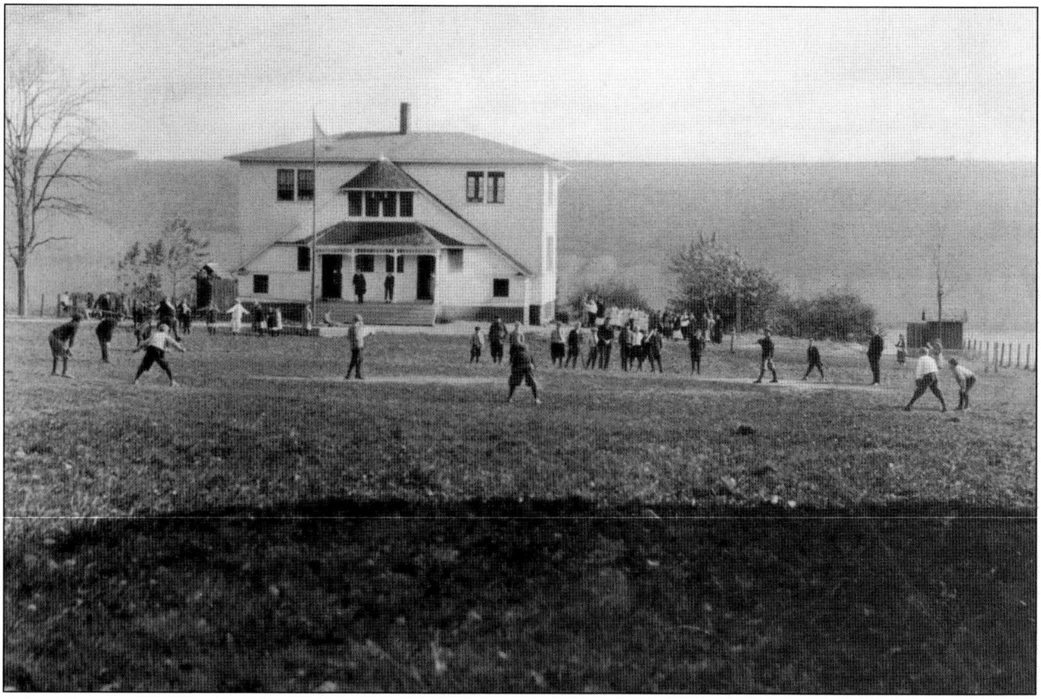

The Union Free School in the center of town served the growing population. In addition to their studies, the students enjoyed recreational activities on the vast expanse of lawn. After centralization of the schools, students in Pulteney either attended Prattsburgh or Hammondsport Central Schools. The current Pulteney Town Hall and library are located in this area.

The old Methodist church is located on County Route 74, the main road in Pulteney. In the late 1800s, the building was struck by lightning. With a dwindling congregation, the Methodist congregation closed the church. The church was eventually sold to Grace Community Fellowship.

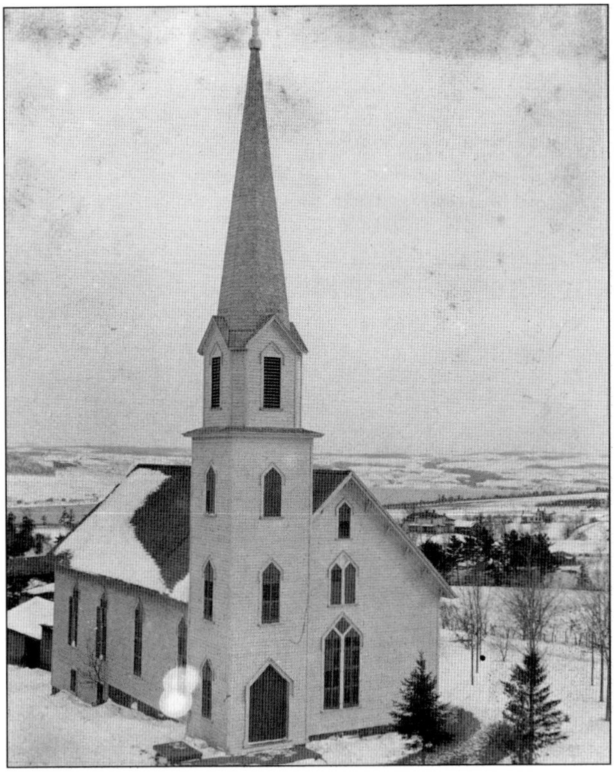

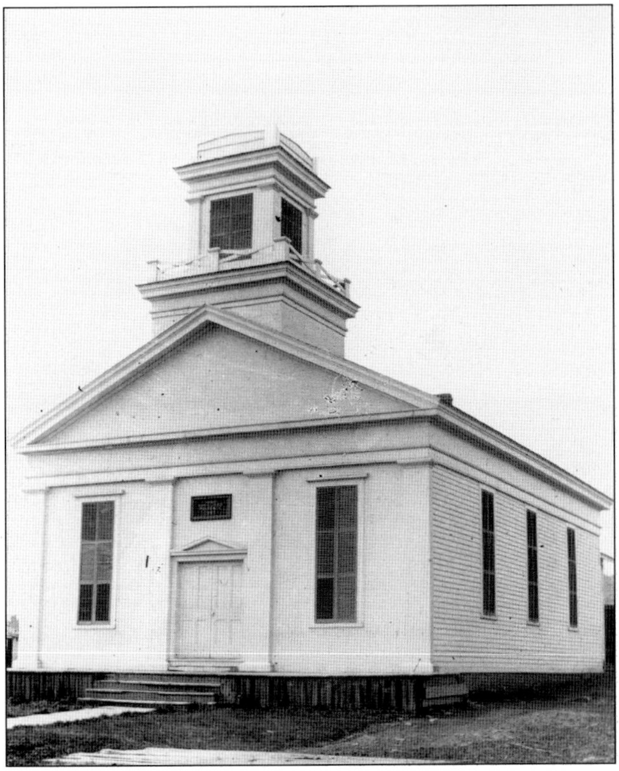

As in other communities, churches were an important part of daily life. The Second Baptist Church, located in South Pulteney, was built in 1867 and served the population for many years.

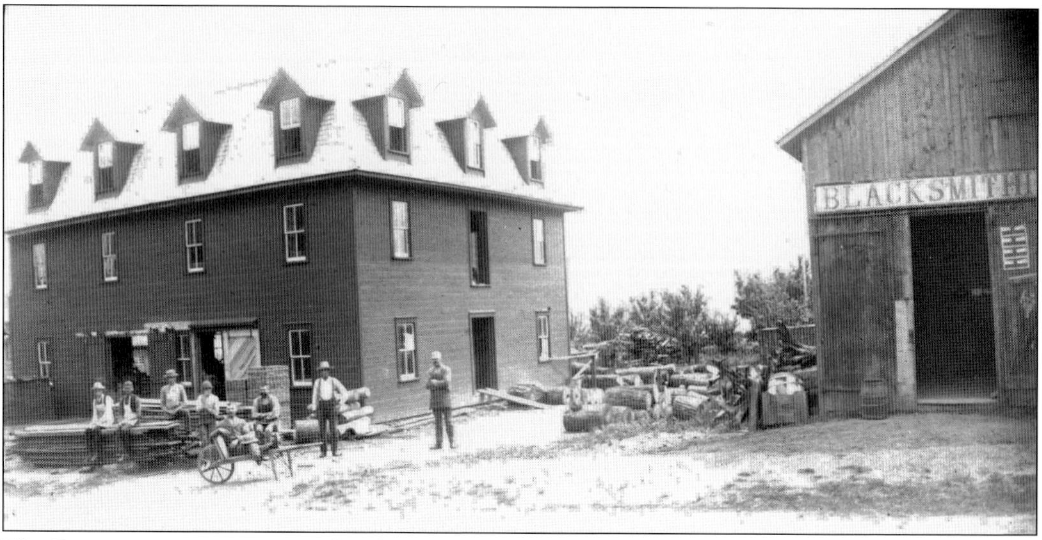

The Retans were a prominent family in Pulteney who settled here in 1820. The family was large and contributed greatly to the town's early development. In 1890, a new basket factory was built by Nelson Retan, giving employment to many people. Nearly three million baskets, which were used for grape and peach packaging, were made in 1891. The Retan Basket Factory burned down twice.

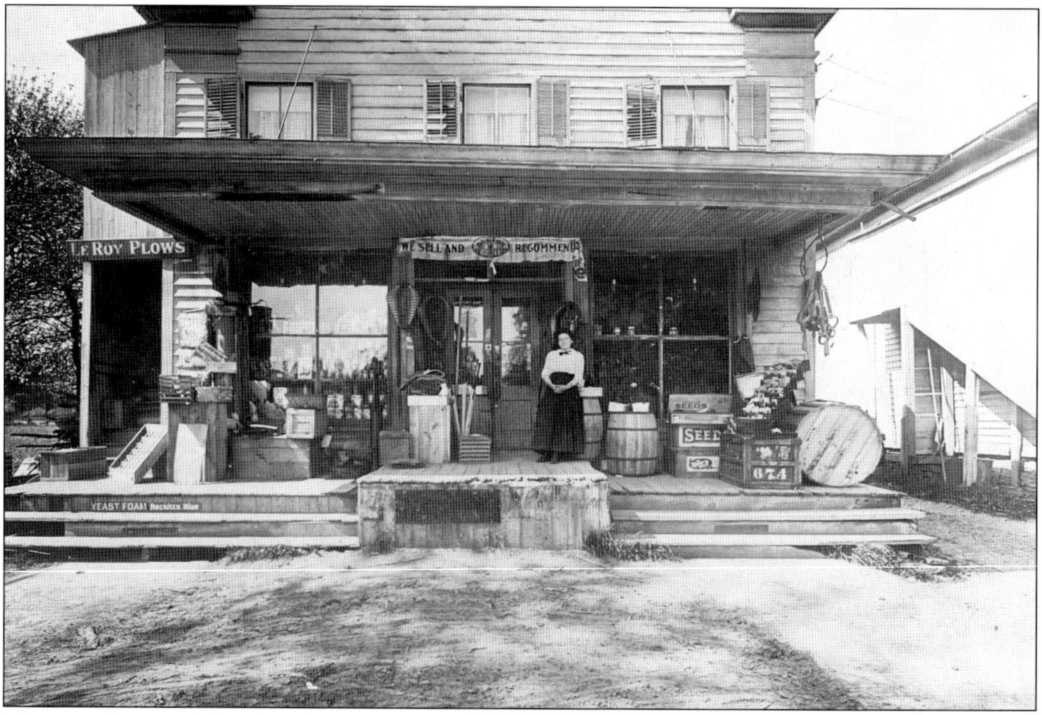

Like most stores of the day, this one served the needs of residents by carrying all of the necessities of daily living. Here, one could purchase canned goods, seeds for planting, horse tack, and dry goods. Many items like pickles and crackers were shipped to the store in barrels, essentially the beginning of bulk food purchasing. These really were one-stop shops run by residents of the town, who often lived upstairs of their stores.

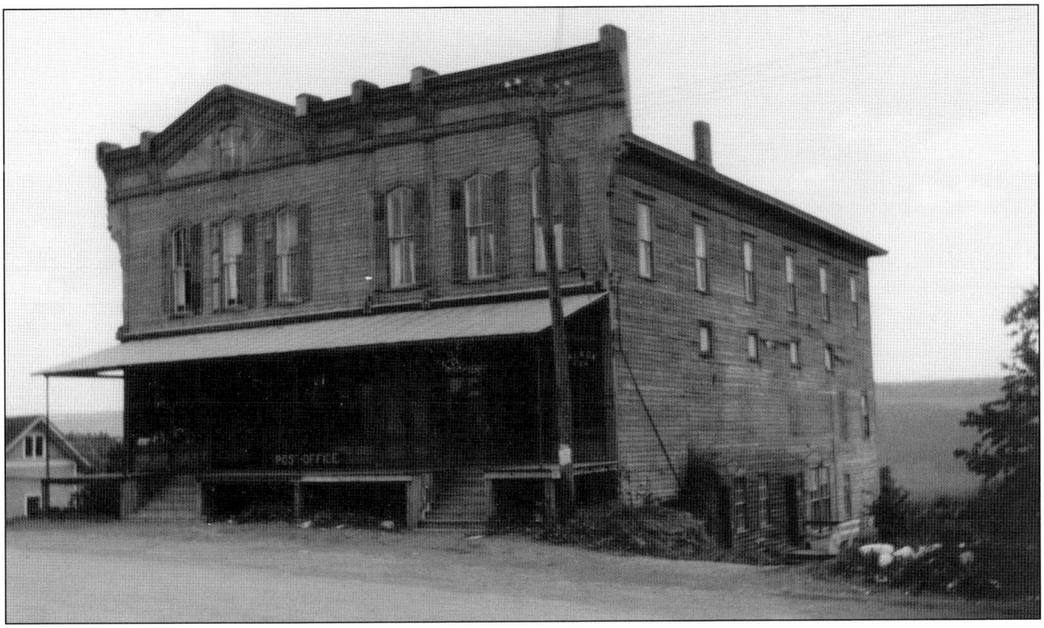

The Nichols Block prior to 1876 was used as a grain storehouse. When Dr. Nichols came to Pulteney, he purchased the building and put in small line of groceries and drugs. Because business was thriving, he constructed a 50-by-70-foot extension on the existing building. The third floor was used as a town hall for social gatherings, medicine shows, meetings, local talent shows, and plays. On any given day, the Nichols Block saw many visitors come through its doors. The building was razed in 1974.

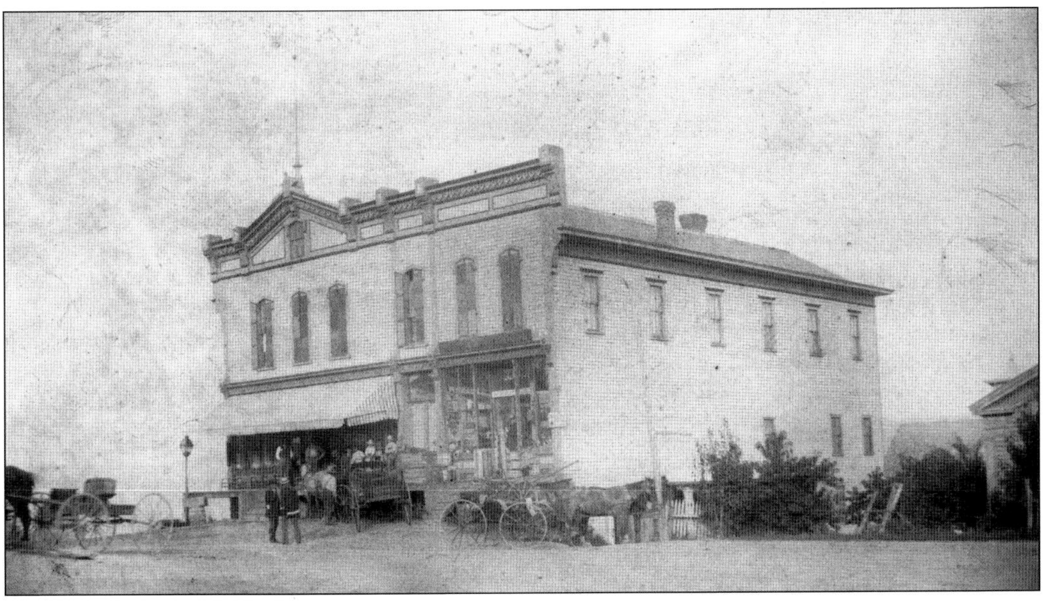

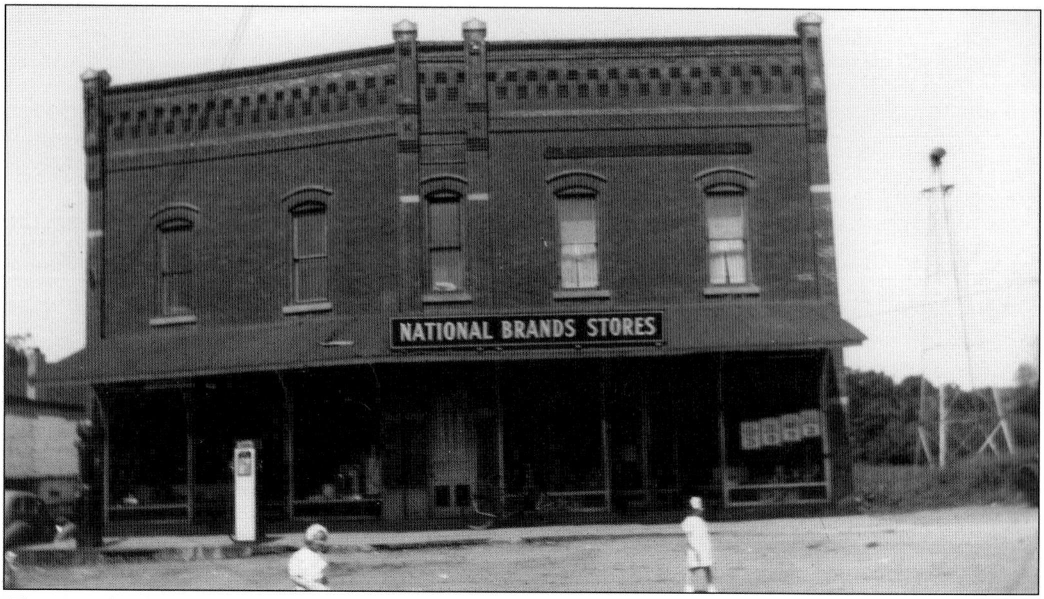

The Goodrich Block on County Route 74 was built in 1890 by proprietors Franklin and Eugene Godfrey Goodrich. Its walls were two feet thick, and different types of merchandise were available, including hardware in one portion of the store. The upper portion had two large halls leased to the Grand Army Post and Odd Fellows. Gas pumps were later added to serve the community. It was the last mercantile building in Pulteney when it was razed in 1992.

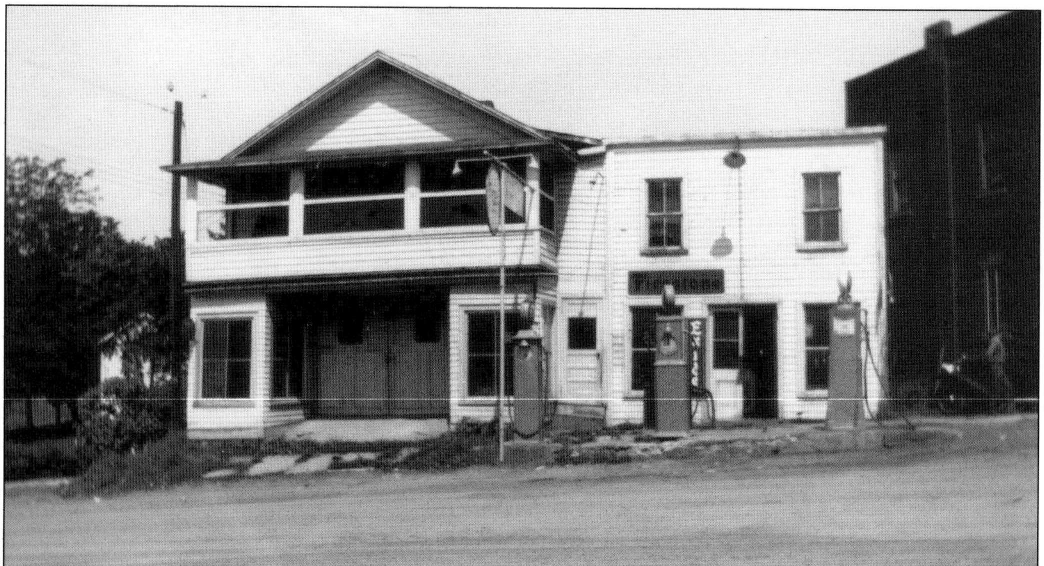

The Wagstaff store stood next to the Goodrich Block and carried a small line of groceries. Later, Ed Nudd ran it as a gas station. As people traveled farther from home to shop, stores like this shut down over lack of business.

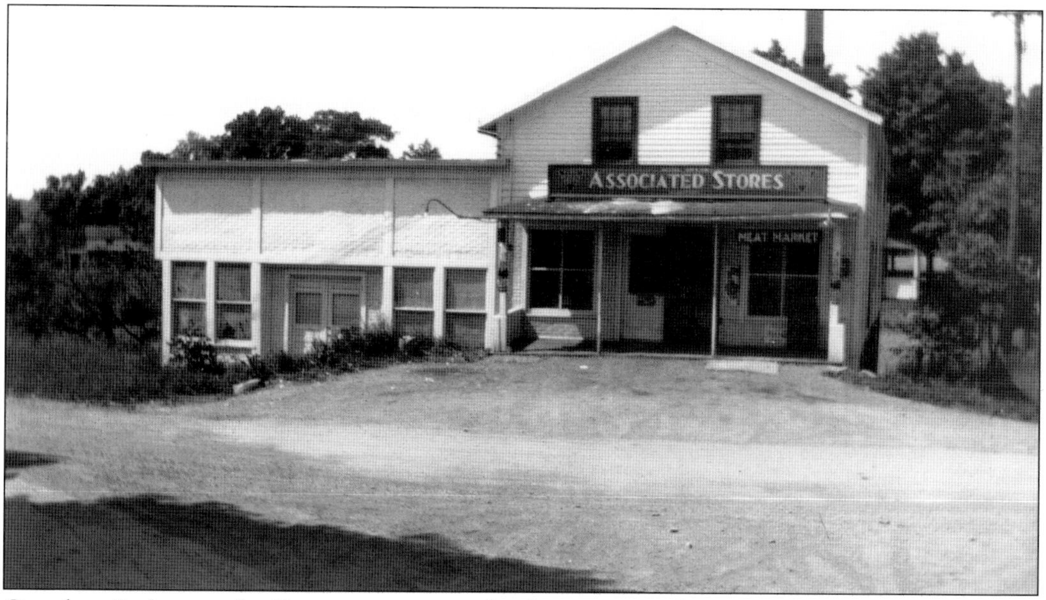

Gretchen Earley ran the Oasis restaurant at the four corners of town, and the grocery store next door was run by her dad. This was a popular place where teens would gather after school and senior citizens would get together for coffee and conversation.

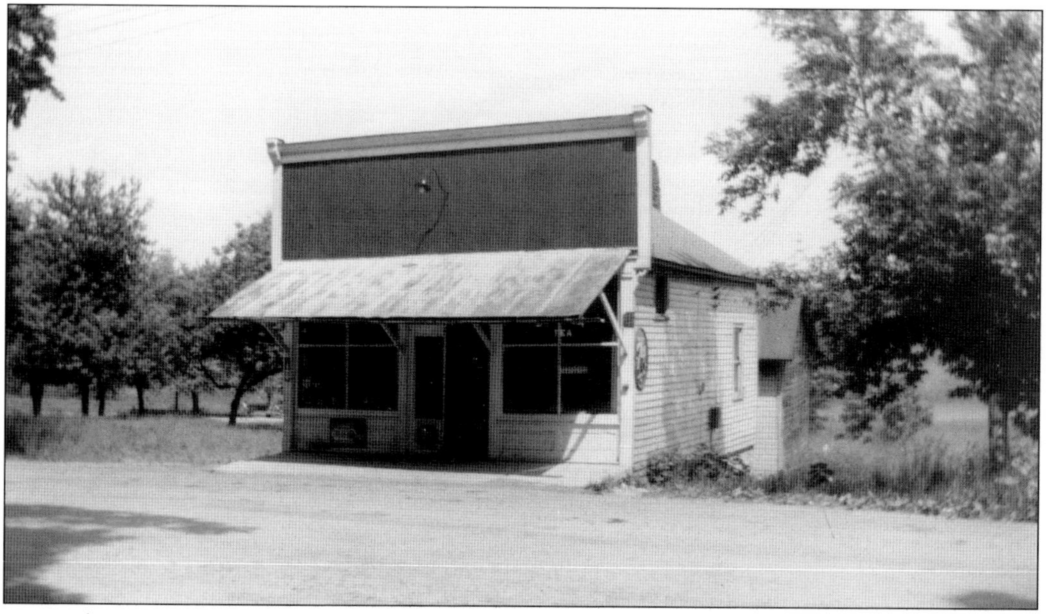

Located down the street from the Nichols Block, this meat market was run by Herbie Keech. The Union Free School is located in the area beyond the view of this building. The building still stands and has been converted into a private home.

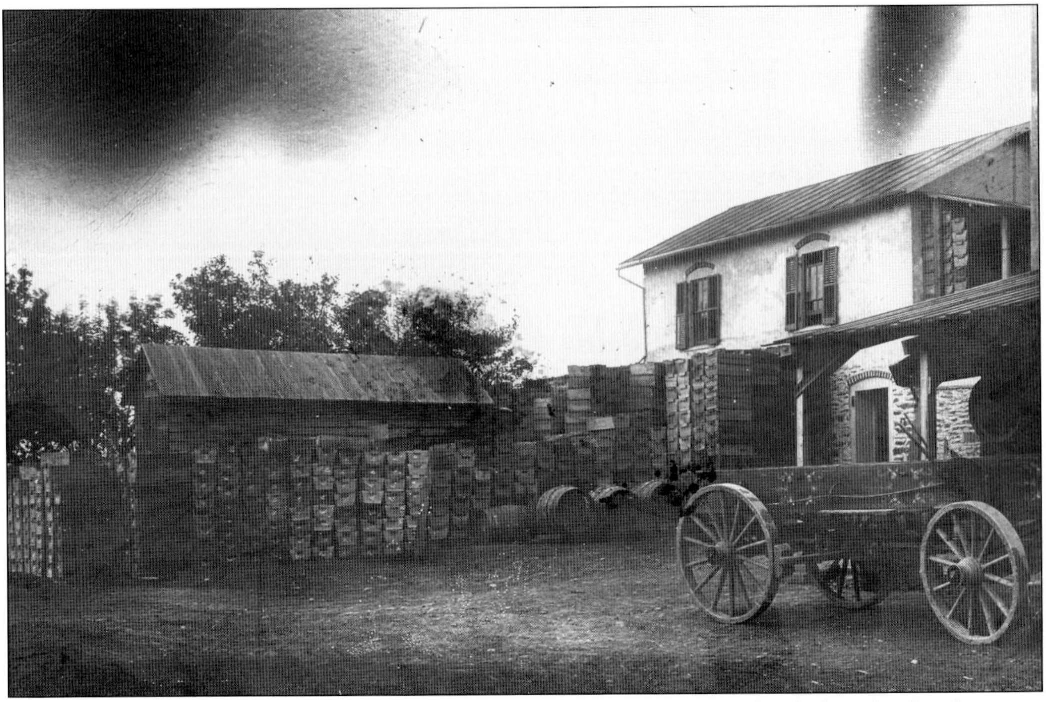

Pulteney's fertile soil lent itself to growing many varieties of grapes. This led to the development of many small wineries in the area. Jepha Foster originally ran this wine cellar. As the photograph shows, one needed many wooden trays to collect the grapes at harvest and bring to the winery. Winemaking continues to be big business in the town.

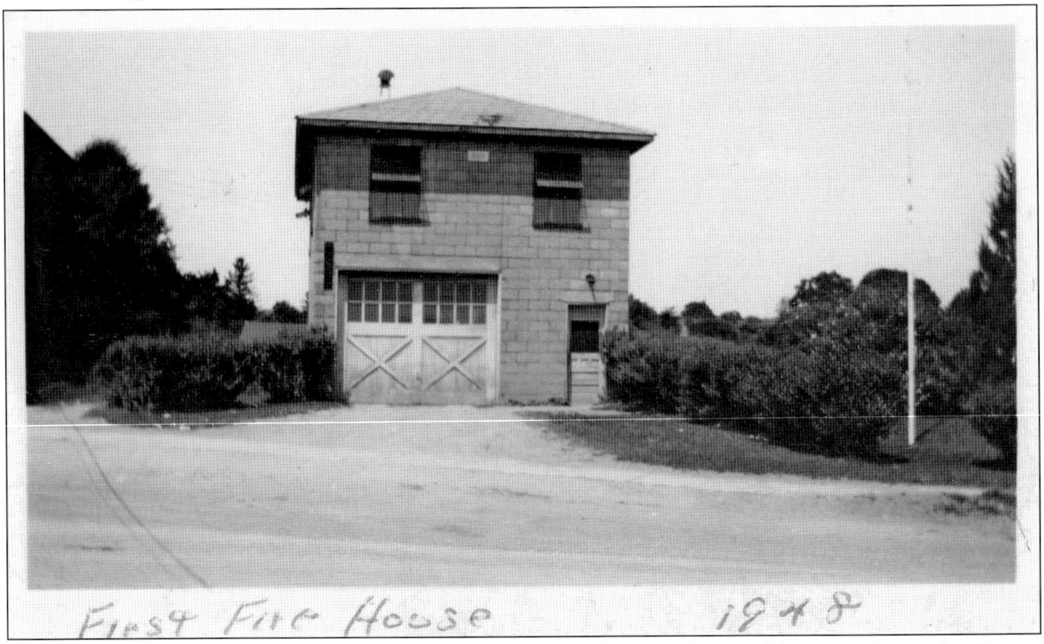

Pulteney's first actual firehouse was built in 1948 on County Route 74 near where the Retan Basket Factory was located. The fire bell was on a tower next to the Goodrich Block. Pulteney now boasts a new firehouse on Brown Road.

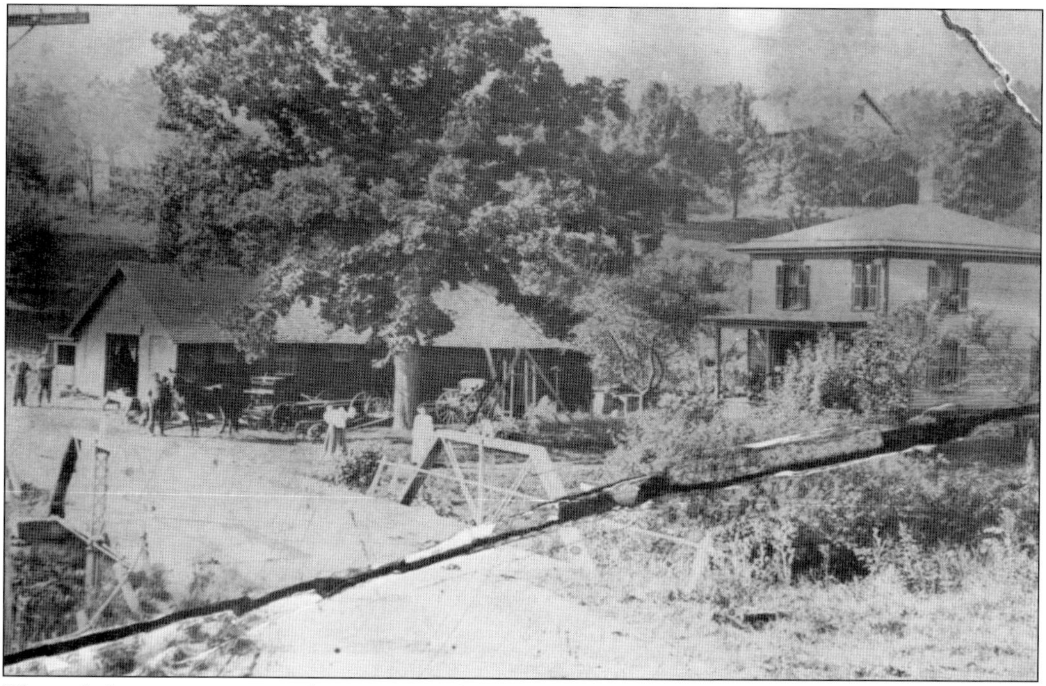

The rickshaw got its start when Reverend Goble, a missionary in Japan, commissioned his old friend and wagon-maker Francis Pollay of Pulteney to design a mode of transportation for his invalid wife. Francis built the carriage and shipped the parts to Japan for assembly in 1869. After it was assembled and used by Goble, a Japanese manufacturer added springs and a hood and mass-produced it for the general population. It quickly became the most popular mode of transportation there.

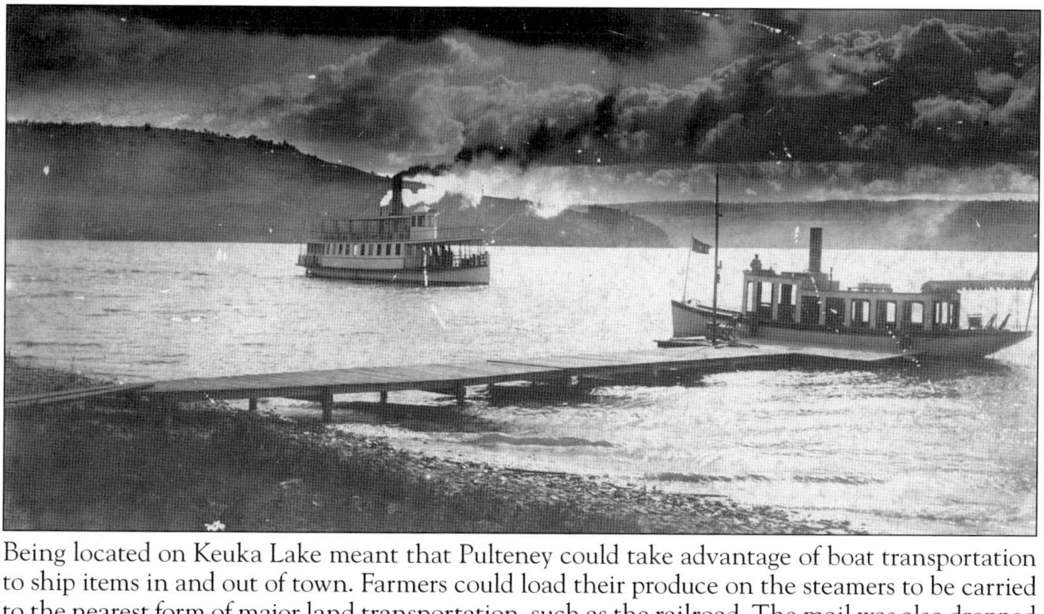

Being located on Keuka Lake meant that Pulteney could take advantage of boat transportation to ship items in and out of town. Farmers could load their produce on the steamers to be carried to the nearest form of major land transportation, such as the railroad. The mail was also dropped off at Gibson Point and picked up by the mail carrier to be transported to the post offices in the surrounding towns.

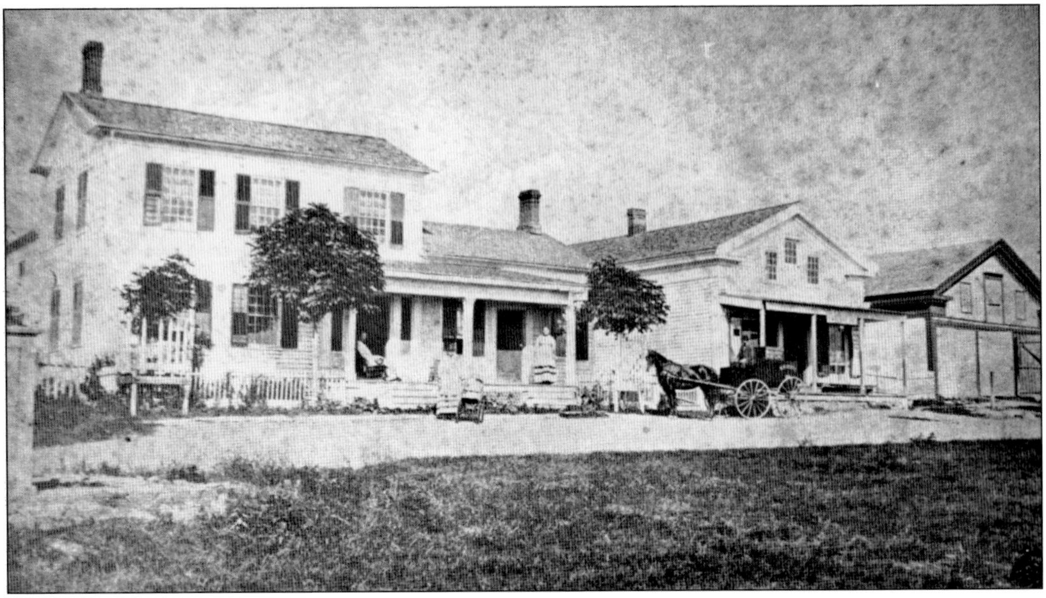

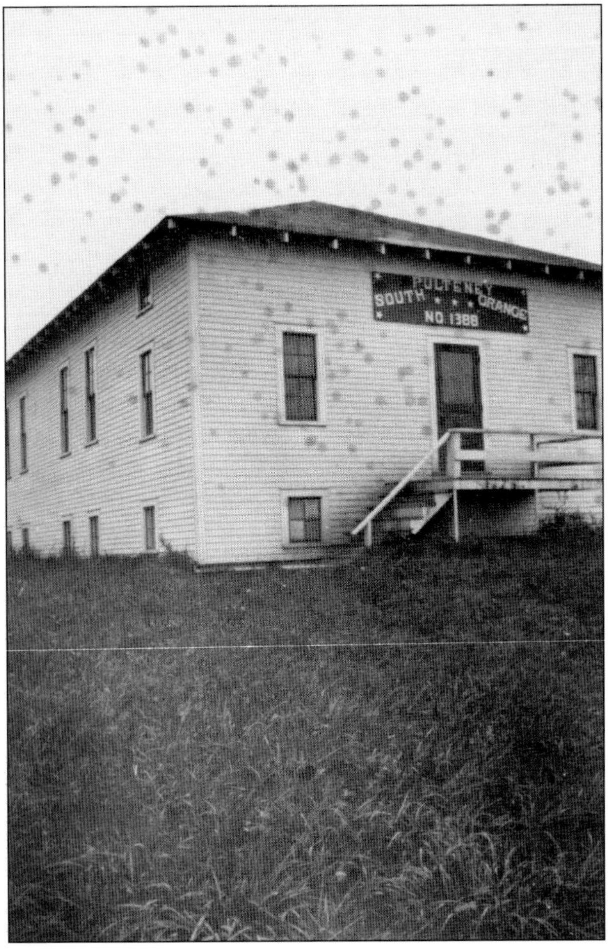

The original Old Hotel was located on County Route 76 on the west side of the street in South Pulteney. The store and post office building next to the hotel were moved south and became the Advent Church. The barn was bought by Hugh Vunck and moved north of Pine Grove and placed on the Vunck farm.

The Grange hall in South Pulteney served as the social hub of the community. Many parties, weddings, reunions, and meetings were held at this building located on County Route 76.

PRIVATE PARTY.

The Company of Yourself and Lady is requested at
A PRIVATE HOP,

At W. W. Scott's, So. Pulteney,

FRIDAY EVENING, JULY 21, 1882.

GOOD MUSIC IN ATTENDANCE.

BILL, - - - - - - - 50 CENTS.

The Grange building in South Pulteney is still standing today but is in much disrepair.

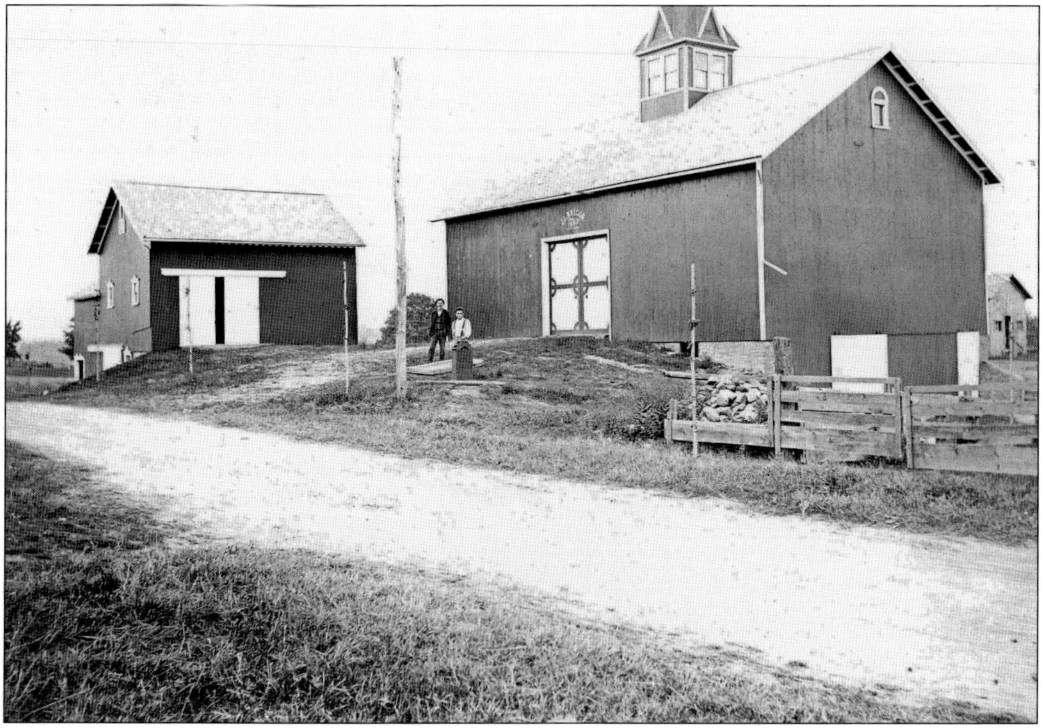

Joe Briggs completed building this farm in 1899, where he lived with his wife, Maria. Joe Briggs received only an elementary education by attending school only in the winter and working on his father's farm the rest of the year. For 48 years, he enjoyed farming his own land until he sold it at age 80 and retired in 1913.

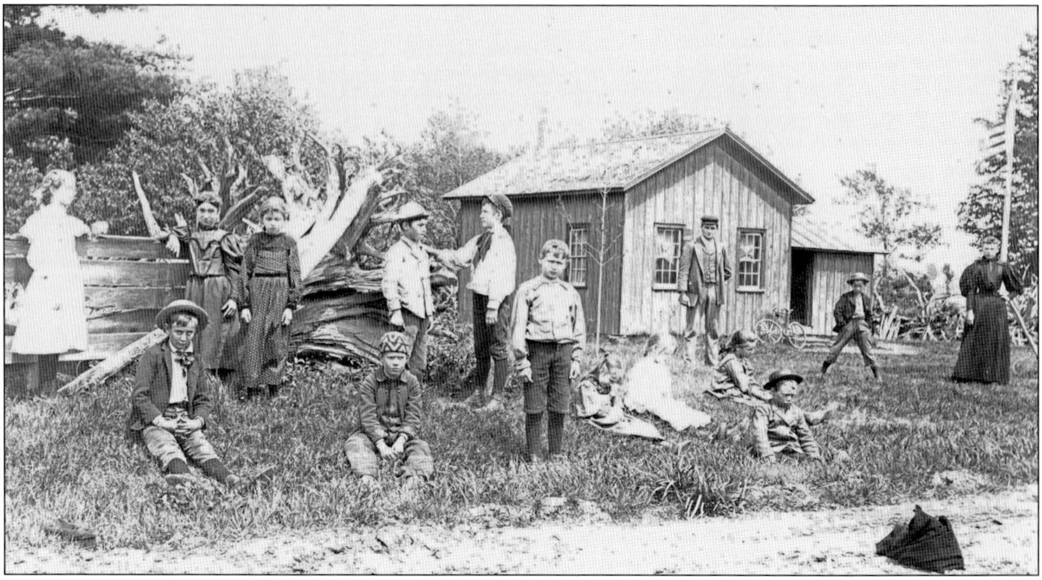

The younger Joseph Briggs, shown here holding the book, was a schoolteacher in Pulteney from 1903 to 1906. Like all one-room schoolteachers, Briggs was challenged with teaching multiple grades.

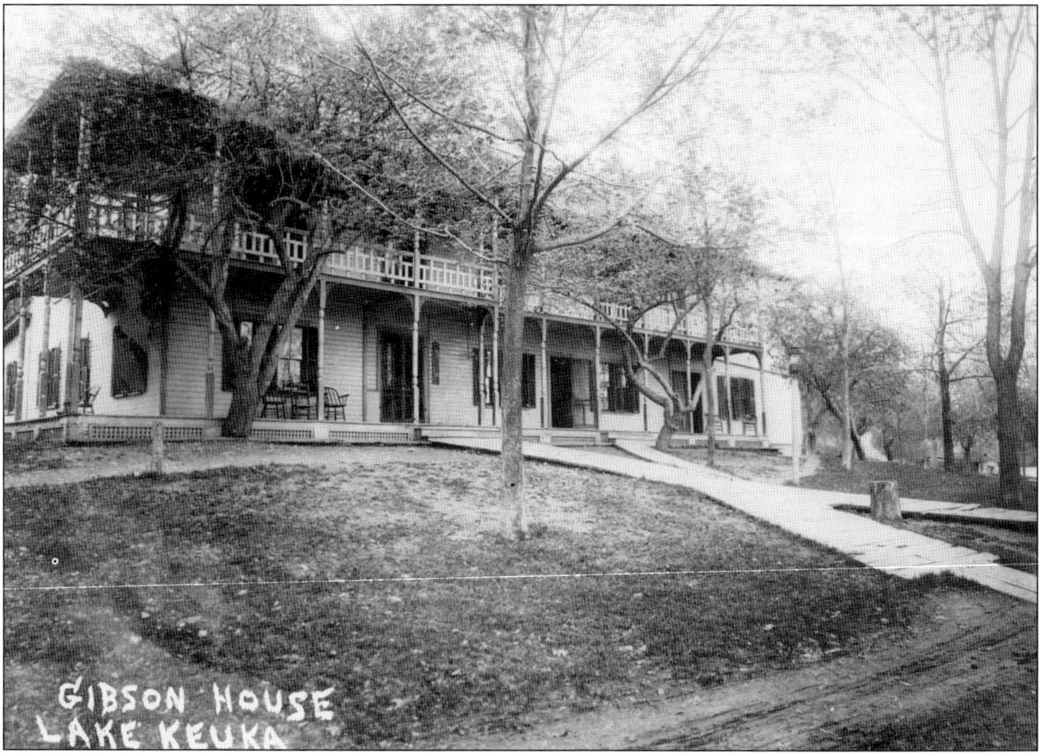

The Gibson House on Keuka Lake was located at the foot of Gibson Hill overlooking the lake. Gibson's Landing served as the point of arrival and departure for the steamers and other boats bringing passengers and other items to Pulteney. The Gibson House was a vacation destination for those seeking recreation at the lake.

Bibliography

Sherer, Richard. *Steuben County, The First 200 Years: A Pictorial History*. Virginia Beach, VA: The Donning Co./Publishers, 1996.

Moon, Elsie Hotchkin, ed. *The Writings of Stephen Bert Merritt 1878–1963*. Prattsburgh, NY: The Prattsburgh Community Historical Society, 1995.

Sesquicentennial Souvenir Booklet. Prattsburgh, NY: The Prattsburgh Community Historical Society, 1963.